T0290461

THE RULES OF PUBLIC RELATIONS

THE RULES OF PUBLIC RELATIONS

Legal and Ethical Issues in Contemporary Practice

CAYCE MYERS

ROWMAN & LITTLEFIELD
Lanham • Boulder • New York • London

Published by Rowman & Littlefield
An imprint of The Rowman & Littlefield Publishing Group, Inc.
4501 Forbes Boulevard, Suite 200, Lanham, Maryland 20706
www.rowman.com

86-90 Paul Street, London EC2A 4NE

British Library Cataloguing in Publication Information Available

Library of Congress Cataloging-in-Publication Data
Names: Myers, Cayce, author.
Title: The rules of public relations : legal and ethical issues in
    contemporary practice / Cayce Myers.
Description: Lanham : Rowman & Littlefield, [2024] | Includes
    bibliographical references and index.
Identifiers: LCCN 2024007704 (print) | LCCN 2024007705 (ebook) | ISBN
    9781538186046 (cloth) | ISBN 9781538186053 (paperback) | ISBN 9781538186060 (ebook)
Subjects: LCSH: Public relations.
Classification: LCC HD59 .M95 2024 (print) | LCC HD59 (ebook) | DDC
    659.2--dc23/eng/20240412
LC record available at https://lccn.loc.gov/2024007704
LC ebook record available at https://lccn.loc.gov/2024007705

Dedication

For my daughter, Cayce Anne Myers

Contents

Introduction

This book began with a series of conversations I had with many public relations (PR) practitioners over the past 10 years. As an attorney, I saw obvious connections between the advocacy of public relations and the advocacy of law. That got me thinking about the issues of litigation, evidence, communication policies, corporate speech, copyright, trademark, trade secrets, and the general philosophical differences between PR and legal strategy. Along the way, I developed a keen interest in ethics of communication as well. Thinking of the law as the lowest level of compliance, ethics present a unique opportunity to go beyond what is mandated toward achieving what is right or just within society. My involvement with ethical research and ethical issues within a PR professional society also made me rethink the relationship between PR and law. From those experiences I began formulating this book in my mind. It is an overview of the laws and regulations that affect PR practitioners—and their clients—provided in broad-brush strokes that are understandable to the lawyer and the nonlawyer alike.

When I would tell people I was working on a book about PR law, my practitioner friends would say that was great, but then they would offer a piece of advice on writing. The refrain could be best summarized as, "Don't bog down the book with a bunch of cases about this court did this and this court did that. Tell us what we need to know. Write about how the law impacts PR practice today." I have taken that advice seriously, and have accomplished what I think is a good primer on the law that affects the twenty-first-century PR practitioner. While there are some cases, and some descriptions of what this and that court did, the chapters focus on the intersection of law and PR practice. I want PR practitioners, students, communication professionals, lawyers, and scholars to see how public relations practice is shaped by legal issues. I also want the reader to know that their work product is directly impacted by the shifting laws on technology and speech that continue to evolve in the 2020s, especially with the rise of artificial intelligence (AI). However, one thing I hope all PR practitioners and students get from this book is an insight into how lawyers think, and why they do the things they do. Public relations practitioners are communicators. Their solutions to problems are rooted in that perspective. Lawyers, however, are trained to be risk averse. They are supposed to see the trial, appeal, and liability way down the road. Because of that, their advice is different, but synergistic with the work of PR practitioners.

There are many things that this book is not. It is not a comprehensive book of all law that affects all of communication. It is not a book designed to get into the ponderous nuances of law with esoteric discussions of niche areas. It tries, albeit with some exceptions, to refrain from offering opinions regarding what the law is or what it should be. This book also has a deliberate U.S. perspective. I am trained in the American legal system, and my expertise resides largely in that area. However, public relations is a global practice, and increasingly PR practitioners are faced with issues that involve the laws and regulations of other countries. So, where appropriate, I provide insight into non-U.S. legal perspectives.

For example, in several chapters, the reader will see an inclusion of European Union law. That is because the European Union is one of the leaders in privacy, technology, and intellectual property regulation. Many businesses based in the United States de facto adhere to EU law when designing products because they must follow that system to have presence there. Additionally, this book touches on the evolution of the law surrounding new technology, specifically digital privacy. The European Union is a leader in that area, and no book about public relations and the law would be complete without an acknowledgement of EU leadership there. My hope is that this book speaks plainly about what and how the law affects modern public relations. Each chapter is dedicated to a specific PR practice theme, and each concludes with questions and discussion points for those who want to have deeper discussions about the contours of laws affecting public relations practice. However, as with all legal scholarship, this book is not legal advice, but education. Readers of all backgrounds, legal or otherwise, should note that when there is a question of law, one should consult an attorney.

WHY DO PR PRACTITIONERS NEED THEIR OWN LAW BOOK?

This is a question I sometimes get from students, and over the years I've come to appreciate how public relations is legally quite distinct from other areas of law. Many times, in the academic world, communication law is taught from a heavily journalistic perspective. There is a lot of content about the First Amendment and journalist privilege. That is important, even for PR practitioners. However, PR practice is different from journalism for all sorts of reasons, obvious and not.

First, PR practitioners, unlike journalists, typically have a client. Those relationships are important and complex, and PR practitioners need to be able to navigate issues of confidentiality, content ownership, and employment with some level of confidence. Second, PR practitioners are content creators. The issues of intellectual property ownership are important, especially because the client relationship may dictate how PR practitioners can use or not use their own work. Third, PR practice is heavily informed by corporate and nonprofit law. For those practicing in publicly traded companies there are special rules that must be followed, and for those in the nonprofit sector there are certain laws within copyright that may affect practitioners in special ways. Finally, PR practice has a lot of unique aspects, particularly in the realm of crisis communication. Knowing what to say, when to say it, and when what you say will get you sued or cross-examined on the witness stand are all important to practitioners and clients.

This focus on PR practitioners includes students. As the future of public relations practice, students need to be aware of the legal challenges they will face in the profession. Many times, students taking a college course in law and ethics don't see the direct connection between what they are learning and how it applies to their future careers. However, I am certain that students entering a professional communications career will experience legal and ethical issues. When confronted with those situations, it is not enough to ask a supervisor or ask a lawyer what to do. Part of being a professional is making decisions, sometimes tough decisions, based on your own knowledge and experience. My hope is that this book provides the type of information that in the future can help students make decisions, identify problems, and create solutions that are sound. As someone who taught many classes in communication law and ethics, I am keenly aware that students may have only one class in their entire education that provides them with formal legal and ethical training. My hope is that this book and its lessons resonate beyond the classroom and stay with students as they enter the dynamic profession of public relations. There will be students reading this book in the 2020s who will be practicing public relations in the 2070s. Therefore it is important for students to have a baseline knowledge of the rules of PR. Having this knowledge provides student with a foundation for decision making and engaging with the technologically complex and evolving nature of public relations.

There are many books out there on media and communication law. Many of them say the same things about the important laws that affect the field. While this book certainly covers legal concepts that may be familiar to readers, it does so in a relatable manner. For each chapter, I try to situate the legal issue within the context of contemporary PR practice. Sometimes this involves hypothetical scenarios that PR practitioners may have to confront. Frequently the book attempts to demonstrate how PR practitioners need to consider a variety of solutions to legal problems. This variety of solutions, as you may expect, means there is not always a clear-cut answer. That is the way much of the law works. There are typically two sides to a case, and sometimes more. There are always multiple interpretations of the same case, statute, or contract. As the saying goes—get three lawyers in a room and you'll get four different opinions.

What I try to do in each chapter is present the options the law provides, and in those options, readers can see there are solutions that may work better than others. What I hope readers take from this is that the role of the PR practitioner and lawyer serve many of the same purposes, and in the PR field, decisions must be made that serve a complex set of communication, ethical, legal, and organizational interests.

PR practitioners also work in a highly complex business. There are such diverse topics for PR practitioners: digital advocacy, reputation management, social media management, big data analytics, corporate communication, nonprofit communication, political communication, corporate social responsibility, corporate social value, social justice, diversity, equity and inclusion, paid media, media relations, earned media, owned media, shared media and, now, if that weren't enough—artificial intelligence. And that just names a few of the specialty areas for PR practitioners. Thus, the laws that affect public relations are as diverse as the field's sectors. That makes it difficult to write a survey book of law for the field, and it also makes practitioners struggle to keep up with what they need to know. Cue in-house counsel.

But reading about public relations and law is not about knowing the answer so much as it is knowing how to recognize the issue. In the following chapters, I try to weave legal content with PR context to illustrate the application of the law to the work of PR practitioners. The work of media relations, social media content creation, social media ownership, requests for proposals, and the legal protection of PR content, both First Amendment and intellectual property, are important items discussed in this book. My intent for these chapters is to showcase how legally complex the field of public relations practice is, and how as the practice evolves—particularly in the era of communication convergence—the more PR practice is subject to an ever-increasing number of laws and regulations.

WHY DOES A PR LEGAL BOOK NEED TO DISCUSS ETHICS?
Public relations as a field is dedicated to ethics. It stems from myriad reasons, but perhaps most important is that ethical communication gives organizations (and practitioners) credibility. Ethics and law are distinct, and when I first began teaching communication law at the university level, I remember making a deliberate decision to only focus on the law. Part of the reason is that ethics deserves its own class. It deserves its own book, and there are many good ones. However, as a scholar about laws that affect PR practice, it would be remiss of me not to include the ethical dimension to this book. Part of the reason is that ethics is a

factor in decision making for PR practitioners. We cannot just think of the legal consequences because that is often the baseline of compliance. Considering the legal along with the ethical makes for better decisions for practitioners, publics, and organizations.

Public relations and ethics have an interesting historical relationship. In the nineteenth century, PR practitioners frequently were publicity seekers who used communications in an ethically questionable way. That foundational history has shaped the arc of the field tremendously. Public relations ethics is frequently a response to these earlier transgressions, and there is an institutional sense that PR practice wants to be above reproach because it sees itself as the ethical conscience of many of those in power. Doing the right thing is a mantra for many PR professionals, and for good reason. The communications that come from PR practitioners will be scrutinized by the press, publics, and stakeholders, not to mention other PR practitioners.

This book's discussion of ethics comes at the end of each chapter, although some chapters present ethical issues alongside the discussion of law. This is not done as an afterthought, but because I want to discuss the legal foundations first and then consider what practitioners may examine as ethical consequences of their actions. While I am a member of several PR organizations that have ethical codes, this book does not represent any specific organizational code. Rather, it represents communication ethics from the proverbial 40,000-foot level. The ethical questions posed in the chapters look at what is required versus what is the right thing to do, assuming there is an obvious right thing. Moreover, the chapters' approach to ethical considerations takes into account that ethics may not be synonymous with the law. As chapter 1 points out, what is legal is not always ethical, and vice versa. Because of that, PR practitioners may find themselves in an ethical paradox when navigating some of the more complex issues of contemporary practice.

What This Book Does

This book analyzes major areas of public relations law. Because of that, chapters are set up not by area of law but by contemporary themes of PR practice: ethics versus law, definitional issues within PR practice,

PR practitioners versus lawyers, transparency in PR practice, reputation management, image management, safeguarding privacy, protecting PR content, and the future of law and PR practice. My hope is these chapters present the relevant information needed for PR students, practitioners, or communicators in general to see the ways that law impacts PR practice as a craft. The deeper objective of each chapter is to show readers the intersection of law with these various communication issues. Each chapter begins with an overview and objectives of the chapter's content, and concludes with discussion questions to help readers explore the topics presented. Additionally, each chapter has extensive notes that include sources for further reading and a few explanatory notes for those who want more granular details of a specific case.

Chapter 1 begins with an overview of law and ethics. Because readers may not be familiar with the intricacies of the legal system, the chapter provides an overview of the sources of law and the various legal approaches of interpretation. These include case law, constitutional law, statutory law, administrative law, international law, and private law. Next, the chapter examines the sources of ethics, including ethical codes, and the Western philosophical underpinnings of ethics, including ethical decision-making processes. The chapter concludes with an overview of the tension between law and ethics, and outlines some of the contemporary challenges for the field, especially in the realm of technology and artificial intelligence.

Chapter 2 explores how the expanding definition of public relations brought about by media convergence has created a new legal reality of PR practice. The chapter begins with the legal definition of public relations under the First Amendment and analyzes how the categorization of public relations under First Amendment jurisprudence has created a segmented legal definition of the field that includes commercial speech, corporate speech, and fully protected speech. The chapter also delves into the unprotected speech categories of fighting words, obscenity, and defamation to illustrate the broad context of First Amendment law. Next, the chapter examines how public relations' complex speech categorization presents unique legal issues for the field, especially in terms of mixed commercial and fully protected speech. The chapter concludes by looking at political PR, and how the fundraising aspect of campaigns has special meaning for PR practice. Additionally, the political context of public relations involves lobbying, and how some PR practice has embraced lobbying as a professional identity, which can create confusion over the field's true purpose. The chapter concludes by looking at the ethical and legal implications for this expanding definition of the field, and how that expansion will lead to an increasingly complex set of laws and regulations for PR practitioners to consider in their practice.

Chapter 3 analyzes the relationship between law and public relations by examining the philosophical underpinnings of each. The chapter begins with an acknowledgement of how the two fields work together in a symbiotic way for clients, frequently providing comprehensive counsel to solve reputational and image problems. There is an overview of the way that lawyers and PR practitioners view communication, and the role communication plays within crisis.

Building from that analysis. the chapter examines the litigation process to demonstrate how legal advocacy differs from that found in public relations, and why lawyers analyze PR communication in the context of admissible evidence, specifically admission by party opponents. This issue of admission of fault is the basis of a section on the role of apology within PR practice, and how apology creates certain issues for PR communication within a crisis context. Next, the chapter turns to the necessity of law and public relations, and how the professions, though distinct, are necessary for successful client representation. Particular attention is paid to the ethical issue of PR practitioner–client confidentiality, and how the legal recognition of that right does not automatically attach to PR professionals without a formal relationship with attorneys. The chapter concludes by acknowledging the distinction between lawyers and PR practitioners while also calling for increased collaboration between the two professions.

Chapter 4 examines the large area of transparency within PR practice. A frequently used term, transparency is subject to much debate because it is an approach that has various levels. A word with a nebulous definition, transparency in the field is frequently overused within ethical discussions of communication practice as a cure-all for reputational problems. This chapter explores the legally mandated transparency of the field of public relations by looking at the mandatory disclosures that must be made in paid communication. This analysis looks at the regulations of the Federal Trade Commission (FTC) in relation to truth in advertising—that is, paid communication—as well as how these regulations are designed to bolster consumer confidence. Issues including substantiation, puffery, regulation of brand influencers, and endorsement disclosures are discussed at length. The chapter pays close attention to paid endorsements and influencers within social media, and how federal regulation has focused on this form of communication to ensure transparency. Next, the chapter examines financial transparency, specifically the regulations of the Securities and Exchange Commission (SEC) with publicly traded companies and transparency within financial reports issued to shareholders. The chapter concludes with suggestions for how PR practice can embrace transparency in its communication with diverse publics, and how this legally mandated transparency establishes a baseline for disclosure practices.

Chapter 5 examines the issues of reputation management, and how this subfield of PR practice is affected by a host of interconnected laws and regulations meant to protect reputations. The chapter provides analysis of defamation, specifically defamation of public figures, officials, and organizations. Specific attention is paid to the difficulty these types of plaintiffs have in bringing successful lawsuits, and how the actual malice standard they must prove creates a significant barrier to legal relief. The chapter also examines how media relations is affected by defamation law, and how media behavior can establish proof of actual malice. The chapter next turns to review sites and their role within reputation management. Specific attention is paid to the liability protection that review sites and online businesses have. Following that discussion is an analysis of reputation management issues related to employee speech, examining the issues with social media policies under the National Labor Relations Act (NLRA). Specifically, problematic social media policies are highlighted alongside their specific legal violations. The chapter concludes with an analysis of the ethical solutions to reputational problems, and how PR practice may have a unique place because legal remedies to reputational problems frequently exacerbate the underlying issue.

Chapter 6 examines the evolving issue of privacy law. The chapter presents a historical account of how privacy development grew in tandem with technological innovation. It then introduces major federal privacy laws alongside privacy torts of appropriation, public disclosure of private facts, and intrusion upon seclusion. The chapter also discusses EU privacy laws because they frequently serve as benchmarks for companies operating in a global market. Specific attention is paid to the EU law of the right to erasure, commonly referred to as the right to be forgotten, and how that law created a cottage industry around online reputation management. Additionally, the chapter examines how transnational data sharing, frequently in the realm of big data analytics, affects how U.S. and EU organizations interact. The chapter concludes with a discussion of how privacy has changed in the 2020s and how AI technology is changing the nature of privacy again for many in the communication field.

Chapter 7 presents an overview of intellectual property (IP) issues affecting public relations practice with a specific focus on copyright, trademark, and trade secrets. The chapter begins with an overview of the requirement of copyright, specifically the types of work protected under copyright and the rights that copyright owners possess. In this analysis, the chapter provides the foundations of infringement and an overview of fair use, with a particular focus on how fair use has dramatically changed with recent U.S. Supreme Court action. The analysis next turns to trademark, focusing on trademark strength and its application to brand identity. Trademark infringement is discussed as well as the issue of trademark genericity and abandonment. The chapter then examines trade secrets by providing an outline of trade secret law, but also looks at how trade secret protections can apply to client lists and media plans. The chapter concludes with an ethics discussion of intellectual property and when to use fair use, how plagiarism relates to copyright, and global issues within IP law.

Chapter 8 concludes the book by examining future legal issues affecting communication practice, specifically AI. The chapter begins with major themes of public relations and the law, examining how the fields are so interconnected. Next, the chapter examines the role of technology and the law, specifically focusing on how AI use within public relations must be tempered with ethical and legal considerations. There is a discussion of how legal standards are evolving for AI, and how the next decade AI's normalization within PR practice will create a new communication reality for practitioners. The chapter next turns to the importance of ethical decision making within public relations, and how PR practitioners are poised to determine the ethical uses of this new technology in the remaining years of the 2020s. Chapter 8 argues that due to the lack of legal standards for new technology in the twenty-first century, PR practitioners are in a unique position to influence the outcome of how AI and other technologies are utilized and normalized within practice. The chapter concludes with suggestions for major areas of law that will likely transform in the coming years, and the role PR practitioners have in that process.

As with any book, there are many people who have helped me produce this project. I want to thank Rowman & Littlefield for allowing me to bring this project to fruition, and specifically Natalie Mandziuk and Yu Ozaki, whose feedback and patience made this book possible. I also want to thank the anonymous external reviewers of this book, and John Santoro, professor of communications at New York University and retired VP of stakeholder communications at Pfizer, for his excellent feedback on several chapters. I also want to thank Holly Hall, J.D., APR, professor of strategic communication at Arkansas State University, and Kathy Fitzpatrick, J.D., APR, professor and director of the ZImmerman School of Advertising and Mass Communication at the University of South Florida, for their kind endorsements of this book. I wish to give special acknowledgement to Robert Denton Jr., emeritus director of the School of Communication at Virginia Tech, for listening to ideas in formulating this book and suggesting I take this proposal to Rowman & Littlefield. I also want to acknowledge Virginia Tech and the School of Communication, which played instrumental roles in providing me the time and resources for this book's completion. I also thank the Virginia Tech Library and its wonderful librarians for tracking down materials, however difficult, to make this book more comprehensive and complete.

I wish to thank my wife, Anne Carroll Myers, who has always been a steadfast supporter when I take on these large projects. She has been there through my entire academic research journey, and her support (and editing) has always made this work possible. Finally, I would be remiss if I did not acknowledge my daughter, Cayce Anne Myers, who has allowed me to work on this project uninterrupted (for the most part). Accordingly, this book is dedicated to her.

DISCUSSION QUESTIONS

1. Why is it important for public relations practitioners to have knowledge of the law?

2. Why do the law and ethics complement each other? How are they different? How are they the same?

3. Think of a time when you faced a situation where you had to make a tough decision. Why did you make that decision? What informed you on what to do?

CASE SCENARIO

Imagine you are a PR practitioner who is working for a client who owns several hotels. The client has a robust social media presence and allows reviews on their Facebook page. One day, you notice a highly critical review about one of the hotels. The criticism states that the hotel lost a client reservation and placed them in a room with two queen beds instead of a room with one king-sized bed, which is what they originally reserved. In the comments following the post, other clients start complaining about the hotel, including room rates, room service, housekeeping, and parking. What should you do as a PR practitioner? What if the hotel asks you to delete the post and block the user? Should you do this? Can you do this legally? What should you do ethically? (See chapter 5 for more about reputation management and public relations).

Legal Requirements and Ethical Expectations

OVERVIEW: TO FULLY UNDERSTAND THE COMPLEXITY OF THE LAW'S impact on the profession, this chapter examines the sources of law with a particular focus on legal interpretation. This explanation is coupled with a discussion of ethical sources from philosophies to professional codes. The chapter argues that law and ethics are distinct but work together to create sound judgment and decision making in the public relations profession.

OBJECTIVES:

- Detail the sources of law in the United States, specifically, case law, statutes, constitutions, administrative laws, international law, and private law.

- Explain the power of each source of law as well as the philosophical approaches to each.

- Discuss the sources of modern ethics from Western philosophies to professional codes of ethics.

- Provide an explanation of how law and ethics work together to inform modern public relations practice.

Public relations practitioners must do the right thing. That means telling the truth, adhering to the standards of the profession, and keeping publics' best interest, however defined, in mind when creating content, developing relationships, or communicating with stakeholders. Doing the right thing frequently means staying within bounds of the law. Similarly, doing the right thing frequently means staying within the bounds of industry, professional, and personal ethics. However, the problem with all these legal and ethical boundaries is that the law and ethics aren't the same thing. The conflation of the two frequently provide confusion over what a practitioner should do in each situation. Consider the following scenario.

Suppose you are a PR practitioner working for a company that has recently experienced major reputational problems. There are ongoing issues with allegations of sexual harassment in the workplace, and there is one sector of the company that has major financial issues. All of this has led to a lowered public trust in the company, and a decline in sales as criticisms of the company have gone viral. You are hired to manage this PR crisis. After receiving the account, you decide you need to research the corporate culture of your client. You do this by conducting a series of one-on-one interviews with the company's executives. During one of these interviews, a senior vice president makes a startling disclosure. He says, "You know . . . all of this was totally preventable. The company knew about those sexual harassment claims and did nothing. And the financial stuff . . . what did the company expect when they could see the issues in the internal reports? It was there in black and white. The higher-ups just chose to ignore it!"

You are now in a position where you know of admissions by the company about their malfeasance, and you are struggling with how to craft a campaign. Soon after your client conversation, another problem arises. You are subpoenaed by one of the plaintiffs in the sexual harassment suit. Their lawyers want you to give a deposition on what you know about the company, and what has been disclosed to you as PR counsel. The question emerges: Do you provide all the information you have during the deposition? Lying under oath is a crime, punishable by prison. Telling your client's confidences is a violation of most PR codes of ethics. Refusing to comply with the subpoena subjects you to contempt of court. What do you do, follow the law, or follow your ethics? It's a bad position to be in, and hopefully most practitioners will never find themselves in this situation. However, this hypothetical scenario shows the real difficulty of law and ethics and the contours of each. Sometimes law and ethics are not necessarily the same—sometimes they are opposites—and knowing the difference can sometimes make all the difference.

In this chapter, the laws and ethics affecting public relations are examined, and the sources of each are explored. The chapter begins with philosophical underpinnings of law versus ethics. Next, the sources of law in the United States are explored, including case law, statutory law, constitutional law, administrative international law, and private law. From that basis, the chapter examines ethics both from the industry codes that shape behavior and the philosophical underpinnings of professional ethics. From those ethical perspectives, the chapter introduces various approaches to ethical decision making, noting that the imperfect process of decision making does at least provide practitioners the ability to better understand the ethical choices they may face as twenty-first-century practitioners. The chapter concludes with contemporary issues of ethics and law that PR practitioners will face in the decades to come.

LAW VERSUS ETHICS

"It's the law," is a phrase most, if not all, people have heard or said. But where does the law we talk about come from? The word "law" includes a lot of complex sources of governance. The *Merriam-Webster Dictionary* defines law as "a rule of conduct or action prescribed or formally recognized as binding or enforced by a controlling authority."[1] However, the law is more complex in its application. Civil violations of the law result in lawsuits where money damages are sought. Criminal violations of the law result in indictments where fines or prison time is sought by the government. In most cases the law is enforced by a governmental entity, such as the police, government agencies, and courts. However, in civil cases the law is enforced by individuals, with some exceptions, who sue someone for a violation of the law. For PR practitioners looking for guidance from the law on what to do, what to avoid, how to defend their property rights, or when to sue, knowing where to look for the "law" is half the battle.

By contrast, ethics is something more nuanced. The practice of public relations is steeped in ethics, as the professionalization of public relations is largely predicated on ethical standards of behavior. Ethics, writ large, come from a variety of sources—experiences, organizations, industry standards, religion, and philosophical traditions, just to name a few. Merriam-Webster defines ethics as "a set of moral principles: a theory or system of moral values."[2] Notice here how the dictionary uses the term "morals" to define ethics. Morality is related to ethics because morals deal with what's "right" or "wrong." Twentieth-century scholar William Durant wrote that "ethics is the study of ideal conduct; the highest knowledge, said Socrates, is the knowledge of good and evil, the knowledge of the wisdom of life."[3] For many, ethics is more visceral than that. It is the gut check. The ability to look your clients and peers in the eye. Ethics provides the guidelines that, if followed, give us the ability to sleep well at night.

Ethics, however, is frequently associated with larger structured approaches to issues, frequently established by organizational codes. For example, the American Bar Association (ABA) publishes the *Model Rules of Professional Conduct* that is established for lawyers and deals with a variety of scenarios that the legal profession faces, from conflict of interest to client interaction. The Public Relations Society of America (PRSA) has its Code of Ethics and the PRSA Member Statement of Professional Values, which details the responsibilities of PR practitioners including transparency, honesty, and responsible advocacy.[4] These codes are ethical guides for the profession, and their elasticity is deliberate, so the codes have longevity and applicability to a variety of scenarios. Their content is made to enhance the profession and to provide guardrails for professional conduct. However, unlike law, their enforcement—like all professional codes—is done by the organization itself, if at all.

Law and ethics overlap. Some of the rules in the ABA *Model Rules of Professional Conduct* or the PRSA Code of Ethics are reflected in the law. For example, many professional codes of ethics include a statement about honesty. The Page Principles, a set of ethical guidelines established by the Arthur Page Society, state "tell the truth" as the first professional standard for PR professionals.[5] However, truth telling has more enforcement than a professional society. The law also embraces truth telling. Defamation laws exist as a deterrent to telling lies about others, and if an individual is the victim of a malicious lie that causes reputational harm, they can sue the liar for money damages. Truth in advertising is a hallmark of creating a confident consumer society. Mandatory disclosures in financial transactions provide for market economies that are more stable, profitable, and beneficial to the public.

However, there are times when ethics and law are at opposite ends of the spectrum. Think back to the scenario at the beginning of this chapter. A PR practitioner is facing a situation where they had been subpoenaed by an individual and were asked to reveal sensitive information about a client. Almost any professional code is going to place a value on client confidences. For example, the PRSA Code of Ethics has a section entitled "safeguarding confidences," which expressly states, "A member shall: Safeguard the confidences and privacy rights of present, former, and prospective clients and employees."[6] However, in the United States there is no law that provides exclusive legal protection for PR practitioner–client communication. It is simply not recognized, and in a situation where a PR practitioner is asked to reveal client confidences or be held in contempt of court, the PR practitioner is at a legal and ethical paradox—break the law or break your code of ethics. Now, there are more nuances this situation. In some cases, if a PR practitioner is working with an attorney for a client's benefit, then attorney–client privilege, which is universally recognized in U.S. law, extends to the practitioner. The International Association of Business Communicators (IABC) Code of Ethics is perhaps the best example of anticipating this dilemma. The code states, "protect confidential information while acting within the law."[7] In sum, these scenarios do not allow for easy decision making. They represent the difficulty of reconciling what is right, what is ethical, what is legal, and what is expected.

Sources of Law

PR practitioners work in a field that is subject to complicated laws. Because of that, it is important to note that "the law" as it is commonly described is not a uniform system of rules and regulations. Instead, it is more diffused, especially in the United States. There are generally six sources of law: case law, statutory law, constitutional law, administrative law, international law, and private law, such as contracts. Each of these sources of law has its own source, and those sources include various levels of government such as the federal and state courts, federal and state legislatures, federal and state agencies, federal and state constitutions, international treaties, and private entities, which includes individual persons and organizations. There are specific areas of law that only one specific entity controls. For example, federal courts have exclusive jurisdiction in lawsuits where the case involves a disagreement between two or more states. State laws typically have statutes prohibiting certain type of personal crimes. Agencies such as the Federal Trade Commission (FTC) specialize in issues concerning consumer protection, specifically in areas like advertising and antitrust. Being able to identify legal problems is as important as identifying solutions.

Common Law

In the United States, the common law tradition is one of the most important and multidimensional aspects of law creation. Common law systems use case law, or appellate judicial decisions, as legal precedent. Those precedents have the force of law within their jurisdictions. Rooted in the medieval legal system of England, common law establishes precedent based on the concept of stare decisis, the concept that once a judge issues a decision, that decision is the law unless overturned. In the United States, case law is discussed regularly in the media, typically in the form of U.S. Supreme Court decisions. For example, famous cases in Supreme Court history such as *Marbury v. Madison*, *Brown v. Board of Education*, and *Miranda v. Arizona* are legal decisions that established various legal precedents in the United States.[8] Stare decisis means these decisions, once rendered, are "law" until they are overturned by a different case. For example, the controversial political case law of *Roe v. Wade*, decided in 1973, was the law in the United States until it was overturned by the Supreme Court in 2022 in *Dobbs v. Jackson's Women's Health Organization*.[9]

Despite media coverage of "hot button" court decisions, case law in the United States is not just decided by the U.S. Supreme Court. There is a federal and state court system in the United States, all of which produce appellate legal decisions that serve as case law. However, unlike the Supreme Court, these lower appellate court decisions are only law in their given jurisdictions. There are 11 federal appellate circuits that encompass multiple states plus the District of Columbia Circuit and Federal Circuit, and can only create case law for their circuit jurisdictions.[10] For example, a state supreme court's decisions are only case law in that state. To complicate matters, in some states there are multiple appellate courts, typically an intermediate court of appeals and state supreme court.[11] Both of those appellate courts can create case law that is binding on their jurisdiction, but a state supreme court can overturn its intermediate appellate court. Judges also vary in number on appellate courts. Since 1869, the U.S. Supreme Court has had nine justices. Federal appellate courts typically hear cases with only three judges, but for certain cases heard en banc, all the federal appellate judges for that circuit hear the case (typically fifteen).[12] States have a variety of appellate judges that depend on a variety of factors including workload. Table 1.1 summarizes the differences between federal and state courts.

An appeal is always about a question of law, not fact. So, case law typically addresses highly important legal issues of constitutionality of law, judicial errors at trials, or statutory interpretation. Appellate courts are not finders of fact; that is the responsibility of trial courts (discussed in chapter 2). However, all appellate courts deal with cases or legal issues that originate at the trial court level. For instance, suppose a PR firm runs a campaign that includes defamatory content about a politician. The politician sues the firm for defamation in trial court (in this case, probably state trial court). The politician wins the suit, but the PR firm's attorney thinks the case should be appealed because the court applied the wrong standard of law. That issue of the standard of law, not the underlying defamation claims, would be the issue the appellate court would decide. The decision of that appellate court would be case law, which could be used as law in another case.

This case law development is why PR practitioners should pay attention to court cases in their jurisdiction of practice and at the U.S. Supreme Court. For example, in 2023 a major Supreme Court decision was published in *Andy Warhol Foundation for the Visual Arts v. Goldsmith*.[13] That

Table 1.1 Federal and State Courts

	Federal	State
Judges	Governed by Article III of the U.S. Constitution. Judges on the U.S. District Court, Circuit Court of Appeals, and U.S. Supreme Court are appointed by the president and confirmed by the Senate. Article III judges serve for a life term and can be removed only by impeachment. Other federal judges such as U.S. bankruptcy judges, U.S. magistrates, and federal administrative law judges are appointed by different processes. These appointments do not require confirmation by the Senate.	Varies by state and can include appointment or election or a combination of both. Most state judges have set terms for which they can be reappointed or re-elected. The appointment of judges is sometimes done by a state's governor with the help of a commission that provides a selection for judges.
Court Type	The federal system has 94 U.S. District Courts (trial court), 13 U.S. Circuit Courts of Appeal, and the U.S. Supreme Court. The federal court system also includes the U.S. Magistrate Courts, U.S. Court of Claims, U.S. Court of International Trade, and U.S. Bankruptcy Courts. Additionally, federal agencies such as the Social Security Administration, Federal Energy Regulatory Commission, and Federal Communications Commission.	State courts are structured similar to federal courts with a state trial court, intermediate appellate court, and state supreme court.* The names for these courts vary by state. State trial courts go by different names such as superior court, district courts, or circuit courts. Famously, New York's trial court is called the New York Supreme Court and the highest appellate court of New York is the New York Court of Appeals. States also have specific courts that handle only one type of case such as probate courts, juvenile courts, magistrate courts, or family courts. States also have administrative law judges having varied levels of authority based on state law.

Appeals	Appeals in federal courts go through the federal appeals system and can be appealed all the way to the U.S. Supreme Court. However, the Supreme Court must grant certiorari to hear a case.	Appeals in state courts go through the state appeals system, typically an intermediate court of appeals and state supreme court. Cases may be appealed from state supreme courts to the U.S. Supreme Court. However, the Supreme Court must grant certiorari to hear a case from a state supreme court.
Types of Cases Heard	Cases that involve: • constitutional issues • foreign treaties • federal criminal laws • federal civil laws, e.g., copyright infringement • disputes between parties in different states (this can include state law issues) • admiralty • bankruptcy • habeas corpus	Cases that involve: • contract disputes • family law issues (divorce, child custody) • state criminal laws (ranging from misdemeanors to capital felonies) • torts (including defamation, privacy torts)

Notes: For a comprehensive breakdown of federal and state court duties, see "Comparing Federal and State Courts," United States Courts, accessed January 20, 2024, https://www.uscourts.gov/about-federal-courts/court-role-and-structure/comparing-federal-state-courts. It is important to note that this chart is an overview of court differences. The types of cases heard are more complex than the chart provides because of the various rules of civil procedure and federal removal under 28 U.S.C. §1441 where state and federal law claims are intertwined, or where the defendant is a foreign state. Similarly, 28 U.S.C. §1332 allows for removal of state law claims to federal court where there is diversity of jurisdiction between the plaintiff and defendant and the amount in controversy exceeds $75,000.

*Nine states have no intermediate court of appeals: Delaware, Maine, Montana, New Hampshire, Rhode Island, South Dakota, and Wyoming.

case involved an interpretation of fair use and its application to transformative use and commerciality. The decision marked a significant change in how fair use analysis would apply in commercial cases. However, that case, like all cases, began with a lawsuit in a trial court, in this case the

U.S. District Court for the Southern District of New York. That case was appealed from the District Court to the U.S. Court of Appeals for the Second Circuit, a federal circuit that includes New York, Connecticut, and Vermont. Then that decision was appealed to the U.S. Supreme Court. This process is not only long, but expensive. The case took approximately six and a half years until Goldsmith prevailed at the Supreme Court, and she had spent more than $2 million of her own money to defend her 1981 copyright.[14]

This backstory of *Andy Warhol Foundation for the Visual Arts v. Goldsmith* illustrates another practical aspect of case law. In civil cases it is very difficult to take cases through the appellate process because of the cost. Parties in a civil case, unlike a criminal case, do not have a right to appointed counsel. They must pay their own legal fees and costs. The trial process is equally expensive. This expense explains why there are fewer trials than settlements; the latest estimate is that 95 percent of cases are settled out of court prior to the trial.[15] Appeals are even fewer, with the Supreme Court hearing only between 100 to 150 cases a year from the more than 7,000 petitions it receives.[16] Moreover, the power of stare decisis, the Latin term meaning "let the decision stand," is a powerful factor in appellate law. Because of that, appellate courts attempt to follow their own precedent closely in deciding cases to provide for logic and predictability in the law. In addition, the Supreme Court also follows a philosophical approach known as the constitutional avoidance doctrine, which essentially is the idea that the court will decide a case on something other than constitutional grounds first so as not create changes to the interpretation of the U.S. Constitution. All of this means that courts are aware of their own power and impact on changes in the law. For the most part, courts attempt to not make drastic changes, if possible, to provide predictability and consistency in American law.

Appellate judges at the federal level are nominated by the President of the United States and confirmed by the U.S. Senate. Those judges can serve for life without any process for reappointment. Removal from the court occurs either by impeachment, retirement, or death. At the state level, appellate judges may be appointed or elected depending on the laws of the state. Those judges typically are not elected for life but are re-elected for terms. While much criticism is made about the life tenure of Article 3 federal judges, the political process of state judges is equally criticized.

Much is made about the politics of judges, and how the judicial branch of government operates in a political way. The term "legislating from the bench" is sometimes a criticism made about appellate judges who create new case law that create radical changes and have great impact to society. So-called activist judges are also said to use their position to fulfill a political agenda. The media frames much of the Supreme Court's decisions this way, especially with the narrative of 5–4 decisions in which the justices break on ideological grounds. However, that narrative is not totally accurate, with roughly one-third of the decisions by the Supreme Court being unanimous.[17] Although split decisions are on the rise, especially post-2020 when there is a conservative-leaning, six to three Supreme Court, the statistic on unanimity illustrates that not all decisions the court makes are the type of ideologically charged cases that would lend themselves to conservative–liberal decisions. This is even more true for lower appellate courts at the federal and state level that handle a much higher volume of cases than the Supreme Court, which has the power to hear or not hear cases through their process of certiorari (a process of allowing a case to be heard). In 2023, U.S. federal courts heard 21,837 civil appeals and criminal appeals topped 9,894. That is in addition to the 4,450 agency appeals heard. Still, that is a small amount compared to the filings in U.S. District Court, the trial courts, which had 353,170 civil and criminal filings (down 8 percent from the year before) with more civil than criminal cases.[18] These statistics mean that the 100 to 150 cases the Supreme Court hears are going to be highly rarified cases that touch on some type of major legal issue. That is why the decisions at that level may be more politically and socially charged and have greater societal impact.

Constitutional Law

Constitutional law is a major part of determining the legality of a particular law or regulation. In the United States, the U.S. Constitution is the supreme constitution, and all federal laws must adhere to it. States also have constitutions, and while they can provide extra constitutional rights to their citizens, they may not provide fewer constitutional rights than what is provided for in the U.S. Constitution. Currently the Constitution has 7 articles and 27 amendments. The seven articles each address a specific area: Article 1 (legislative branch and how laws are made), Article 2 (executive branch and qualifications), Article 3 (legislative branch, judicial review, and jurisdictions), Article 4 (relationships between states and citizenship between states), Article 5 (constitutional amendment process), Article 6 (supremacy clause establishing the U.S. Constitution as supreme law), and Article 7 (ratification process of the U.S. Constitution).[19] While this may seem like an academic point, these articles have major implications for PR practice. For instance, Article 1, section 8, clause 8 establishes the right of copyright, something the framers of the Constitution were keenly interested in, especially because they were creators of copyright themselves.

The 27 amendments of the U.S. Constitution address various rights. The first 10 amendments are known as the Bill of Rights: First Amendment (speech, religion, assembly), Second Amendment (arms), Third Amendment (prohibits quartering troops in private homes), Fourth Amendment (prohibits unreasonable search and seizure), Fifth Amendment (criminal defendant rights, prohibits self-incrimination and double jeopardy), Sixth Amendment (criminal defendant right to public and speedy trial, jury of peers, right to counsel), Seventh Amendment (right to jury trial in federal civil cases), Eighth Amendment (prohibits cruel and unusual punishment, prohibits excessive bail and fines), Ninth Amendment (protects against rights not enumerated in the Constitution), and Tenth Amendment (limits powers of the federal government to those enumerated by the U.S. Constitution).[20] Since the Constitution originally applied to the federal government, these 10 amendments did not originally apply to the states. However, since the passing of the Fourteenth Amendment in 1866, several, but not all, of the first 10 amendments also apply to states through a process called incorporation. Currently the First, Second, Fourth, Fifth, Sixth, Seventh, and Eighth Amendments have been incorporated. The Third, Ninth, and Tenth Amendments have not. What all of this means is constitutionally, amendments that apply to communication, namely the First Amendment, apply to the federal and state regulations in the field.

Philosophical Approaches to Case Law

There are philosophical approaches that appellate judges apply to many of the constitutional issues they analyze. While lower appellate courts are bound to follow the precedent set forth by higher courts, for example, the U.S. Court of Appeals for the First Circuit must follow the precedents of the U.S. Supreme Court, there are instances where novel issues are addressed. At the highest level, the Supreme Court addresses cases that have a high level of novelty that likely have major constitutional implications. Because of this, philosophical approaches to analysis are important to understand. While a case may have implicit or explicit political overtones, courts do not decide cases based on pure politics. The legal rationales provided are rooted in larger philosophical understandings of the law. Some of these major constitutional philosophies are textualism, originalism, structuralism, doctrinarism, pragmatism, and living constitutionalism.

To understand the political culture of legal decision making, it is important to have a working knowledge of how philosophical approaches work. Those in the communication field are affected, especially in First Amendment cases, by these philosophical approaches. One of the most discussed approaches is textualism. The philosophy of textualism is a conservative interpretive philosophy that argues the plain text of the law without looking at the intent behind the drafter's words. Textualism is not only concerned with looking at the absolute words in the law (that is the approach found in strict constructionism). Rather, textualists look at the plain meaning of the law, such as a statute, in concert with the time at which it was written. Going beyond the text, such as looking at legislative history including legislative debates, is impermissible according to textualists, as that is not part of law.[21]

A philosophy related to textualism is originalism, which looks at the original intent of the framers when interpreting the Constitution. The two approaches, while used by conservatives, are not interchangeable. Originalism is a constitutional interpretive theory advanced by conservative legal thinkers and jurists, notably the late Supreme Court Justice Antonin Scalia, that argues the meaning of words are fixed in a specific period. Because of that, originalism looks at legal issues, specifically constitutional ones, from the lens of the original intent. Justice Scalia's 2008 decision in *District of Columbia v. Heller*, which evaluated the constitutionality of Washington, DC gun laws considering the Second Amendment, is an example of originalist analysis of the law.[22]

Pragmatism is a judicial philosophy at odds with originalism and textualism. In this tradition, a jurist looks at the law in context with the current times considering contemporary needs and issues.[23] In this sense, pragmatism has an essence of changing public opinion in its judicial approach. Critics argue it makes for unpredictable outcomes and shifting legal standards. However, the philosophy is outcome based and cases that use this philosophy are more concerned with the result of the case rather than internal legal logic. Legal pragmatism has long roots in the judicial system with Justice Oliver Wendell Holmes, who served on the Court from 1902 until 1932, being a large proponent of the philosophy.[24] Today the approach is largely associated with jurists, such as Judge Richard Posner of the U.S. Court of Appeals for the Seventh Circuit, whose interpretation of constitutional issues take into account contemporary attitudes and beliefs.

Another judicial philosophy is living constitutionalism, which argues that as a living document, the U.S. Constitution should be subject to different interpretations based on the changes in society. The landmark abortion case *Roe v. Wade* is a classic example of living constitutional philosophy with the U.S. Supreme Court holding that the Fourteenth Amendment's Due Process clause protects the right to an abortion. That right was inferred from the interpretation of the ban on the government "depriving any person of life, liberty, or property without due process of law."[25] In this case, liberty was interpreted to mean privacy and, in turn, the right to abortion access. This type of interpretation is at odds with an originalist or textualist perspective. An originalist would argue that the drafters of this clause never intended for it to include privacy or abortions, as the Fourteenth Amendment was a post–Civil War amendment enacted in 1868 meant to establish the citizenship of the formerly enslaved in the United States, providing due process under the law and giving them equal protection under the law.

Other approaches to judicial interpretation of the Constitution include moral and ethical interpretivism, which argues that moral and ethical principles should inform the decision making of courts.[26] Doctrinarism is yet another view that advocates that stare decisis should always be deferred to in application and interpretation of law. Structuralism is a philosophy that looks at the construction of the Constitution and the relationship between the parts of the document to create a holistic interpretation of constitutionality.[27]

What does this mean to those looking to the law as it applies to communication? These philosophies demonstrate that legal interpretation is not a science. It is rooted in a philosophical interpretation that varies. Just as each lawsuit has two sides, judicial interpretation varies depending on the judge. The law is not a book of concrete answers. Most of the time, the interpretation of legal precedents will be a byproduct of the interpretive decisions of the courts. To further complicate matters, there are few, if any, purists in legal interpretation. Jurists may use an amalgamation of philosophies to interpret the law and apply the Constitution. This is what makes for the evolving nature of court decisions, and why legal scholars and the public watch what courts decide.

Statutory Law

Statutory law is the law made through a political process in which legislatures pass bills that are then signed into law by an executive, for example, a governor or president. The process in which bills become law is complex and varies depending on the rules the legislature has for review. Statutory changes occur at a glacial pace because of increased polarization in the United States, and frequently what the media covers as a change in the law at the federal level is something that is the result of an executive order or agency regulations. Take, for example, the rapid evolution of artificial intelligence and the way laws are trying to address the negative consequences of AI technology for privacy, discrimination, and human decision making. As of this writing, the law on those issues is largely coming from federal agencies and executive orders from the

President of the United States.[28] Congress, by comparison, has conducted inquiries into these areas, but has not passed comprehensive legislation on the topic. There are practical implications for this longevity. Legislation, that is, statutes, have staying power. Executive orders do not. Because of that, PR practitioners or lawyers looking to long-term laws on the governance of any topic need statutory laws to help make decisions about the legalities of their actions and use of AI.

Looking at the political process for statutory creation, it is easy to see why law changes slowly. For example, in the U.S. Congress, bills go through committee reviews before they go to the floor for a vote. The term "dying in committee" is a common euphemism for bills that don't make it out of committee for vote by the full chamber. In bicameral legislatures, that is, legislatures with an upper and lower chamber—usually a House of Representatives and Senate—a bill must be passed in its exact form by both chambers (only Nebraska has one chamber, known as a unicameral legislature). Only then can a bill be presented to the executive to be signed into law. Even then, the executive has the right to veto a bill, thus ending its chance of becoming law. Statutes once enacted are indexed into state or federal codes. For example, federal statutes are in a code known as the United States Code, which currently has 54 titles published by the Office of Law Revision Counsel in the U.S. House of Representatives. States have similar codes in which statutes are published in a state-specific code.

This process is even more complex because, as mentioned above, the process for statutes to become laws is a political one. Political negotiations are frequently part of the process of lawmaking. Committee chairs have a large role in what is considered. There are parliamentary procedural issues, and sometimes straightforward powers like vetoes can be different. For example, according to Article I, section 7, clause 3 of the U.S. Constitution, the President of the United States has veto power that can be overridden by a two-thirds vote of both houses in Congress. Many governors have line-item veto powers where they can veto certain parts of a bill while signing others into law. Even more complex is how legislatures reconcile the items in similar yet distinct bills passed in the House and Senate through a process called a conference committee. All of this is done also within a system where lobbyists are trying to influence the outcome of a vote.

To nonlawyers, it may seem that statutory codes provide a clear-cut answer to legal questions. However, that is not always the case. Statutory interpretation is a major component of case law development. Judges and lawyers frequently struggle to interpret what the true meaning of a statute is, especially if the statute is unclear or silent on an issue. Statutes are also subject to the U.S. Constitution and state constitutional analysis. Sometimes courts strike down statutes for being a violation of a certain section of a constitution.

When interpreting a statute, there are some philosophical and interpretive conventions that are followed by judges and lawyers. The overall goal of statutory interpretation is to know what was meant by the law itself. One of the plainest forms of interpretation is a literal interpretation, which is the plain meaning of the text itself.[29] A related concept is the fixed meaning interpretation, where a statutory word's definition is fixed as the meaning of the time in which it was written.[30] When looking at words within the statute, one approach is *noscitur a sociis*, Latin for "known by its associates," which looks at a word in context with the works surrounding it or other words closely associated with the word in question.[31]

Purposivism, or purpose approach, is an interpretive philosophy where a judge looks at the purpose of the statute itself.[32] The context of the law is important in purposivism because it demonstrates the true meaning of the law. The issue with purposivism is that it uses nonlegal materials, such as legislative histories and debates, to determine the legal meaning of a term. An adherent of *noscitur a sociis* would argue purposivism ignores the fact that legislatures, when creating laws, had the opportunity to put in whatever definitions they wanted at the time. Another text-based approach to statutory interpretation is *expressio unius est exclusio alterius*, termed a "negative implication canon," another Latin phrase that means "the expression of one thing is to the exclusion of another."[33]

These interpretive conventions have power even beyond statutes. They can be used to interpret a whole host of content from statutes, federal regulations, or even company policies. For example, suppose there is a policy that says employees of a company must communicate with supervisors on leave requests via email. That policy under *expressio unius est exclusio alterius* excludes other forms of communication for supervisor requests, such as telephone or in-person meetings. Another interpretive approach is the "distributive phrasing canon," the Latin *reddendo singula singulis*, which means "by interpreting distributive terms as distributive."[34] This approach is important because it tries to ascribe meaning and order from a statement that lends itself to broad interpretation. For example, a company has a policy stating that the chief communication officer and the human resources officer have control over communications and employee management. Under *reddendo singula singulis*, the interpretation would be that the chief communication officer has power over communication and the human resources manager has power over employee management.[35] Otherwise, a broad interpretation of the rule would give both the chief communication officer and the human resources manager power over both communications and employee management equally.

Professional communicators know the power of words and their meanings. Interpretations of statutes include many more approaches than what is listed here, but knowing these different approaches can help PR practitioners understand the importance of clarity of the law. It is also important to note that there are devotees of certain statutory interpretations. Certain types of judges or legal systems tend to lend their interpretations to a particular camp over others. However, those professionals involved with statutory regulations should note that there is a wide array of approaches (some not listed in this chapter) that judges can and do use. This makes for interesting legal analysis when facing a novel issue of statutory law.

Administrative Law

PR practitioners regularly work using digital social media and, very recently, AI platforms. All these entities are regulated by administrative law. If a PR practitioner wants to stay up to date on the legal changes that most affect their industry, knowing the alphabet soup of federal agency acronyms and their regulations is essential. The role of government agencies has increased exponentially in the regulation of communication in the past 50 years. Agencies such as the Federal Trade Commission (FTC), National Labor Relations Board (NLRB), Securities and Exchange Commission (SEC), Food and Drug Administration (FDA), and Equal Employment Opportunity Commission (EEOC) create and apply regulations that directly impact communication. States also have agencies that mirror many of the same areas that the federal government regulates.

In the field of communication, agency law is perhaps the most prevalent type of law affecting the field. That is why agency regulations are discussed at length in over half of this book. Social media regulation, for instance, has been a major component of the FTC in the past 20 years. Issues surrounding disclosure, transparency in purchasing, and disinformation have been a mainstay of FTC regulation. Social media policies and workers' rights have been a topic of great interest to the NLRB since the 2010s, and that agency has led the discussion on what is legally permissible to regulate in employee speech. The SEC has a long-standing history of regulating communication related to markets, specifically the quiet period that is required prior to a company listing its stock for the first time, known as an initial public offering (IPO).

Agencies also enjoy a great deal of autonomy in regulating specific areas. When Congress creates an agency, that statute has an enablement clause that provides the agency with the ability to put their regulations into effect. This provides the agency the power to create regulations and set up an adjudicatory process in which to appeal agency decisions. Cases involving procedural due process in agencies allows the agency to create different systems in which issues are resolved. Some of these allow for various levels of internal agency appeals and sets the standard for hearings. Administrative law judges (ALJs) are part of the agency hearing process in many cases. A person wanting to appeal an agency decision must first exhaust all internal agency appeals before their case can be heard at a trial or appellate court.

Agency rulemaking is completed through an internal system that is governed by the Administrative Procedure Act (APA).[36] That act requires an agency to identify a need for a rule. Next the agency drafts a proposed rule, which is then reviewed by the agency leaders, frequently by the Office of Management and Budget (OMB). Next the rule is published in the *Federal Register*, which allows the public a set time frame to comment on the rule, typically 30 to 60 days. Once the comment period is over the rule is eventually published within the *Federal Register* with an enactment date, typically 30 days from publication.

Agency rules can be challenged, but challenging federal agency rules presents unique issues. The approach the U.S. Supreme Court designed for reviewing federal agency rules was set forth in a landmark 1984 case, *Chevron USA v. National Resources Defense Counsel.*[37] In that case, the Supreme Court held that in a challenge to an agency's rule, courts defer to the agency's interpretation of its own rule unless that interpretation is unreasonable. This had led to increased power of agencies; critics argue that this has led to judicial abdication to agency interpretation of rules. The practical result of this decision is that agency power is high, and when dealing with agency interpretations of rules, the agency likely wins when challenged in court. This may change, however, as there are currently legal challenges to this 40-year precedent.[38] However, at the time of this writing, Chevron deference remains intact.

International Law

For PR practitioners—particularly those working in social media, digital communication, AI, or big data—international laws, in the form of non-U.S. laws and treaties, have a major impact on the field. Topics like data privacy and intellectual property are regularly the subject of global standards of practice, which directly impact the digital content production and data analysis that has become a mainstay in PR practice. International law's relationship with domestic U.S. law is complex, and largely follows what is known as a dualist philosophy. That is, domestic U.S. law and international laws are distinct, and they do not formulate a solitary system of governance. This is different than monism, such as is the case in the European Union (EU), where international and domestic law form a singular legal system. There are international legal influences in the United States both directly and indirectly. The U.S. government enters international treaties with other nations that constitute the law, as noted in the Supremacy Clause in the U.S. Constitution.[39] For example, the United States is part of Berne Convention for the Protection of Literary and Artistic Works.[40] Created in 1886, the Berne Convention sets the standards for copyright protection internationally. The United States joined the convention in 1989 and had to change some domestic copyright law to join. There are other international laws, known as executive agreements, such as the U.S.–EU safe harbor network that regulates personal data, which has approximately the same force as a U.S. Senate confirmed treaty. There are also international court decisions, which do not have the same impact on U.S. case law that domestic courts do, but can be influential.

Indirectly, there is the so-called importation of foreign law into the U.S. legal system. The way this works is courts may use foreign legal precedents or philosophies to interpret domestic law. Another way importation occurs is when the economic power of a trading partner is so strong that compliance with their domestic laws is a prerequisite of doing business. This is particularly seen with U.S.-EU trade where EU laws require much stricter forms of privacy than that mandated under U.S. law. Known as the Brussels Effect, the EU's trading power is so great that many countries adhere to EU standards to be able to engage in trade.[41] In the United States the influence of EU law is even seen in state laws, such as in California, which has mirrored many of the privacy protections found in the EU General Data Privacy Regulation (GDPR).[42] As the practice of communication grows more complex with the advent of AI, there should be an expectation among practitioners that the role of international law will increase. Knowing the contours of a global communication marketplace will become more important than it ever has in the field of PR practice.

Private Law

The work of PR practitioners is impacted by private law almost daily. Client contracts, employment contracts, request for proposals, and nondisclosure agreements are examples of how private law impacts and shapes the relationship within communication practice. Despite its importance, private law is an area that many people overlook when thinking about the law, even though it constitutes the most frequent form of lawmaking. Contracts are agreements between parties, individuals, and organizations that enumerate terms of an agreement. When one party breaches the contract, the other party can sue using the court system to enforce it. Damages can be awarded for nonperformance and, in some cases, the contract's terms can be enforced even when there is disagreement. Still, in other situations, contracts that may seem legally enforceable are not because a contract convention was not followed; for example, a contract over a certain amount violates the statute of frauds because it was not written.[43] Other requirements for contracts exist such as capacity to enter a contract, presence of mutual exchange (consideration), genuine agreement without duress or fraud, and legal purpose, that is, a contract to commit a crime cannot be written.

Interpretations of contracts vary according to case. The four corners doctrine of a contract typically govern the interpretation of its meaning. The use of parol evidence, that is, evidence of agreements or discussions that preceded or were contemporaneous with the contract's execution not but explicitly part of a contract, is typically (but not always) prohibited. Other conventions in contract interpretation include tenets such as ambiguity in a contract is interpreted against the drafter,[44] implied terms are interpreted in the way an industry defines them, specific clauses are preferred over general clauses, and the context of an entire contract is part of any interpretation (i.e., no single clause of a contract is interpreted independently from the whole).

There also legal principles that are present in some, but not all, contract laws that protect parties who may be wronged by a strict interpretation of the contract. Promissory estoppel is a principle in law that states that if a person relies on a promise made to his or her detriment, that promise is legally enforceable even when there was no consideration (i.e., exchange) made in the contract. Another principle in equity is unjust enrichment, where one party is unjustly enriched at the expense of another. For example, if an employer overpays the employee, under the employment contract the employee may be required to return the overpaid amount.

It is important to note that contract law in the United States largely assumes the parties are competent to enter into an agreement, especially if those parties are professionals or organizations. Looking at the content of the contract is important because that is the basis for how the agreement will work. Trying to amend a contract after the fact will require agreement between all parties in the contract. Because of that, it is best to negotiate terms upfront and carefully read all the (fine and bold) print.

Sources of Ethics

Public relations ethics are important because practitioners have a host of fiduciary duties to clients, publics, media, fellow practitioners, stakeholders, and the profession itself. Because of this, the actions of PR practitioners are highly informed by ethical principles. As noted in the beginning of this chapter, laws and ethics are different. Unlike laws, which can be rigid applications of rules, ethical codes serve as guardrails for behavior, decision making, and professionalism. Ethical decisions are rooted in a variety of sources such as ethical codes, philosophical traditions, personal values, and formalized decision-making processes.

Codes of Ethics in PR Practice

Ethical codes serve as guideposts for professional conduct. Public relations professionals have multiple codes from a variety of organizations that attempt to provide standards for ethical dilemmas. Codes are not a new phenomenon, however. In ancient Greece, the physician Hippocrates (460–370 BCE) established ethical principles for doctors, which resulted in the modern-day Hippocratic oath and its famous derivative maxim, "first do no harm."[45] By the nineteenth century, ethical codes were established in two learned professions, medicine and law. The American Medical Association (AMA) founded in 1847 and the American Bar Association (ABA) founded in 1878 created codes of ethics for members to follow.[46]

The public relations field has its first major ethical canons published at the turn of the twentieth century. Ivy Lee's Declaration of Principles, published in 1905, was the first attempt to codify the ethical codes of public relations.[47] He advocated for transparency, honest promotions, accurate information, honest dealing, fair dealing, and that public relations had a role to play in the common good of society. It came at a time when American businesses were incorporating the PR practitioner into corporate. Legal regulations at the turn of the twentieth century coincided with the growth of ethical considerations for communicators. Legislation such as the Tillman Act of 1907, which regulated campaign finance, and the establishment of the FTC in 1914 forced American businesses to think in terms of ethics in communication.[48]

Communication ethics were a major issue in the early twentieth century. The 1920s saw some high-profile issues emerge surrounding ethics and communication. From 1928 to 1935 the National Electric Light Association (NELA) was investigated by the FTC because of its communication on public ownership of electric companies. NELA's work in the 1920s was considered the epitome of propaganda, as the association paid professors to write pro-NELA textbooks and give tours of electric companies to gain public support for utility companies.[49] The 1930s saw increased criticism of corporations and their communications. Scott Cutlip and Allen Center, two luminary PR educators, noted that in 1949 *Fortune Magazine* stated that public relations practitioners did not possess the "ethics of a profession."[50] Professional growth in public relations continued in the 1930s and 1940s, with the first public relations professional association, the National Association of Accredited Publicity Directors (NAAPD), founded in 1936.[51] The American Council on Public Relations (ACPR) in 1945 created the *Public Relations Journal* as its official publication, and in 1947 the ACPR merged with the National Association of Public Relations Counsel to form the Public Relations Society of America (PRSA), one of the largest PR member organization in the United States.[52] By 1950 PRSA established its first ethical code, and the revised code was published in 1953, 1959, 1963, 1977, and 1983. In 1962 PRSA established a nine-member Grievance Board, which was changed to the Board of Ethics and Professional Standards (BEPS) in 1983.[53]

PR organizations worldwide developed professional codes through the 1950s and 1960s. PRSA created the Accredited in Public Relations (APR) credential in 1964, which was a PR accreditation that included ethics competency.[54] Country-specific public relations organizations also passed codes of ethics from the 1940s through the early 1960s: PRSA (1947), Canadian Public Relations Society (1948), *Club de la maison de verre* (France, 1950), Public Relations Institute of South Africa (1957), *Deutsche Public Relations Gesellschaft* (Germany,1958), and the Hellenic Public Relations Association (Greece, 1960).[55] Organizations such as the International Public Relations Association (IPRA) establishing the first international code of PR ethics, known as the Code of Athens, in 1965 with amendments in 1968 and 2009.[56] By the early 1970s many countries adopted the Code of Athens, making it a highly influential ethical code. Unlike many public relations codes, the Code of Athens is explicitly tied to human rights and was crafted expressly with the Universal Declaration of Human Rights as a benchmark for communication.[57] Ethics became an issue within PR research, with industry standards being the subject of the Declaration of Barcelona Research Principles published in 2010. Among the research guidelines, the Barcelona Principles states that practitioners should engage in transparent research so results are rooted in ethical measurement that embraces the standards of "integrity, honesty, and openness."[58]

The Philosophy of Ethics

Still, there are other dilemmas where there is neither applicable law nor an ethical code to guide decision making. In these scenarios, philosophical approaches to ethics may guide an PR practitioner's decision. This may include considering ethical decision-making frameworks that are rooted in ethical traditions for consequentialism, nonconsequentialism, and agency. These more esoteric forms of ethical reasoning are rooted in complex philosophical approaches. While these approaches typically are not readily identified by the public or professionals, they do serve as an underpinning of how many professional codes and ethicists think about ethics.

Consequentialism in Public Relations Ethics

Consequentialism is an approach that approaches ethics from the standpoint of the consequences of an action. Approaches within the consequentialist tradition include the common good approach, utilitarianism, and egoism. Common good is an ancient approach to ethics rooted in Platonic and Aristotelian philosophy. The basic premise of ethical decision making is predicated on what type of good can be done for society.[59] The common good is the good of the community. This philosophy can be seen in initiatives, such as public works, that benefit large sectors of a community. There is also a concern with decision making for the betterment of others. This type of ethical approach can be seen in the idea of PR practitioners operating in a manner that is beneficial to various publics, and the idea that PR practitioners have a fiduciary duty to the public to act in an ethical, open, honest, and transparent way.[60]

One major example of Aristotelian common good initiatives is the sustainability movement within companies. PR practitioners play a major role in sustainability efforts by communicating these initiatives to the public and shareholders. The authenticity of these efforts is important, and communicating how sustainability helps a company's image is at the core of many shareholder conversations. These sustainability efforts require long-range planning and prioritization of community, climate, and environment over short-term monetary gains. Companies such as the clothing manufacturer Patagonia have made sustainability a major part of their corporate identity, and this sustainability effort has become infused within their corporate culture, going so far as self-imposing a 1 percent Earth tax on their products, which is then donated to grassroots environmental organizations.[61]

Utilitarianism is perhaps the best-known and used of the consequentialist approaches. Rooted in the teachings of eighteenth-century English philosopher Jeremy Bentham and nineteenth-century English philosophers John Stuart Mill and Henry Sidgwick, utilitarianism advocates that the most correct decision is the one that produces the greatest good.[62] The appeal of this approach is that is allows for ethical decisions when there are large groups of people with divergent viewpoints and needs. Good in the utilitarian tradition is viewed as having equality among all people. To decide, a person only needs to know how the "good" can be maximized. Utilitarianism has been refined over the years, and is subject to many criticisms, chief of which is that, taken to an extreme, utilitarian decisions can lead to outcomes that are wrong and require great sacrifice of those who are not in the majority. Moreover, utilitarianism also discounts the motivations behind actions themselves, with decision makers focusing exclusively on maximized outcomes. However, the impact of utilitarianism in society is immense. In PR practice, utilitarianism is seen as the root of most crisis communication strategies, particularly with product recalls. The famed Tylenol recall in 1982 occurred when product tampering resulted in the cyanide deaths of seven people in the Chicago area. Johnson & Johnson, the owner of Tylenol, made the decision to pull all Tylenol from stores nationwide for fear that consumers could be killed. The decision cost Johnson and Johnson $100 million in 1982, a substantial sum now and even more so then.[63] There was serious discussion of whether the brand Tylenol, then was a top medicine brand in the United States, could survive the negative publicity around the Tylenol murders. However, the brand did survive and rebound in large part because of the decisions of Johnson & Johnson and the corporation's utilitarian approach to pulling products and losing money for the greater good for the whole. In many respects, this underscores the long-term benefits associated with public trust and careful reputation management. That is why the Tylenol case, as its frequently called, has become a mainstay in PR literature.

Egoism is another consequentialist approach that traces its philosophical roots to ancient Greek Sophists, particularly Thrasymachus, who advocated that leaders were infallible. Thomas Hobbes, a sixteenth-century British philosopher, was also in the egoist tradition as was famed author and Russian American libertarian thinker Ayn Rand, who wrote the popular novels *The Fountainhead* (1943), *Atlas Shrugged* (1957), and her appropriately named 1964 book, *The Virtue of Selfishness: A New Concept of Egoism*.[64] In *The Virtue of Selfishness* Rand in a collection of essays argues that a reason-based self-interestedness actually helps society because it allows individuals to achieve uncompromised self-fulfillment and self-sufficiency. For Rand, these qualities actually elevate society because self-sacrifice, charity, and altruism facilitate a passiveness in individuals so they do not reach their full potential.[65]

Contemporary egoism has been associated with a type of cynical nature toward others with self-interestedness being a core characteristic of the approach. However, that is an oversimplification of this philosophical tradition. Instead, the self-interestedness of egoism serves as a tool to create benefits for others by creating a self-sufficiency in society that then allows for greater societal benefits. These ideas can be seen in the laissez-faire economics advocated by economists such as Nobel Prize winner Milton Friedman, who argued that businesses making money for shareholders was the primary goal of any firm. Though not a pure egoist, Friedman advocated for a type of economic approach that promoted self-interest (although he did not advocate for self-interest at the expense of others as a classical egoist would). One major example of his self-interest philosophy is his view of corporate social responsibility (CSR). For Friedman, CSR was a distraction from the core purpose of business, and business and society would be better off if firms focused exclusively on revenue and profit generation.[66] In public relations, an egoist ethical approach would be reflected in campaigns promoting content that appealed to the self-interestedness of the individual and would emphasize that individual self-preservation was the responsibility of all individuals. Similarly, the PR practitioner who emphasized the supremacy of corporate revenue and profits to shareholders would be representing free market egoism.

Non-Consequentialism in Public Relations Ethics

Non-consequentialism is a response to the ends-based focus of consequentialist ethics. For a non-consequentialist, the good or bad result of an ethical process is divorced from the process itself. In other words, a good result may be bad ethics if the result is obtained by unethical means. A major philosophical approach in non-consequentialism is the deontological ethics associated with Immanuel Kant.[67] For Kant, ethical choices were about intentionality of the person. Regardless of the outcome, the universal ethical law—or as he put it, the categorial imperative—that drives all decision making is sacrosanct. Kant famously wrote, "Act only according to that maxim by which you can at the same time will that it should become a universal law."[68] Similarly the Kantian ethical formula can be expressed as "So act as to treat humanity, whether in your own person or in another, always as an end and never as only a means."[69]

What does this mean? Truth telling, for instance, is a popular illustration of Kant's categorial imperative. Telling the truth is a virtue, and lying is not. A person under the deontological approach to ethics never lies, even if the lie would help someone stay out of danger. In obeying this moral law, we have achieved a rational ethical decision. Of course, the criticism of this is the results. Protecting a person from an intruder bent on murdering them requires a lie. For Kant, this result was irrelevant to the ethical purity of deontology.

PR practitioners may think this type of analysis is the type of esoteric discussion that ethics devolves into, making it impractical for those working in industry. However, Kantian ethics has something particularly useful for those in multiple industries. First, Kantian thought and deontology has filtered into mainstream society's thinking. For example, deontology has led to the establishment of many ethical codes because there is an inherent assumption that there are universal right and wrong approaches to ethical issues.[70] It has also emphasized individual reason-based decision making, which is typical of how profession-based ethical guidelines are structured. Deontology is also the basis of many of the ethical approaches that emphasize rights and obligations of individuals.

PR practitioners are frequently confronted with difficult choices that pit the ethics of Kantian deontology against utilitarian outcomes. Nowhere is this more evident than in the conflict between legal counsel and PR practice. Take the example of a product recall. Ethical codes (deontological) may require a transparent result to a dangerous product that may injure consumers. The public relations professional wants immediate disclosure and the issuance of a statement that claims responsibility for the defective product. Conversely, legal counsel may argue (utilitarian) that the product recall may result in massive financial losses, and that an admission of guilt by the manufacturer will serve as direct admission of wrongdoing that will be brought up as evidence in later product-liability lawsuits. These types of conversations are commonplace in the communications world and demonstrate how an otherwise esoteric theory, like

Kantian deontological philosophy, is actual present in many boardroom discussions and decisions.

The Role of the Individual in the Ethical Decision-Making Process

Many decisions in life are not made by ethical codes, but by personal values. In public relations practice, there is literature that talks about doing the right thing. Nowhere is the experience and beliefs of an individual more present than in the world's religions. Religion frequently serves as a moral compass for individuals and their decision making. In eastern religion, the role of harmony in decision making is found in the teachings of Confucius. He stated that a person's virtue is important to all decisions, and virtue ethics requires that an individual create *ren* that encompass virtuous behavior such as benevolence, loyalty, and respect for others.[71] If a person has these qualities inherent within them, they will make better and more ethical decisions. Such decisions bring people into a more perfect harmony with the world by focusing on the needs of the community rather than the individual. Christianity has a similar approach to ethics as a reflection of personal qualities and emulation of the infallible behavior of Jesus Christ including humility, love, integrity, compassion, and justice. Both the Jewish and Christian traditions embrace the prescriptive moral code of the Ten Commandments, which Moses brought forth on Mount Sinai, to bring order to the Israelites. Similarly, in the Muslim religion, teachings of the Quran and Hadith (teachings of Mohammed) require virtuous behavior in action to strive toward righteousness.

Individual morals are frequently the byproduct of religious teachings. There are delineated right and wrong, good, and evil, and righteousness and transgressions. In ethical decision making the morality of the individual decision maker is frequently the core reason why a decision is made. Personal integrity and initial reactions are often the byproduct of a core set of religious or spiritual beliefs that manifest themselves in individual decision making. The perception of a problem and its definition, which is typically the first step in ethical decision making, is frequently framed by these inherent moral characteristics. And it is this morality and values of an individual that is the most likely to remain unchanged through life.

Another contributor to individual perception of ethics is a person's unique life experiences. Individual experience is one of the largest factors in making decisions. The past serves as a roadmap to the present and future, and experience in situations is a standard resource for making decisions.[72] In fact, according to some behavioral scientists, too much reliance on experience can actually be a bad thing because it allows us to use the perspective of the past, which may be flawed in innumerable ways, to understand the present.[73] However, the role of experience and the core values that are inherent to a person are important.

Frameworks for decision making vary by person and industry. Brown University's Science and Technology Studies lists four factors that emerge in ethical decision making: obligation, impermissibility, permissibility, and supererogatory.[74] A sense of obligation to make an ethical decision implies that not only is something good to do, but it is wrong not to do it. For example, a company recalling tainted milk from consumers is the right thing to do, but not conducting a recall is conversely wrong. Impermissibility is the concept that an action is wrong and that not doing the action is right.[75] For example, a communication professional who fabricates evidence of the effectiveness of a drug is doing something wrong. Abstaining from falsehoods and exaggerations is the right thing to do. Permissibility looks at the gray area of ethics. Permissible ethical decisions are neither right nor wrong; they are value neutral. This presents perhaps the most complex area of ethical decision making because this is a value judgment on behalf of the decision maker. For example, a PR practitioner can maintain a social media presence for a company and regularly post updates on multiple platforms. While that is a "good" thing, it is not necessarily bad that certain platforms go unused. That is a judgment on the part of the practitioner and the practitioner's organization. Finally, there is the supererogatory aspect of ethics. Supererogatory is the idea that a person goes beyond the norm in ethical behavior to achieve truly exceptional results. While this is the goal of many professionals, it is aspirational for many.[76] It also presents unique challenges in terms of resources, time, and effort. A classic example in public relations can be found in the CSR efforts of many organizations, particularly those actions that are self-imposed restrictions, such as Patagonia's 1 percent

Earth tax. In the field of public relations, the mentorship programming that goes on within professional organizations or internally within a corporation is an example of going beyond and giving back to the profession. None of these types of behaviors are required, or even expected. There is no ethical obligation to perform them, yet people and organizations consistently engage in supererogatory actions for the benefit of others. There is some evidence that such actions help organizations gain reputation-increasing trust from publics because of altruistic actions that are not related to return on investment (ROI).

The Ethical Decision-Making Process

In the law, the process for legal application is defined by either criminal or civil procedure. The application of law typically follows a standard process and legal transactions usually follow a standardized format, be it an employment contract, settlement agreement, will, or purchase. These standardized processes make legal decision making more straightforward (although litigation does have its surprises). Ethical decision making, however, does not have a standardized approach. There are many applications of ethics to PR decisions, and this chapter will detail a few of those, but this list is nowhere near exhaustive. Many people who make ethical decisions also follow no process. Such decision making is sometimes referred to as instinct or "gut" decisions based on experiences, perceptions, and general mood of the decider. This is not without merit. There are those who believe that making intuitive decisions frequently get good results because their highly developed internal process leads them to make the right choice.[77] In fact, a study by Deloitte states that "emotional fortitude," via an internal assessment process, of CEOs is a major force in its decision making, particularly during high-uncertainty problem solving. This requires a heightened level of self-awareness that takes place during the process of metacognition, which focuses on the "thoughts, intuitions, and feelings" of the decision maker.[78]

Individual ethical decisions in public relations are also rooted in the environment in which public relations is practiced. The psychology of executives is a major aspect of ethical decision making. According to business psychologist Merete Wedell-Wedellsborg, when transgressing ethical boundaries leaders are frequently guided by certain psychological traits of omnipotence (all knowing), cultural numbness (desensitization to the organization's norms of transgression), and justified neglect (ends justify the means).[79] These factors lead to what social scientists refer to as the spiral of silence, which postulates individuals are less likely to share countervailing ideas to a group if they perceive that no one else shares their view. This leads to ethical transgressions because of the unwillingness of individuals to speak up so they can fit in a group dynamic.[80] In essence, the spiral of silence argues that "public opinion as social control" provides both incentives and disincentives for agreement with the majority opinion, especially the opinions of superiors.[81] For example, suppose a company's CEO makes a mistake during a press conference on a minor detail about the company's financial forecast. The CEO is known as a difficult person to work with and is overly sensitive to being corrected. She has an icy relationship with the communications team. Should the company's chief communication officer (CCO) tell her about the mistake? Should she issue a correction? Not doing so would constitute an ethical and legal issue, but the dynamics of omnipotence, cultural numbness, and justified neglect could create an outcome where the CCO says nothing. This is the spiral of silence at work.

Setting aside the internal metacognition of decision making, there are several approaches to ethical decision making. As detailed earlier in this chapter, there are ethical processes rooted in ethical philosophies such as consequentialism, deontology, and virtue ethics. However, there are also more formalized processes. Many of these processes are industry specific. For example, nurses, counselors, human resource officers, and police, just to name a few professions, have guidelines that are provided for ethical decision making.[82] Similarly in the PR industry there are ethical decision-making models, such as the one articulated by the Board of Ethics and Professional Standards (BEPS) in PRSA.[83] That model, written by legal and ethical scholar Kathy Fitzpatrick, gives a six-step process for ethical decision making in a PR context. It states:

1. Define the specific ethical issue/conflict.

2. Identify internal/external factors (e.g., legal, political, social, economic) that may influence the decision.

3. Identify key values.

4. Identify the parties who will be affected by the decision and define the public relations professional's obligation to each.

5. Select ethical principles to guide the decision-making process.

6. Make a decision and justify it.[84]

The six-step process works in concert with the PRSA Code of Ethics, and the fourth step emphasizes the PR practitioner's obligation to key publics and stakeholders. The decision-making process ends with the decision, which leaves it open to the decision maker to have an answer that is justifiable but is ultimately up to their own judgment.

The underlying philosophy of the PRSA model of ethical decision making is found elsewhere. For example, the Josephson Institute, a nonprofit organization dedicated to ethics, outlines seven steps for ethical decision making that begins with thinking about the problem seriously before making quick and poorly planned decisions.[85] Laura Nash created a 12-step model for ethical decision making that was designed to examine ethical question from a diversity of viewpoints that culminated with a decision that was informed, well intentioned, and considerate of the diverse experiences of the decision makers. In a 1981 *Harvard Business Review* article, Nash described her 12 steps as a "process of ethical inquiry that is immediately comprehensible to a group of executives and not predisposed to the utopian, and sometimes anticapitalistic, bias marking of much of the work in applied business philosophy today."[86]

For Nash, the 12-step approach to decision making has a purpose: to analyze the issue from multiple perspectives to gain a fully understanding of the issue. Inherent in her approach is the assumption that ethical decisions are not binary, but are multidimensional problems that require an in-depth understanding. Built into that approach is the recognition that the outcome cannot and likely will not be "one size fits all" and that certain parties may be disadvantaged by the decision. Nash's process begins with problem definition, but the second step requires a business-person to define the problem from a perspective opposite of their own to allow for a comprehensive understanding of the issue. Beyond that, the decision-making process requires examining how the issue occurred, who does the organization, or whom the decision maker is loyal to; analyzing intentional outcomes and who is injured by the decision; and examining what lines of communication are available to the other side, whether the decision will work long-term and who can you tell about this decision, whether your decision will be understood, and whether there are exceptions that should be considered.[87] While not a prescribed decision process, Nash's guidance provides guardrails for ethical discussions, and it serves as a process that turns over ideas and facts to generate a sound result. It also mandates the input of others in the organization, but also provide a boundary to discussion. Nash argued between balancing pure altruism against pure profit motivation. A realistic boundary within ethical discussions provides a balance between the two, which she said would result in a solution that benefitted both sides of the argument.[88]

Of course, these two approaches represent a small subset of ethical solutions. However, they serve as illustrations of two different styles of ethical decision making. Fitzpatrick's approach is process-oriented and leads to a decision based on established ethical principles centered on public relations professionals. Nash's approach is more reflective, taking into consideration a wide array of divergent viewpoints that seek to understand the complexities of a problem and its possible solution at the C-suite level. Both approaches have great merit for PR practitioners. And both approaches demonstrate a respect for the impact of ethical decisions within the communication and business fields. Too often there is the sentiment within all industries that ethical discussions are impractical, esoteric endeavors that do not fully appreciate real-world implications. One important thing to note in ethical decision making is that the outcome is not a guarantee of success. Individual decisions require the decision maker to consider that their ultimate choice may not work. Additionally, ethical decision makers sometimes make unethical choices. The Global Business Ethics Survey in 2021 found that despite widespread support for ethical corporate culture, the pressure to compromise ethics and the observation of ethical transgressions has increased since 2017.[89] In public relations, perception of an organization or action always runs the risk of inaccuracy, particularly given the ease and accessibility of disinformation. Well-intentioned and grounded ethical decisions on complex matters can be interpreted through a variety of lenses, which may not accurately reflect the reality of a situation.

CONTEMPORARY ISSUES AND TENSIONS BETWEEN LAW AND ETHICS

As this chapter shows, law and ethics complement each other. There are many instances where they overlap, but they have distinct differences, especially in their implementation. Law and ethics have fundamental differences in scope, enforceability, implementation, and flexibility. Laws are more rigid and their implementation hinges on the legal system in which an individual or organization is operating. Ethics, by contrast, have more flexibility, and their implementation largely depends on the individual or organization's selection of values. Because of this, it is incumbent for those in the communication field to have a good grasp of both. It requires the PR practitioner to understand the law, but also root themselves in an ethical perspective. The former is based on the area of practice, the latter is based on values.

The biggest issue legally and ethically for any communication professional is an area where there is little law and unsettled ethics. In the 2020s, this is evident in two areas: AI and diversity, equity, and inclusion (DEI). The reason for this uncertainty in both fields is their widespread use and adoption within the communication field. The law either has not fully caught up, as is the case with AI, or is undergoing challenges to its approach and philosophy, as is the case with DEI. Ethical issues abound for both areas of communication, and they serve as examples of the difficulties in reconciling ethics and law in a fast-paced and evolving communication practice.

The proliferation of AI platforms and the widespread acceptance of AI within the communication field has created a situation where ethical judgment is going to be of paramount importance. Part of the reason for this is rooted in the contours between law and ethics. Governments are struggling to develop regulations that will regulate the excesses of AI. Issues such as liability, disinformation, discrimination, privacy, and the role of human decision makers are top of mind for lawmakers. In 2023, President Joseph Biden's administration presented a "Blueprint for an AI Bill of Rights" that addressed many of these issues and pointed to AI as a major concern for the 2020s.[90] Similarly, federal agencies have referred to AI as the next "civil rights frontier," pointing out that the discrimination and bias of AI can lead to unjust consequences. The European Union has also expressed concerns about the role of AI in privacy and as of the time of this writing is crafting laws to regulate privacy rights within AI.[91] Moreover, AI organizations are stating that they are creating AI guardrails to protect users and society from the potentially negative consequences of AI. Despite this concern, AI remains an area that is largely unregulated. It will be up to the ethical norms of each profession to determine how and when it will be used. PR practitioners will have to make some difficult decisions concerning AI and ethics without the mandates of the law. For example, does a practitioner need to disclose to a client that some of the content produced in a campaign is AI generated? What is the due diligence of a PR practitioner to verify the content produced by AI? In what way should PR practitioners use generative AI for ideas, and how does a practitioner charge for those services when AI, not the practitioner, is creating strategy for a campaign? These questions highlight the importance of ethics in considering communication strategy, content, and execution.

DEI initiatives have become a corporate norm in the 2020s, and the growth of DEI programs and officers has brought a large amount of attention to this area of communication. DEI practices are designed philosophically to foster change and awareness on a variety of issues within an organization. The programs and related content include a wide array of issues ranging from inherent bias to accessibility for those with disabilities. The basis of DEI is three pronged, with diversity (cultural, cognitive, experiential), equity (access, opportunity, fair dealing), and inclusion (listening, belonging, environmentally welcoming). As a result, DEI initiatives have a series of outlets that include recruitment, retention, transparency, trainings, mentorship programming, and the establishment of affinity groups, among many other things. Because of the complexity of DEI, it can be described as an ethical and philosophical approach that requires a continual commitment and implementation for an organization. The ethics surrounding DEI involve issues such as inclusion and exclusion, authentic gestures of inclusivity, and a value system that embraces the tenets of diversity. Legally, DEI can be subject to some scrutiny, especially around hiring practices. While the ethical commitment of an organization to DEI may be genuine, legal parameters present boundaries in some initiatives. For instance, diversity recruitment is a goal of the diversity prong of DEI. However, hiring practices that use race as a standard to hire individuals is disallowed under federal law, specifically Title VII of the Civil Rights Act of 1964.[92]

Compounding the issue of DEI is the 2023 U.S. Supreme Court rulings in *Students for Fair Admissions Inc. v. President and Fellows of Harvard College* and *Students for Fair Admissions Inc. v. University of North Carolina* holding that race-based admissions decisions are a violation of the Fourteenth Amendment Equal Protection Clause.[93] The immediate result of this decision is a change in college admissions processes, but some court watchers predict there could be implications for DEI initiatives within corporations.[94] There are even warnings from state attorney generals warning about the constitutionality of DEI programs considering the Supreme Court's decision.[95] However, that seems unlikely if DEI stays in a category of training and inclusive programming as opposed to a guidepost for hiring practices. As mentioned above, Title VII of the Civil Rights Act of 1964 prohibits hiring discrimination based on race, color, religion, sex, or national origin. So, if a corporation used a DEI program to produce a hiring result based on those factors, that would be illegal. However, DEI as currently structured in corporate America does not do that.[96] Nevertheless, it is highly likely that cases targeting DEI will increase, and there may be constitutional challenges to this ethically based approach.

AI and DEI are just two examples of the complexity of law and ethics. While AI shows the important of ethical guides in the absence of actual legal regulations and guidelines, DEI shows the limits that ethical approaches may have because of legal boundaries. Moreover, both illustrate the shifting nature of ethics and law within the communication field. Static ethical guidelines are sometimes criticized because they can be difficult to apply to contemporary issues. However, having elasticity within ethical codes or principles allows for long-term utilization. Conversely, the law is famously inflexible and slow to change. However, as the DEI illustration shows, there can be sudden changes in the law, especially surrounding hot-button social issues such as affirmative action. It is the role of the communicator to be able to navigate these changes within the industry and utilize both law and ethics to make changes. It is also important that PR practitioners understand the limits of both the law and ethics. Neither will be able to provide clear-cut answers in all circumstances. That is why analysis of the law and ethics is so important. Sometimes these help refine the issue and present a solution. However, sometimes in a legal or ethical paradox, the best that can be hoped for is not an answer, but simply the ability to ask a better question.

DISCUSSION QUESTIONS

1. What is the most applicable ethical tradition to public relations?

2. Why are ethics and laws at odds? If there is a conflict, why should law trump ethics?

3. Which form of judicial interpretation appeals to you when reading a case? Pick a case in this chapter and argue it from the originalist and textualist perspective.

4. Suppose a statute states that "no speeches can take place in a public park after 10:00 pm." Argue statutory interpretation of the term "speech," "public," and "park" using the statutory interpretations listed in this chapter.

5. Is the law's glacial pace of change good or bad when dealing with developing technology, such as AI?

CASE SCENARIO

Suppose you are a PR practitioner working as in-house counsel for a soft drink manufacturer. Your work is centered around promoting a diet soft drink that is targeted toward Generation Z. Your work gains national attention, and you are eventually recruited to go to a boutique public relations firm in the fashion sector. Your specific job is to create PR work targeting Generation Z. Can you use your insights from your time at the soft drink company about Generation Z at your new job with the PR firm? Suppose the firm has a new soft drink client that is a competitor to your old soft drink client. Can you work on the new soft drink account? What measures should the firm take, if any, to screen you from the account? Suppose you have a nondisclosure agreement that prohibits you from discussing your work at your previous soft drink employer. Does that change how you can work with the new PR firm? Does it matter?

CHAPTER 2

The Expanding Definition and Legal Implications of Public Relations

OVERVIEW: PUBLIC RELATIONS PRACTICE HAS A LARGE AND COMPLEX definition that continually expands with technology. Today's PR practice embraces content and strategies from all forms of communication including what has traditionally been advertising and marketing. Because of that, this chapter examines how the expanding definition of public relations has created a profession subject to multiple legal standards. Specific attention is paid to the speech regulation of public relations. The chapter begins with an overview of First Amendment speech categorization, paying particular attention to how public relations is included in political, commercial, corporate, and political speech.

OBJECTIVES:

- Identify the various categories of speech and the legal implications of each for PR practice.

- Discuss the role of commercial and fully protected speech in PR practice and the impact this categorization has on the profession.

- Detail the categories of speech that are unprotected, with a particular focus on defamation law as it applies to PR practice.

- Analyze the political protections of speech in PR practice specifically with fundraising and lobbying.

What is public relations? In 1958, Scott Cutlip and Allen Center wrote in the second edition of their seminal textbook, *Effective Public Relations*, that "the public relations function is the planned effort to influence opinion through acceptable performance and two-way communication."[1] Cutlip and Center's definition is broad and encompasses a lot of types of PR practices. It gives a nod to ethics and law implicitly in the "acceptable performance" part of the definition.[2] However, Cutlip and Center recognized that even in the 1950s, like today, the PR function and role within an organization was complex—so complex that it frequently caused confusion about what the field was compared to other forms of communication practices. For its time, public relations was both a functionary role and a managerial profession. That identity included a seat at the management table and C-suite status and access that levelled up the profession from mere technical skill. However, the viewpoint remained that PR was the support staff, which reduced public relations to output-based communication run by functionaries rather than leaders. These debates of management versus skills have become more complicated in today's converged media society. The rigid definitions of public relations, marketing, and advertising still exist, but have been largely eroded by technological change. Today the PESO model of public relations has been widely incorporated into academic and professional literature on the field.[3] PESO, an acronym for paid-earned-shared-owned media, encapsulates the tactics and outlets PR practitioners must operate within. That definition is quite expansive and has definitional implications. Using PESO, the PR industry now can be said to operate in way that includes advertising, journalism, social media management, digital content creation, public relations, media relations, web content design, and almost anything else you can think of that pertains to communication in the twenty-first century. Moreover, the field of public relations includes managerial decisions as well as tactical execution. Because of this, PR practitioners in the era of PESO are frequently making strategic decisions using a multifaceted tactical approach. This change in the definition of public relations and the increase in PR management functions has legal consequences in that public relations is subject to many more regulations that PR practitioners may realize, particularly those who still hold to the traditional definitions of PR. This is compounded by the rise of decision making that considers the impact of communication choices on a diverse group of publics.[4] This approach, sometimes labelled stakeholder theory or public engagement theory, is a proactive decision-making model that seeks to address issues in a way that prevents legal problems. That way organizations are not placed in a position to engage in reactive PR, which is ultimately a disadvantage for the practitioner and organization. Being able to anticipate the legal consequences for action and inaction positions PR practitioners to anticipate issues and communicate from a strategic advantage.

Most communicators who have a college degree in a communication field likely had a major that was very discipline specific, such as journalism, public relations, advertising, or marketing. Today's majors have expanded somewhat, and more recent graduates may be the products of converged majors, such as strategic communication or just simply communication. Those monikers reflect a change in the identity of public relations and professional communications, and mirror some of the job descriptions the industry uses. Regardless of major, many undergraduate students take courses in their respective field of public relations, journalism, or advertising, but then take a comprehensive communication or media law course. However, those law courses may not present the complete depiction of the laws that affect PR because of the complicated identity that PR has in the twenty-first century. In addition, PR practitioners also operate in a First Amendment reality in which their speech falls into multiple categories that receive varying degrees of protection. Therefore, it is important for PR practitioners to know the legal identity of the field, because those labels on type of speech have different rights associated with the profession.

It is also important to note that public relations' own definition of itself, regardless of whether it subscribes to Cutlip and Center's early definitions or the ubiquitous use of PESO, is largely irrelevant to the conversation about PR's legal definition.[5] Judges and the law typically do not differentiate between the self-definitions of communication professionals, nor do they turn to industry definitions and terms of art to describe different categories of speech. Rather, the law that evaluates what a PR practitioner can say has more to do with content, specifically what is said and where it is said. Because of that, public relations has enjoyed a rather complex legal identity that ranges in its protection. This has some practical implications for the way modern public relations is practiced. Many organizations use lawyers as spokespersons because they want communications that limit liability. Lawyers typically are not trained in PR practices, so this choice of lawyers as de facto PR practitioner can result in communications that are legally sound but poor PR. Literature within public relations emphasizes that PR requires relationship management and two-way communication to create effect communication that resonates with publics. However, this encroachment of lawyers into the space of public relations is a reality that practitioners should be prepared to address with their clients or organizations. Communication created to limit liability can create unintended consequences for public opinion. Because of this, the communications of an organization facing legal troubles should utilize and respect the perspectives of legal counsel and PR practitioners. Both professions' skills are essential to successful organizational strategy.

This chapter begins with an overview of the First Amendment and the establishment of speech categories. It details the categories and the legal tests associated with them. Next, the chapter delves into commercial speech regulation, a legal space where much of the content of PR work resides. Insight is provided regarding what the ever-expanding definition of public relations means for practitioners, and how those definitional arguments largely do not impact the legal and regulatory world in which public relations operates. Finally, the chapter wrestles with some of the ethical issues facing PR definitions today—specifically, what role public relations plays within the larger discussion of free speech, disinformation, and political communication in the United States.

FIRST AMENDMENT AND SPEECH CATEGORIES
The First Amendment of the U.S. Constitution states:

> Congress shall make no law respecting an establishment of religion or prohibiting the free exercise thereof; or abridging the freedom of

speech, or of the press; or the right of the people peaceably to assemble, and to petition the Government for a redress of grievances.[6]

The First Amendment is arguably the most important amendment in the Constitution as it lays the foundation for a democratic society. Within it there are five distinct rights (religion, speech, press, assembly, and government petition), but the freedom of speech is the one most involved with PR practice. However, what does it mean to have freedom of speech? Is that only verbal or written speech? What about behavior, like picketing? What about the space in which speech can take place? What about money as speech in a political campaign? All of these are issues that have been the subject of U.S. Supreme Court cases for over 100 years, and it is in this case law that speech is defined.

Even though the First Amendment was in the Bill of Rights that was ratified in 1791, it was not until the twentieth century that the U.S Supreme Court began issuing case law on the Amendment. In fact, it was not until 1925, some 134 years after the ratification of the First Amendment, that it applied to the states in the case *Gitlow v. New York*.[7] It is important to note when speaking about the First Amendment that there are certain parameters. All too often in society we hear of people speaking about their First Amendment rights. Imagine that a company's employee, Bob, makes derogatory comments about a group of coworkers by saying that the coworkers are "lazy and stupid and don't care about anything but payday and quitting time." Bob is later fired for those comments by his supervisor Jane. Bob is enraged and says "I can say whatever I want, Jane. It's my First Amendment right!" Technically Bob has First Amendment rights, but Jane firing him is not necessarily a violation of his rights because in this situation it is the private company, not the government, firing Bob. This is an important point going forward in this chapter. When the law speaks about First Amendment regulation and laws, it is talking about restraints placed on the government. Now, what the government is can be complex. The role of a state actor can depend on the status of a person or of an organization.

First Amendment Development

First Amendment law has developed over the past century in tandem with the historical and technological advances in society. Wartime is one event that seems to bring about great levels of societal change, and the First Amendment's modern contours were created from concerns that emerged during World War I. During that era, the U.S. Supreme Court began looking at the First Amendment and making distinctions between types of speech. The Court established its "clear and present danger" standard, which was one of the first attempts to delineate speech that was constitutionally protected and speech that could run afoul of the law.[8] During World War I there was a concern about domestic criticism of the war effort, and in response Congress sought to criminalize behavior that would harm the government and military. In 1917 Congress passed the Espionage Act, which criminalized giving aid to the enemy, interference with military recruitment, and interference with military operations. The Espionage Act criminalized speech activity that fell into these categories. This was what was at issue in the case *Schenk v. United States*, in which Charles Schenk, the general secretary of the Socialist Party, was convicted for distributing 15,000 flyers that advocated for resisting the draft. He appealed his conviction all the way to the U.S. Supreme Court, arguing that the Espionage Act of 1917 violated the First Amendment.[9] The court unanimously held that the Espionage Act did not violate the First Amendment. Writing for the Court, Justice Oliver Wendell Holmes presented the first of what would become speech tests the Supreme Court used to evaluate whether speech could be constitutionally regulated by law. He wrote:

> The question in every case is whether the words used are used in such circumstances and are of such a nature as to create a clear and present danger that they will bring about the substantive evils that Congress has a right to prevent. It is a question of proximity and degree. When a nation is at war many things that might be said in time of peace are such a hindrance to its effort that their utterance will not be endured so long as men fight and that no Court could regard them as protected by any constitutional right.[10]

This application of the Espionage Act of 1917 to speech continued in another 1919 case, *Abrams v. United States*.[11] The Abrams case involved only two leaflets, one in English and the other in Yiddish, that spoke out against sending U.S. troops to impede the Russian Revolution. The court held these convictions were constitutional under the "clear and present danger" outlined by Holmes in *Schenk*. Interestingly, Justice Holmes disagreed. In what is perhaps one of the most cited dissents in Supreme Court history, Justice Holmes argued that criminalizing thoughts and speech were antithetical to the First Amendment, and that speech in the United States was part of a marketplace of ideas in which good ideas could overcome the bad without legal intervention. He wrote that "the best test of truth is the power of the thought to get itself accepted in the competition of the market."[12]

After World War I, speech cases focused on the constitutionality of content-based restrictions on speech. The Supreme Court would begin creating tests on types of speech laws to evaluate their constitutionality. In 1925, the Supreme Court in *Gitlow v. New York* held that the First Amendment rights extended to the states through the Due Process clause of the Fourteenth Amendment. Gitlow also established the criteria in which speech could be criminalized by the states.

After the First World War, the Supreme Court began hearing First Amendment cases more regularly. Over the next century, the court carved out certain types of speech for protection, and established norms for constitutional analysis of speech laws. It would grapple with issues that ranged from what type of content should be protected to when is a law about speech without explicitly mentioning speech. The result is a complex system of First Amendment jurisprudence that examines when and how speech can be regulated.

Vagueness, Prior Restraint, and Overbreadth

Speech regulations must meet certain baseline requirements to be constitutional. For those in the communication field, being able to understand the law and being compliant with it means having a grasp of the boundaries of the First Amendment. One issue the court directly addressed after World War I was the presumptive unconstitutionality of certain laws that were vague, overbroad, or served as a prior restraint. Constitutional lawyers use vagueness and overbreadth arguments consistently when challenging speech laws and often couple these with arguments surrounding the constitutionality of how laws are applied. In 1926, the Supreme Court held that a vague law is a "statute which either forbids or requires the doing of an act in terms so vague that men of common intelligence must necessarily guess at its meaning and differ as to its application violates the first essential of due process of law."[13] Overbreadth is related to vagueness, but it is distinct in that it focuses on a law that is written so broadly that it includes both protected and unprotected speech.[14] The issue with overly broad construction of a speech law is the chilling effect the law has on otherwise legally protected speech.[15]

Prior restraint is yet another argument that makes certain speech laws presumptively unconstitutional. Laws that operate as a prior restraint are presumptively unconstitutional because they stop speech before it can begin. The Supreme Court held that laws operating as prior restraints are unconstitutional in the 1931 case *Near v. Minnesota*.[16] This doctrine was later affirmed in the so-called Pentagon Papers case, *New York Times v. United States*, in which the Supreme Court, 6–3, held that the *New York Times* could publish material from top secret documents given to the newspaper by former military analyst and RAND Corporation employee Daniel Ellsberg.[17]

The importance of understanding these nuances of First Amendment protections is rooted in the idea that PR practitioners and other professional communicators need to know what the law is to follow it. Vague and overbroad laws create compliance issues, and PR practitioners that cannot understand or apply the law results in a stifling of discourse and advocacy. Prior restraint is particularly insidious to PR work that relies on timely and strategic releases of information. Laws that craft prescreening and preapproval of content limits the effectiveness of the profession. PR practitioners have a responsibility to advocate for their profession. Examining new laws that seem to suppress free speech is always an attack on the PR profession, which values the free exchange of ideas.

Content-Specific Speech Regulation: Fully Protected Speech

While there are presumptively unconstitutional structures of speech laws, there are also types of speech that are protected on a continuum of unprotected to fully protected under the First Amendment. In the past century, the Supreme Court has divided speech into three categories: fully protected speech, commercial speech, and unprotected speech. The category that public relations mainly fall into is commercial speech, but it regularly falls into fully protected speech as well, especially when the PR is done in a political context. Of course, sometimes PR falls into unprotected speech, namely defamation, when practitioners do not use standard care, professionalism, or ethical considerations in their work. Understanding these three categories demonstrates that it is necessary to see how PR practice is affected by First Amendment jurisprudence. As the sections that follow show, fully protected speech receives the most protection under the law. It is the category of speech that is the most difficult to regulate. Commercial speech is slightly easier to regulate than fully protected speech, and it is because of this status that PR communications are subject to laws and regulation. Unprotected speech receives no First Amendment protection, and for that reason that type of speech can be outlawed or punished by the law.

Fully protected speech receives the greatest constitutional protection, and laws that regulate the content of fully protected speech are typically unconstitutional. The fully protected speech category is defined in many ways by what it is not. It is neither unprotected nor commercial speech. In other words, it is a broad swath of speech. This book would be considered fully protected speech. A sermon in a church, a novel, or a personal diary would likely fall into this category as well. Because of the importance afforded to fully protected speech, the Supreme Court held that it may be regulated in only very specific circumstances. When the government passes laws that are content-specific regulations of fully protected speech, the legal threshold the government must prove (and almost never does) is strict scrutiny. The strict scrutiny standard has three basic requirements; the government must show that the law:

1. *Serves a compelling state interest*: This is a high threshold in which the government almost always loses.

2. *Is narrowly tailored*: This standard means the law is written in such a way that it directly advances the compelling government interest. It cannot be overly broad or imprecise in how it applies to speech.

3. *Uses least restrictive means*: This standard means there cannot be any other method for regulating this speech that is less restricted to achieve the same compelling government interest.[18]

Because of this high threshold, the government almost always fails in proving strict scrutiny on content-specific speech regulation. However, there are exceptions where the government prevails. Terrorism is one example of a compelling state interest, according to the Supreme Court.[19] Another is the integrity of the legal process, in which the Supreme Court upheld a law banning judicial solicitation of funds for elections.[20] These cases are the exception and not the rule. As Justice David Souter wrote in his dissent in *City of Los Angeles v. Alameda Books*, "strict scrutiny leaves few survivors."[21] However, sometimes strict scrutiny is not even necessary when the discrimination is based on gradations of protection of fully protected speech. According to the Supreme Court, compelling a type of speech or providing different standards based on the fully protected content of speech are presumptively unconstitutional. For example, a town ordinance banning signs had varying standards for religious signs versus political signs and was held to be unconstitutional because the law discriminated based on fully protected content.[22]

This protection given fully protected speech is important to PR practitioners. Frequently PR campaigns center on awareness and social causes. Those types of public relations communications are textbook examples of fully protected speech. Where the issue gets to be more complex is when PR communications are discussing social causes or public concerns on behalf of an organization that uses those issues to create a corporate identity. This is found in communications around corporate social responsibility (CSR) or corporate social advocacy (CSA). In those cases, there is content that is arguably commercial speech blended with fully protected speech. Courts sometimes use various tests to examine those admixtures of speech. Sometimes they look to the main point of the speech. Sometimes courts will parse out sections of the speech and evaluate those independently. The big takeaway for PR practitioners is that when speech is fully protected, there are fewer government restrictions placed on it. As the next section shows, unprotected speech can essentially be banned outright. PR practitioners should never be in a situation where they are engaging in that type of speech. However, PR practitioners will find themselves and their work product to be fully protected. Knowing the legal benefits of each speech category is important when navigating how regulation affects content.

Content-Specific Speech Regulation: Unprotected Speech

While fully protected speech receives the full protection of the First Amendment, unprotected speech receives no protection. The legal implication is that the government can pass almost any laws banning unprotected speech. This is why an individual cannot say anything they want, and have it protected by the First Amendment. The principle of unprotected speech dates to the U.S. Supreme Court's decision in *Schenk v. United States* in which Justice Oliver Wendell Holmes wrote, "The most stringent protection of free speech would not protect a man in falsely shouting fire in a theatre and causing a panic."[23] Unprotected speech falls into three general categories: fighting words, obscenity, and defamation. The PR practitioner must be aware of all three types of unprotected speech, but it is likely that defamation will be the most applicable to day-to-day PR activities.

Fighting Words

Fighting words is a speech category that the U.S. Supreme Court has determined is without value in society because it is the immediate incitement of violence. Established in the 1942 case *Chaplinsky v. New Hampshire,* the Supreme Court held that certain words have no value under the U.S. Constitution and should not be afforded any protection. Writing for the majority, Justice Frank Murphy wrote:

There are certain well-defined and narrowly limited classes of speech, the prevention and punishment of which have never been thought to raise any Constitutional problem. These include the lewd and obscene, the profane, the libelous, and the insulting or "fighting" words—those which by their very utterance inflict injury or tend to incite an immediate breach of the peace.[24]

The Supreme Court later refined the concept of fighting words in 1949 as "likely to produce a clear and present danger of a serious substantive evil that rises far above public inconvenience, annoyance, or unrest."[25] The Supreme Court has also examined the type of laws that prohibit fighting words, especially considering viewpoint discrimination. As a result, the Court has held that least restrictive means be used in creating laws prohibiting fighting words.[26]

It is difficult to imagine a PR campaign or content centered on fighting words. However, content does matter, and its interpretation by readers is something PR practitioners need to keep in mind when they create content. This is particularly true in grassroots activist campaigns or even modern political campaigns where fighting words on behalf of an organization or candidate is used to galvanize public response. Some have claimed that former president Donald Trump's words on January 6, 2021, which galvanized Trump supporters to storm the U.S. Capitol, constituted constitutionally unprotected fighting words.[27]

Obscenity

The next category of unprotected speech is obscenity. A standard of obscenity was something the Supreme Court struggled with in the 1960s and 1970s. Justice Potter Stewart famously wrote that he could not define obscenity but pronounced, "I know it when I see it."[28] U.S. laws regulating obscenity were local until the 1970s. Local ordinances and morals committees could evaluate whether a film was allowed to be shown in each community. Laws going back the nineteenth-century Comstock Act, passed in 1873, banned using mail to distribute obscene materials.[29] By the 1950s the Supreme Court took up the issue of obscenity in *Roth v. United States* in which the court defined obscenity where the "dominant theme taken as a whole appeals to the prurient interest."[30] In 1966, the Court in *Memoirs v. Massachusetts* created another obscenity test that incorporated the idea that obscenity was "utterly without redeeming social value."[31] Later the Supreme Court created a new standard in the 1973 case *Miller v. California*, which stated obscenity was present based on:

1. whether "the average person, applying contemporary community standards," would find that the work, taken as a whole, appeals to the prurient interest;

2. whether the work depicts or describes, in a patently offensive way, sexual conduct specifically defined by the applicable state law; and

3. whether the work, taken as a whole, lacks serious literary, artistic, political, or scientific value.[32]

This standard was to be of help to prosecutors of obscenity to provide standards for juries. However, the net effect of the Miller test, as it became known, was far fewer prosecutions of obscenity post-1973. However, obscene material is not protected under the First Amendment, even if the obscene material is provided only to consenting adults.[33] The Miller test has also been criticized by some for providing a catchall in the third factor, which essentially allows almost anything to be considered exempt for some type of value.

Obscenity is not a catchall term. It has specific meaning. The term "pornography" is not the same as obscenity, as pornography can be defined broadly as sexual content. Some pornography may be obscene under the Miller standard, but much of it is not. The Supreme Court has held that hard-core violence in and of itself is not legally obscene.[34] Despite the impact of the Miller test on the production of pornographic material, there is still legally obscene material that is prosecuted federally and at the state level. Obscenity prosecutions do occur, specifically within state jurisdictions.[35] Although the Miller test has been unwieldy to apply, the court has not developed a test to replace it. The application of the Miller test was the major issue in the Telecommunications Act of 1996, the Communication Decency Act, which provided screens for children against obscene material online. The Supreme Court found the CDA's definition of obscenity too broad, and it was later recodified in the Children's Online Privacy Protection Act (COPPA) of 1998.[36] That was also challenged in court, but the obscenity standard in COPPA was held constitutional in a landmark case, *Ashcroft v. Civil Liberties Union* (ACLU II).[37]

Obscenity's application to public relations is complex because it affects both communication in international campaigns, where community standards may vary from those in the United States, and in the type of content, specifically digital content, that can be used. There also are considerations surrounding content for target audiences that may be considered vulnerable by the law, such as internet content targeting children. Community standards is also a vague term, which may have some level of impact of the scope of content used in a PR campaign. This is particularly true in televised content in which the Federal Communications Commission (FCC) prohibits obscene, indecent, and profane content.[38]

Defamation

Defamation law is one of the most important issues facing content creators because it directly deals with reputational harm. In fact, defamation can only be proven if there is proof of reputational harm to an individual, or, in the case of product disparagement, a good or service. Defamation is unprotected by the First Amendment, and states allow civil cases for money damages when a person is defamed. The elements of a defamation case are straightforward, yet proving them, particularly the degree of fault, can be challenging. Proving a case requires the plaintiff to show the following:

1. A statement was made;

2. Published to at least one other person;

3. Required degree of fault (negligence or actual malice depending upon the status of plaintiff);

4. Damages from reputational harm.

However, the development of defamation law in the United States balances the issue of fame and defamation within the context of the freedom of speech. Essentially, under U.S. law, the more famous a person is, the more difficult it is for them to be able to prevail in a defamation suit. It is also important to note that defamation is state law tort, and because of that states may have idiosyncratic interpretations of defamation law (although all must adhere to the standards put forth by the U.S. Supreme Court on the First Amendment).

Prior to the 1960s, U.S. defamation law mirrored that of British common law. Historically defamation included libel (written defamation) and slander (spoken defamation). There was also libel per se, libelous statements that were presumptively defamatory such as criminal behavior, questioning professional ability, stating someone had a loathsome disease, or any type of statement that suggested moral turpitude on the part of the subject. Contrast that with libel per quod, which was a statement that was not obviously defamatory on its face. Today defamation subsumes these older categories of libel and slander, and courts use the term defamation as an all-encompassing term. Additionally, criminal libel is something that exists in some state statutes, but it is rarely part of a court case. Defamation is almost exclusively a civil matter where a plaintiff—the person bringing the lawsuit—is asking for money damages based on reputational harm. Damages in some jurisdictions were presumed.[39]

The *New York Times v. Sullivan* case was a watershed moment in U.S. defamation law and First Amendment jurisprudence.[40] It created the actual malice standard for plaintiffs that fell into a specific status. The Court's reasoning was that for the press to be able to engage in robust discussion of public officials, there had to be a higher standard of proof for public figure defamation suits. Actual malice is committing defamation with "knowledge that it was false or with reckless disregard of whether it was false or not."[41] The court later extended their actual malice standard to public figures in 1967.[42] A public figure was defined by Chief Justice Earl Warren as one "whose views and actions with respect to public issues and events are often of as much concern to the citizen as the attitudes and behavior of 'public officials' with respect to the same issues and events."[43] Later the court held that states were free to establish whatever standard they wanted in dealing with defamation of private individuals so long as the standard was not strict liability, or no fault. Currently, most private-figure defamation requires only negligence to prove a defamation case. The justification for the private person versus the public figure status was the access and power a public figure has. Writing for the majority, Justice Lewis Powell wrote:

> More important than the likelihood that private individuals will lack effective opportunities for rebuttal, there is a compelling normative consideration underlying the distinction between public and private defamation plaintiffs. An individual who decides to seek governmental office must accept certain necessary consequences of that involvement in public affairs. He runs the risk of closer public scrutiny than might otherwise be the case. And society's interest in the officers of government is not strictly limited to the formal discharge of official duties.[44]

The issue of public figures and the criticism they receive in the press continued in the U.S. Supreme Court case *Hustler Magazine v. Falwell*.[45] In this case, the court held that statements that were hyperbole and no reasonable person would assume were facts are protected under the First Amendment, even when those statements could cause emotional distress.[46]

Defamation laws have real impact on PR practitioners who work representing famous clients (discussed at length in chapter 5). Celebrities and public officials should expect to have untruthful information circulating about them, sometimes from seemingly legitimate news outlets. The problem with the actual malice standard is that the media is highly protected against lawsuits regarding defamatory content. That is not to say it is impossible for public-figure defendants to win (UK jurisdictions traditionally have been far more favorable to public-figure plaintiffs because of their libel standards). Public relations practitioners should make note that this heightened standard of proof makes a successful lawsuit exceedingly rare. Because of this, it is probably a better strategy for reputation management to directly combat the disinformation. A lawsuit may be able to do that, but an effective PR campaign may, in some respects, have a better result.

The liability of individual making defamatory remarks falls into three categories: the primary publisher, the secondary publisher, and the republisher. The primary publisher is usually the person sued in a defamation case because it has complete control over the content. In the context of a lawsuit, a primary publisher could be a person who makes a social media post, or a person who verbally makes a defamatory claim in a public way. A republisher is a person who shares the content from the primary publisher. This is very easy in the contemporary world of social media where sharing information is easy and is the actual basis for social media exchanges. A secondary publisher is an entity that may host or dispense the defamatory content, but they are not responsible for the content's creation. An internet service provider (ISP) or an online website would be a secondary publisher.

In the United States, online secondary publishers are legally protected against lawsuits as secondary publishers of defamatory content. The Communications Decency Act, section 230, provides this immunity for an "interactive computer service," such as a social media site, because they are not considered traditional publishers.[47] The issue of the CDA 230's protection has become a political hot-button issue on both the right and left. President Donald Trump attempted to strip certain social media companies of CDA 230 protection because of alleged screening of conservative content.[48] Democratic lawmakers have also criticized section 230 because they think it provides too much protection for large internet companies, such as Facebook. However, CDA 230 is here to stay at least for the foreseeable future. In 2023, the Supreme Court was presented with cases that could have determined the constitutionality of the act.[49] However, the Court sidestepped the issue, and the only opportunity for its elimination comes from Congress. The issue of eliminating the protection is essentially a fear of the unknown. Because the internet was created with the CDA 230 in place (the act was part of the Telecommunications Act of 1996), there is a large degree of uncertainty on how the elimination of the protection would impact the internet's function.[50]

There are some affirmative defenses to defamation. An affirmative defense is one the defendant, the person being sued, can present at trial to directly counter the underlying lawsuit. In defamation cases, truth has been a longtime established affirmative defense. While falsity is not part of the prima facie case of defamation, proving the truth is an option a defendant may present in a trial. Truth by its very nature cannot be defamatory. The second major category of affirmative defense is the privileged status of the speaker. In some circumstances, such as in congressional debates or courts of law, defamation laws do not apply. For example, in court a lawyer may make an argument that another person is guilty of a crime. That accusation in a regular setting would be defamatory, and in fact is libel pe se. However, in a courtroom, defamation law does not apply because the court system is such that lawyers are able to make whatever arguments they can in support of their client (so long as the judge permits). The third major affirmative defense is opinion. An opinion is not defamation because defamation laws apply to statements that purport to be fact. That is why those statements cause reputational harm. In the case of an opinion, there is not a factual basis. However, opinions are not always exempt as defamation. The Supreme Court has held that opinions that may imply a basis of fact can be defamation.[51] There are also some jurisdictions where reporters may have special privileges that immunize them from defamation, such as when a reporter is presenting two sides of a story (neutral reportage) or when a reporter is working on a matter of public interest and follows normal journalistic standards (responsible communication defense). It is important to note that a retraction is not grounds for a defense to defamation, but it can mitigate damages.

COMMERCIAL SPEECH AND CORPORATE SPEECH

Public relations practice is largely under the umbrella of corporate or commercial speech categories. Because of this, it is important for PR practitioners to understand the difference between these two areas of speech and the rights afforded to PR content under these speech categories. Corporate speech is an umbrella term that includes commercial speech and political speech, but is frequently used to refer to fully protected speech made by corporations. Commercial speech is economically motivated speech that is used to promote or sell products and services. As the following section will demonstrate, there is a heightened complexity in commercial and political speech when they are mixed, as is the case in many corporate social responsibility (CSR) campaigns.

Fully protected speech and unprotected speech represent two poles within First Amendment jurisprudence. However, at the center of that continuum is commercial speech. Commercial speech receives some protection under the First Amendment. However, it also does not receive as robust of protection as fully protected speech. Because of that, the government has an easier time regulating commercial speech than fully protected speech.[52] In fact, the government when regulating commercial speech follows what some call an intermediate scrutiny, not quite at the level of strict scrutiny, as outlined in the U.S. Supreme Court case *Central Hudson Gas & Electric Corporation v. Public Service Commission.* Known as the Central Hudson test, it requires the government to prove the following when determining whether a commercial speech regulation is constitutional:

1. Is the communication in question constitutionally protected?

2. Is there a substantial government interest in regulating this speech?

3. Does the regulation directly advance the government's interest?

4. Is the regulation no more restrictive than necessary to advance the government's interest?[53]

This differs from strict scrutiny for fully protected speech. Note that the Central Hudson test only requires a substantial interest (not compelling), a direct advancement of the interest (not narrow tailoring), and no more restrictive than necessary (not least restrictive means). All of this means that the government does not have carte blanche to regulate commercial speech, like it almost does for unprotected speech. However, it is far easier for the government to regulate commercial speech than fully protected speech. As Justice Lewis Powell wrote, "Consequently, there can be no constitutional objection to the suppression of commercial messages that do not accurately inform the public about lawful activity. The government may ban forms of communication more likely to deceive the public than to inform it."[54]

So, what is commercial speech and how do courts recognize it? Some classic examples of commercial speech include things like television commercials, billboard advertisements, signage, and product endorsements. Many people think of commercial speech as advertising. However, as discussed at the beginning of this chapter, public relations has expanded its view of itself to include the PESO acronym. The P stands for paid, which is historically advertisement. Because of this, public relations in the twenty-first century is certainly involved in commercial speech.

Commercial speech is relatively new to First Amendment analysis. Until the 1960s commercial speech was unprotected, just like defamation, fighting words, and obscenity. It had no protection under the First Amendment, so it could be banned outright by laws.[55] This is why whole swaths of advertisements, such as attorney advertising, were banned until the late 1970s.[56] The Supreme Court first acknowledged limits on commercial speech regulation, therefore giving commercial speech some legal protection in 1975 in *Bigelow v. Virginia* and in *Virginia Board of Pharmacy v. Virginia Citizens Consumers Counsel* in 1976.[57]

The identification of commercial speech is not as easy as one might think. Imagine this scenario. A company that manufactures outdoor tents has a PR campaign highlighting the company's CSR efforts that focus on environmentalism. In the campaign the company discusses climate change and responsible care for the outdoors. It provides facts on pollution and plastics' impacts on the environment. It provides tips for campers on how to leave a smaller carbon footprint. It also includes information about the sustainability of its products, especially the material that is used in the tents. Part of this campaign includes social media posts on the company's official social media page that is boosted by paid promotions. It also includes a grassroots letter-writing campaign such as letters to the editor to certain magazines and trade journals. The company also engages in earned media by pitching stories about environmental issues and the company's sustainability efforts. All of this is detailed on a company website and digital newsroom.

What type of speech is this? Commercial? Fully protected? It looks a lot like an ad campaign. It looks paid. And it looks like there is an economic motivation. However, it is not that simple. Environmental issues are a public concern and a political concern. There are all types of content here that has various outlets that is paid, earned, shared, and owned. How do you know when something is commercial speech? The short answer is that it is difficult to tell.

The Supreme Court has a three-part test that examines when speech can be identified as commercial speech. Known as the Bolger test, established in *Bolger v. Youngs Drug Products*, the test looks at three factors, none of which are dispositive, to determine commercial speech.[58] They are the commercial nature of the speech, specific reference to a product, and the speaker or sender's economic motivation.[59] In a case where all three are present, then it is likely a court will determine that the speech is commercial and subject to commercial speech regulations.

In the latter half of the twentieth century, the Supreme Court continued to provide protections on commercial speech.[60] Laws regulating commercial speech, even if well-meaning such as for public health, were struck down as unconstitutional.[61] Outright bans of advertising were likewise struck down as unconstitutional. However, the First Amendment protection of PR content has not been addressed by the U.S. Supreme Court.[62] The differentiation of communication types, such as marketing, advertising, or public relations, has never been part of the Court's method of analysis. Those definitions are largely industry or academic distinctions, and it is important for PR practitioners to know that they do not factor into the Court's analysis of public relations. The closest the Court has ever come to determining whether public relations is considered commercial speech came in the early 2000s in the case of *Nike v. Kasky*.[63]

Nike v. Kasky addressed Nike's campaign regarding its use of so-called sweatshops in its manufacturing of Nike products. The case began in the late 1990s when Nike was receiving immense criticism for the use of sweatshop labor. This criticism reached an apex after the TV show *48 Hours* and numerous newspapers including the *Financial Times*, *New York Times*, and *San Francisco Chronicle*, among others, alleged that

Nike's products were made in factories that utilized sweatshop labor. Nike at that time manufactured much of its apparel in factories in southeast Asia and had a memorandum of understanding that it was responsible for its subcontractor's compliance with labor laws in those respective countries. In 1997, a spot inspection of a Nike subcontractor in Vietnam found that 77 percent of the workers had respiratory problems stemming from atmospheric pollution. Another independent agency, the Hong Kong Christian Industrial Committee, conducted a study showing that in China subcontractors made workers work 11- to 12-hour days, made them work overtime, violated minimum wage laws, and exposed the workers to toxic levels of dust and fumes. The same study showed that there were workers in those factories under the age of 16.[64]

In response, Nike created a PR campaign that countered this narrative. It used press releases and a letter to college athletic directors, who are major purchasers of Nike products, refuting the claims about Nike sweatshop labor. Specifically, Nike made six claims about its manufacturing labor practices: (1) Nike did not have workers subject to corporal punishment or sexual abuse, (2) Nike complied with wage and hour laws, (3) Nike complied with health and safety laws, (4) Nike paid line workers two times the minimum wage in southeast Asia, (5) Nike provided healthcare and free meals to workers, and (6) Nike paid a living wage.[65]

Marc Kasky, a California consumer rights advocate, sued Nike in California Superior Court under a state law that allowed individuals to bring a case for consumer deception. Nike argued that these laws did not apply to the type of speech it engaged in because the company's speech was fully protected speech. The Superior Court and the California Court of Appeals agreed with Nike, stating that the speech in question was fully protected. The California Supreme Court disagreed, stating that just because Nike was speaking about labor practices, a public concern, in the context of its own commercial speech promoting Nike did not make the speech noncommercial. Moreover, the California Supreme Court pointed out that commercial speech, which the U.S. Supreme Court gives some level of constitutional protection, does not have protection when it is misleading or false.[66]

This case was appealed to the U.S. Supreme Court, which granted certiorari, only to reverse itself, citing that the case did not have a final disposition at the trial court level.[67] The case was then settled out of court with no U.S. Supreme Court decision on the issue of public relations and commercial speech status. This led to a nondefinitive answer as to whether public relations were commercial or fully protected speech. However, the answer to this is that PR is commercial speech when it meets the elements of the Bolger test. When there is commentary that is mixed with public concern, such as labor laws or any other political issue, the speech becomes mixed. In the years since *Nike v. Kasky*, California courts have cited the California Supreme Court's decision regularly. However, the approach of mixed commercial and fully protected speech has led to a resolution where courts either parse out the protected speech or consider the main thrust of the speech when analyzing it for constitutional purposes.[68]

The *Nike v. Kasky* case serves an example for PR practitioners that positioning clients' goods and services by entering public debates is not a strategy for avoiding commercial speech regulations. More importantly, it serves as a cautionary tale about ethical communication. While the legal issue here was about commercial speech status for a company to get out of a lawsuit based on misleading information, the ethical issue here is why a company would engage in disinformation to protect a problem that was being exposed at multiple levels. The sweatshop allegations did not go away because of the *Nike v. Kasky* lawsuit or Nike's victories at the trial and intermediate appellate court level. The issue persisted, and the awareness of work conditions on outsourced manufacturing is a topic still relevant today. What the case shows is that Nike's PR campaign was misplaced in its approach, and that Nike could have avoided a legal problem had it rooted its promotions in an ethical approach.

POLITICAL SPEECH

One of the most controversial areas of speech regulation is political campaign contribution laws. This may not seem like a First Amendment issue, but courts have held that financial contributions to campaigns are equal to political speech. Moreover, as communication firms and corporations become more actively involved in politics directly, this area of speech has proliferated in the past few election cycles after the 2010 landmark decision in *Citizens United v. Federal Election Commission.*[69] What the laws in political communication illustrate is that for the past 60 years, the U.S. Supreme Court has grappled with the power of money in politics equating campaign contributions to speech. Public relations professionals actively work in political communication and, as this chapter will show, sometimes the role of a PR practitioner and lobbyist is blurred, causing legal confusion. Understanding how lobbying laws and political communication/fundraising is regulated is important for PR practitioners because it demonstrates how specific sectors of public relations have unique rules that apply in highly fact-specific circumstances.

In the past 20 years, particularly since 2010, the Supreme Court's decisions have led to a high-water mark for the rights of corporations to speak in political matters. Going back to the turn of the nineteenth century in the famous Supreme Court case, *Dartmouth College v. Woodward*, which established the rights of corporations to enter contracts, U.S. law has recognized that corporations have many of the same rights as individuals.[70] In the 1860s, corporate rights were increased, especially after the 1868 ratification of the Fourteenth Amendment of the U.S. Constitution. Meant to give rights to newly freed slaves, the Supreme Court used the interpretation of the word "persons" to include juristic, or legally created persons, personhood for corporations. This interpretation of rights given to corporate personhood was taken as unquestionable truth in the 1886 Supreme Court case *Santa Clara County v. Southern Pacific Railroad, Co.* in which the court held that applying the equal protection clauses to corporations was so self-evident that the court did not even need to decide that principle of law.[71]

Campaign finance issues have traditionally been intertwined with the concept of balancing contributions against undue power and influence. There is a long history of campaign finance regulation that highlights a tension between being able to use donations to demonstrate political support while tempering the corrupting influence of donations within the political process. It is a tension that has been pushed and pulled for over a century, sometimes with the law erring on the side of allowing greater donations and sometimes the law restricting them. The current regulatory environment can be described as pro-donor, but that may change given the increased concern over the cost of elections. For example, for the 2020 presidential election there was $14 billion raised and spent in aggregate, making it the most expensive election to date.[72]

In the United States, campaign finance issues go back all the way to the eighteenth century when the Virginia House of Burgesses placed a ban on giving away alcohol during a political campaign. However, the issue of campaign finance and speech did not become a major political and legal issue until the twentieth century. Beginning with the Tillman Act in 1907, Congress sought to place bans on campaign contributions. In 1911, the Federal Corrupt Practices Act capped expenditures in political campaign. The Supreme Court became involved in campaign finance issues in 1921 in a case *Newberry v. United States*, holding that a Michigan state law that capped campaign expenditure in general and primary elections to 25 percent of congressional salaries was unconstitutional.[73] Other cases concerning the constitutionality of campaign finance laws continued. In *Burroughs v. United States* the Supreme Court held that the Federal Corrupt Practices Act's reporting requirements were constitutional.[74] In the 1930s and 1940s, campaign finance laws were passed by Congress including the Public Utility Holding Company Act (PUHCA), which banned utilities from making political donations; the Hatch Act in 1939, which placed limitations on civil service employees engaging in the political process; and the Taft–Hartley Act in 1947, which placed prohibitions on union contributions to political campaigns.[75]

By the 1970s campaign finance laws would emerge, making the field of campaign contributions more regulated. The Federal Election Commission (FEC) would be created in 1974.[76] That agency created political contribution limits, capped campaign spending by individual candidates, and created recordkeeping requirements. However, these laws were challenged on First and Fifth Amendment grounds, and the Supreme Court in the landmark 1976 case *Buckley v. Valeo* held that much of the FEC's regulations and its establishment was constitutional.[77] There began to be challenges to laws that banned corporations from donating to specific candidates and causes. These donations had a speech component in that this money would be giving a corporation the ability to "speak" on behalf of candidates. In 1978, the U.S. Supreme Court in *First National Bank of Boston v. Bellotti* held that corporations had the right to speak on political issues, and state laws that restricted corporations from speaking on issues that only affected the corporation was unconstitutional.[78]

In the 2000s, there was a political movement to rein in the excess of campaign expenditures. The Bipartisan Campaign Reform Act of 2002 (BCRA), better known as the McCain–Feingold Act, became law.[79] It placed restrictions on advertisements, specifically stating that candidates had to identify the source of an ad. It also raised the contribution levels for individuals, but severely limited parties and candidates from accessing nonfederal money from state parties. This was challenged in a lawsuit, which ultimately made its way to the U.S. Supreme Court. That case, *McConnell v. FEC*, challenged the soft money provisions in the BCRA under the First and Fifth Amendments.[80] The court upheld the constitutionality of the BCRA, paving the way for other types of political organization, notably the so-called 527.

Post-*McConnell*, the Supreme Court began regularly striking down laws that prohibited fundraising and corporate speech. In the 2007 case *FEC v. Wisconsin Right to Life*, the court held that the BCRA's restrictions on corporate-funded issue advertisements during pre-federal election periods was unconstitutional.[81] In 2010 the Supreme Court held in the highly controversial decision *Citizens United v. FEC* that the BCRA's restrictions on corporations and unions using independent expenditures—that is, their own money–and running advertisements within 60 days of an election violated the First Amendment.[82] The consequence of this decision was to change political campaigns and the law of corporate speech significantly. It permitted corporations and unions to fully engage as speakers within political elections. *Citizen's United* and the decision *SpeechNow.org v. FEC* created a legal environment in which the popularly termed "super PAC" emerged as a political force in U.S. elections.[83] Later in 2014, laws that restricted donors' aggregate contributions was also struck down by the Supreme Court in *McCutcheon v. FEC*, paving the way for highly expensive U.S. elections in which PR practitioners/political consultants play a major role.[84]

PUBLIC RELATIONS AS LOBBYING?

In the twentieth century PR practice has embraced expanded definitions that include public affairs and political communication. Lobbying, which is sometimes part of a larger umbrella of government relations, has been embraced by some in the PR industry. In fact, the distinction between lobbying and public relations is sometimes blurred, creating problems for "typical" PR practice. Lobbying also presents a unique analysis of public relations because it demonstrates the interconnectivity between ethics and law. The laws of lobbying frequently reflect ethical concerns. For example, major pieces of legislation that regulate federal lobbying, the Ethics Reform Act of 1989, the Lobbying Disclosure Act of 1995, and the Honest Leadership and Open Government Act of 2007, were passed to ensure transparency and disclosure of lobbying activities.[85] While a comprehensive discussion of lobbying is beyond the purpose of this book, there are some things that are important for public relations practitioners to note in how the lobbying field is legally defined. In fact, it was in lobbying efforts that the Supreme Court first recognized the constitutionality of PR work.

Prior to World War II, lobbying in the United States was largely unregulated at the federal and state level. In 1946, the Federal Regulation of Lobbying Act went into effect, mandating the registration of lobbyists. That law was ultimately upheld, largely on First Amendment grounds, in that it only applied within a narrow context of when there was "direct communication with members of Congress on pending or proposed federal legislation."[86] This decision came just a year after the Supreme Court held that lobbyists did have some protected privacy rights and did not forfeit them just because of their profession.[87]

In the 1960s, the issue of lobbying again made its way to the Supreme Court in *Eastern Railroads President's Conference v. Noerr*.[88] In that case, 41 Pennsylvania truckers sued 24 Eastern railroads, the Eastern Railroads Presidents Conference, and the public relations firm Carl Byoir and Associates. The truckers alleged that:

the [Eastern] railroads had engaged [Carl] Byoir to conduct a publicity campaign against the truckers designed to foster the adoption and retention of laws and law enforcement practices destructive of the trucking business, to create an atmosphere of distaste for the truckers among the general public, and to impair the relationships existing between the truckers and their customers.[89]

While the railroads did admit they engaged in a campaign to promote railroad business and influence state laws on trucking, they claimed they did not engage in a campaign designed to harm the trucking business. The question before the court was whether the railroads and by extension their PR firm had violated the Sherman Antitrust Act in their lobbying efforts. The Supreme Court held that this type of public relations campaign meant to influence legislation cannot be considered a violation of the Sherman Antitrust Act, and that these types of communications were protected under the First Amendment. Later, the Supreme Court would hear another case involving lobbying and antitrust law, *United Mine Workers of America v. Pennington*.[90] In that case, the court reaffirmed that lobbying efforts did not violate antitrust laws when those efforts were designed to influence public officials about regulating industries. These cases taken together established what is now called the Noerr–Pennington doctrine, which states that organizations may petition the government, including using lobbying and PR efforts, without fearing a violation of antitrust laws. The doctrine would be extended to courts and administrative adjudications in 1972 in *California Motor Transport Co. v. Trucking Unlimited*.[91] However, these lobbying efforts must be sincere, and cannot be a veiled campaign whose true meaning is to interfere with the business practices of a competitor. Such "sham" campaigns do not protect organizations and their PR/lobbyists from antitrust liability.[92]

The PR practitioner behind the *Noerr* case, Carl Byoir (1886–1957), was famous for groundbreaking work in the field of corporate communication. During World War I he worked on the Committee for Public Information (CPI), known popularly as the Creel Committee. During his work with the Eastern Railroads, Byoir created highly negative advertisements about truckers. The conflict later became dubbed the

"Railroad–Truckers Brawl." Byoir died in 1957 before the resolution of the case in 1961, predicting his side would prevail in court.[93]

By the 1970s lobbying was impacted by many of the campaign finance reform laws that went into effect post-Watergate. *First National Bank v. Belotti* allowed corporations to engage in ballot initiative campaigns, which presented new opportunities for corporate lobbyists.[94] *Citizens United v. FEC* likewise provided greater opportunities for lobbyists to engage in political campaigns and fundraising through super PACs and corporate political speech. As opportunities for financial support grew in the 2010s, lobbying became a stronger force within U.S. elections.

However, the understanding of lobbying versus traditional public relations has created some legal issues for the industry. For example, in 2016 the state of New York passed a law aimed at regulating press contacts between lobbyists and editors that was written in a way that would have turned rank-and-file PR practitioners into lobbyists for reporting purposes (the law eventually was challenged and was overridden by ethics legislation).[95] The moral of that legislative journey is that public relations with its expanded definition can be thought of as forms of communication that are not explicitly PR. Lobbying is one of those forms, and its highly regulated practice makes lobbying an expensive business. PR practitioners being included in the definition of lobbying is an example of how the unintended expansion of PR work has made the PR industry vulnerable to increased, and expensive, regulations.

Ethical and Legal Implications of Expanded Public Relations Practice

Public relations practice has always been a unique admixture of skills: relationship management, reputation management, media relations, customer relations, stakeholder communications, organization communications, organizational conscience, and jack of all trades. Because of this, the legal identity of public relations is just as complex as the job. Some of the speech that public relations is engaged in is fully protected, some of it is commercial speech, some is corporate speech and, unfortunately, some of it is occasionally unprotected speech. From an ethical standpoint public relations values certain types of communication approaches. For example, transparency has been a hallmark of good public relations for decades. That transparency is an industry standard and is the basis for good two-way communication. However, it is also a legal standard, especially when dealing with consumers and digital media. The history of the First Amendment's development also shows that public relations practice does not neatly fit into a category. Like the *Nike v. Kasky* case shows, public relations is a mixed bag of communication types. Because of that it is sometimes unclear what public relations is.[96] However, some of the ethical guideposts that the industry has created around truthfulness and honesty provides guardrails for PR practice.

One of the important things to note about the identity of public relations as a form of speech is that the First Amendment evaluates speech from a unique philosophical viewpoint that is not necessarily found in other western democracies. Looking at the freedom of speech, the U.S. system evaluates speech from a marketplace of ideas approach. As shown in chapter 1, that philosophical approach is rooted in the ideas of John Stuart Mill. It assumes that within communication, the best ideas rise to the top. Under this philosophical approach, the field of speech is an even playing field. Good ideas win over bad ideas. However, the neutral-value approach of U.S. speech laws is criticized by many who think that speech is reflective of the power dynamics within society. In fact, courts and lawmakers have struggled with this in their analysis of campaign contribution laws. If money equals speech, ergo, the people with the most money have the most speech. Their ideas rise to the top (and they might not necessarily be the best). This is an example of where PR practice has an important role to play within democratic society. By mandating that PR practitioners be honest and forthright in their communications and to consider the impact on numerous publics and stakeholders, the PR profession ethically strives to be a positive force within the large societal dialog in the United States. Good PR, in this sense, is good for democracy. Moreover, public relations must have professional oversight by the press. Organizations that speak untruths will eventually be uncovered. This system of a free press ensures that bad communication will be called out.

However, the communication system in the United States is more complex than that. Currently we live in a society where disinformation is weaponized to create societal discord. This has been accelerated through the proliferation of social media and through the technological evolution of artificial intelligence, which creates seamless fake realities. Hate speech, a type of speech that attacks others based on characteristics such as race, gender, ethnicity, sexual identity, and religion, is largely protected under the First Amendment, unless it constitutes fighting words. While international agreements, such as International Covenant on Civil and Political Rights (ICCPR), exist to combat hate speech, U.S. law cannot prohibit it outright. The same is true for communication that constitutes disinformation. Unless the disinformation constitutes defamation that, too, is largely protected speech regardless of its harmful impact on society. The digital sphere provides an outlet for both insidious forms of communication, and it is only through the community standards of those platforms that such speech can be contained. That too is problematic, as critics point out selective enforcement of such standards and the weaponization of fact checkers in content that is highly subjective, particularly in political discourse. This gap in the law demonstrates the need for the PR practitioner to adhere to professional ethics and personal morals when communicating. It also shows that merely adhering to the legal parameters of communication may permit unethical and unprofessional communication.

As the twenty-first century enters its third decade, the law of communication in the United States will have many things to consider, particularly with the proliferation of content. However, it is highly probable, almost certain, that the First Amendment's delineation of speech categories will endure. Despite the criticisms of the marketplace of ideas approach the First Amendment has toward communication, that philosophy will also endure as the underpinning of speech laws. PR practitioners will do well to continue to adhere to their own ethical and professional standards and acknowledge the complex role they play within communication law and society.

DISCUSSION QUESTIONS
1. What type of speech is public relations most of the time?

2. Suppose you are a new PR practitioner working for a firm that handles PR for a major restaurant chain. One day you're chatting with one of the firm's division heads about how you like working for the firm, especially on the restaurant account. You say, "I love working on the account because I actually eat at their restaurant. One time I made a mistake and ate at one of their competitor's places and got really bad food poisoning." The division head says, "Really . . . well, you should post a review about that on the competitor's site. That type of thing helps our client, and it's not like you're lying. It's the truth." What should you do? What are the legal and ethical considerations you should consider? Suppose a few days later you see a post that looks a lot like your story, but you don't recognize the name. Should you talk to the division head? Could that post be defamation? Why or why not?

3. Is the expansion of the definition of public relations a good or bad thing?

4. Should commercial speech have limited protection under the U.S. Constitution? Why couldn't it be fully protected?

5. How should online companies protect against defamation? Should they have CDA 230 immunity? If that law were revoked, could the internet still function?

CASE SCENARIO

Suppose you are working for a company that manufactures frozen fish for retail sale in supermarkets. Recently, there have been numerous reports about mercury levels in fish, particularly frozen fish products, and the media have mentioned several companies—not yours—that produce frozen fish products. Your company decides to enter into the public discussion on mercury levels in fish and posts a series of blogs on the company website speaking about the dangers of high mercury in fish. Part of the blog contains a statement about how your company sources its fish from areas low in mercury. Later, a reporter writes a story about how your company's frozen fish has high levels of mercury. The story is true. Can your company be sued for false advertising because of the blogs? Are the blogs corporate or commercial speech? What legal implications are there for the blog content being commercial speech versus corporate speech?

CHAPTER 3

Balancing the Perspectives of Public Relations

OVERVIEW: THIS CHAPTER LOOKS AT THE PHILOSOPHICAL DIFFERENCES between lawyers and public relations practitioners. Understanding the differences in the legal profession's approach provides insight into how PR practitioners can engage with legal strategy and identify some pitfalls of communication strategy, particularly in a litigation process. Since PR communication often is used during times of crisis, this chapter details the legal process of trials and appeals with a focus on how lawyers examine communication content from an evidentiary perspective. Specific attention is paid to the use of apology as a communication strategy, and how apologies and statements can be used as evidence during trial. The chapter also examines confidentiality issues between PR practitioners and clients, and how attorney–client privilege can attach to PR practitioners in certain circumstances.

OBJECTIVES:

- Provide an overview of the U.S. trial and appellate process for civil cases, focusing on how this process informs legal approaches to communication.

- Discuss apology and how it impacts litigation as a form of evidence and admission of fault.

- Analyze issues relating to PR practitioner confidentiality and how attorney–client confidentiality can attach in specific circumstances.
- Discuss how lawyers and PR practitioners can work together for the benefit of clients.

Law and PR professionals work together a lot. Reputation management, crisis communication, issue management, compliance with communication regulations, organizational communication, and corporate social responsibility all are areas of PR practice that have significant legal overlap. Knowing the laws of public relations is essential for any communicator to effectively do their job. The laws of the twenty-first century affect the content, structure, and delivery of PR communications. Knowing these laws gives practitioners the ability to make legally sound and justifiable work for their clients.

This chapter discusses some of the biggest legal issues facing PR practitioners in the 2020s. Legal and PR work performed in house sometimes pits legal and communication strategies against each other. The law is a profession rooted in risk aversion, that is, limiting legal exposure and minimizing potential lawsuits. The law also is a profession that is set up as adversarial. Each civil lawsuit has at least one plaintiff and one defendant, and, except for purely transactional law, there is usually a resolution to a lawsuit in which one party prevails over another. By contrast, public relations is a communication profession that is rooted in relationship management and two-way communication. Dialogue and information dissemination is the main purpose of most PR work, and because of that, the solutions PR practitioners present usually involve transparent engagement. This does not mean that law and PR cannot coexist or even share the same strategies. What it does mean is that these are two distinct entities that approach problems with different tools and philosophies. In many ways, they complement each other, and a good communication and legal strategy frequently has a synergistic power that helps clients and organizations through difficult times.

This chapter will look at law and public relations in the context of their guiding philosophies, particularly in terms of practice and ethical decision making. The chapter begins with an overview of the litigation process. This context is important because it illustrates what lawyers think about when dealing with potential cases, especially those cases that involve organizational crisis involving liability. Next, the chapter examines litigation strategy using civil procedure to show the ways lawyers and PR practitioners work together during organizational crisis. The chapter also examines evidentiary issues within public relations, noting that evidence is frequently produced by an organizations' own communication. Of particular importance is the role of apology and mortification strategies within communication, and how apology can be construed as an admission of fault at trial.

The chapter also looks at the relationship between PR practitioners and their clients, specifically within the ethical context of safeguarding client confidences. This unique area of law presents certain logistical questions, and it demonstrates how lawyers and PR practitioners need each other during organizational crises to maintain confidentiality. Building on these areas of law, the chapter concludes with an analysis of how client interests are better served when there is a strong relationship between PR and legal professionals because each approaches problem solving in a unique, yet essential way.

PR VERSUS LAW: UNDERSTANDING TWO PERSPECTIVES ON COMMUNICATION

Imagine that a corporation manufacturing bicycles has just found out that one of its most popular models made in one specific factory has a defect that may cause the brakes to stop working. The company does not know if this defect has affected all bicycles or just the ones from this factory. The repair for the brakes is minimal, but many of these bicycles are shipped all over the United States. The company does not have a robust social media presence because it is mainly in the wholesale industry. The retailers of their products could be a source of information, but their communication strategies are diffused. This defect may or may not cause injury and, in rare circumstances, could cause death, but again this hasn't happened yet. To date there have been no issues reported. The brake failure was noticed by employees of the company testing one specific bicycle. This scenario (product defect causing harm, lots of contingencies and communication issues, followed by a series of communication scenarios that make unified communication difficult) is the basis for many classic crisis communication case studies that are analyzed each year in college classrooms, and is a scenario examined by a large body of literature in PR research.[1]

The answer to this type of question always starts from the standpoint of what type of communication works best. Should the company issue a recall? Who should the company tell first? Should the company issue an apology? How does the company stay on message? Who should be the spokesperson for the company? How does the company effectively communicate with its publics? What communication channels should the company use? Notice that all these questions are communication questions. That should not be a surprise. PR practitioners are communicators, and communication is the key to an effective PR strategy. Lawyers, however, are not trained as communicators. They are trained as legal experts representing clients, and, as such, one of their fiduciary duties to a client is to follow the boundaries of the law.

For lawyers, this scenario will present a list of different questions.[2] Exactly how was the defect noticed? What does the warranty on the bicycles say? Who were these employees? Did they perform a test? How accurate was the test? To whom did they report? What did they specifically notice? How was the bicycle manufactured? Was any part of the manufacturing done by a subcontractor? If so, who? What was the subcontractor's expertise? Were any express claims made about the bicycle to retailers? What do the retailers say about the bicycle to customers? You get the point. It's about liability, litigation, contracts, lawsuits, third-party responsibility, commercial goods, and evidence. And that is just about the incident. When factoring in what the company says, there are a whole host of legal questions that arise, especially if communicators use certain crisis communication strategies. Suppose the communications team wants to send out a notice that includes an apology for the inconvenience of having to have the bicycle fixed. Compounding this situation is the fact that several people have experienced some non-life-threatening injuries that may require a doctor's visit. A lawyer may begin to consider a whole new set of questions about the communications. Is this statement a true admission of fault? How will these statements be viewed by opposing counsel, the judge, or the potential jury? Suppose there's a major injury, could the statements establish negligence on the part of the manufacturer? While the advocacy of an attorney requires communication; the purpose of these communications is delicate. Lawyers think of the law and legal implications, just like the PR practitioner thinks of communications and the consequences of what is said to the public.

In this context, the lawyer and the PR practitioner differ in their solutions. Traditional PR practitioners view the court of public opinion as the primary means of navigating a crisis, whereas the lawyer sees the actual legal system as the proper space to manage crises. As a result, traditional PR and standard legal practice are sometimes at odds because their orientations toward crisis management focus on two divergent places to communicate. PR practitioners want to effectively manage a crisis by engaging with publics in a way that guides the organization through the end of the crisis. A lawyer wants to effectively manage a crisis by effectively engaging with the legal system to produce the best legal result for the client. Looking at it this way, the PR practitioner and lawyer both want what is best for the organization, but the lens from which they see that objective is different. This difference of perspective may be one of the reasons why lawyers and PR practitioners have a level of tension in their management of communication. Their objectives in the big picture are the same, but their means of achieving it are different. Their concerns are also different, and the boundaries in which they frame the issue come from two different professional perspectives.[3]

Despite their professional differences, there are advantages to the legal and PR counsel working together. Not only does it provide a more robust and integrated approach to issues, but attorney–client privilege can attach to PR practitioners when working with legal counsel.[4] Currently federal law does not recognize a PR practitioner–client privilege, which means that a PR practitioner can be called to testify and reveal client confidences despite the ethical guidelines provided about client confidentiality. However, lawyer–client privilege is a strong right that has long-standing recognition within the law. Unlike any other profession, attorney–client privilege cannot be waived unless done so by the client.

Most importantly, that attorney–client privilege can extend to those professionals working with legal counsel for a client. Integrating the legal and PR work for an organization provides this benefit. Because this relationship with legal counsel is so important, it is not enough for PR practitioners to be aware that there is a legal department; they also need to have a working knowledge of the law. This gives PR practitioners the ability to create communications that are legally sound, but also gives them the knowledge to better situate themselves within the management function of an organization.[5]

The Legal Process: Adversarial Advocacy

To fully understand an attorney's viewpoint on representing crisis, it is important to understand the legal process. When attorneys deal with issues affecting public relations and organizations, these lawsuits typically involve civil cases. For this reason, this section focuses on the civil process of law. This is important to note because civil suits in the United States differ from criminal cases. Within the media, civil suits are largely underrepresented in both news and entertainment. Because of that, many people confuse the processes and may ascribe criminal procedure to civil lawsuits. As such, the following sections provide a comparison of the two systems, focusing on the civil.

Lawsuit: The Beginnings

All cases in U.S. law, criminal and civil, begin with a set of facts that lead to a lawsuit. In criminal law a crime occurs, and an individual is usually indicted by a grand jury. The indicted person is then prosecuted by the state or federal government (depending on the crime), and the case goes forward to trial. Before the trial begins the individual, known as the defendant, can either plead guilty or not guilty. If they plead not guilty, the prosecutor (the individual handling the case for the state) goes forward with the case. Evidence is gathered, a trial date is set, and pre-trial motions are made. Prior to the trial date the defendant may take a negotiated plea and, if accepted by the judge, no trial is made and the trial phase ends. If the defendant goes to trial, then the case will proceed to a judge or jury to decide. A bench trial is where a judge decides the case, and a jury trial is where usually 12 jurors decide the case.

There is a standard procedure for state and federal criminal trials. Jury trials begin with voir dire, a process whereby attorneys question potential jurors and then select them based on a series of strikes. These strikes are for some reason, typically bias, but cannot be for reasons such as the race of the juror. After a jury is selected, or in the case of a bench trial the judge is ready, the prosecution and defense present opening statements, the state presents its case, the defense presents its witnesses (though not required), closing statements are made, jurors are given instructions by the judge, and then the jurors deliberate. After deliberation a jury may come back with a verdict of guilty or not guilty or, if they are unable to reach a verdict, they are deadlocked. Once the trial is over and if the defendant is found guilty, the appellate process can begin.[6]

Like criminal cases, civil cases begin with an action, typically an event such as a contract dispute, intellectual property infringement, or an action of negligence. That event causes a person or organization some type of monetary harm that prompts them to bring a lawsuit. The plaintiff makes a series of claims known as a complaint. The defendant—the person being sued—is sent the complaint and must answer the complaint within a set period, typically 30 days. The defendant can enter the response to a civil complaint by admitting the claims are true, denying the plaintiff's claims are true, or neither admitting nor denying the plaintiff's claims because of insufficient knowledge. A defendant then may make motions to dismiss for legal reasons, such as lack of jurisdiction. However, if the defendant fails to answer the lawsuit the plaintiff is then able to make a motion for a default judgment, or a judgement is made that awards money damages to the plaintiff because of the defendant's failure to respond. This need to answer is why all defendants usually deny allegations made in plaintiffs' complaints.[7]

Lawsuit: Pretrial Discovery

After the civil defendant answers the complaint, the process of discovery begins. In civil cases, discovery is a major part of pretrial work. It is where both parties gather evidence for the client. This can take the form of subpoenas for documentary evidence, depositions of testimonial evidence, or interrogatories of witnesses. Each of these discovery tools are different. Subpoenas for documentary evidence may include any type of document, and this sometimes leads to massive amounts of documents being combed over by lawyers and their assistants. In this phase lawyers are sometimes "buried in paperwork," which delays the discovery and eventual trial process. Depositions are a way to gain testimonial evidence from individuals who are witnesses in the case. These depositions are given under oath with a stenographer, and both parties are present for the testimony. These depositions can last for a short or long time depending on the issue and the witness. Lawyers can object to certain questions during this process. However, the depositions serve as a basis for what the witness may say at trial. If the testimony at trial differs from that given in the deposition, then the witness's deposition testimony can be used to impeach the witness on the stand. Last, interrogatories are used to find out information from a witness. However, unlike subpoenas, these are written responses that are typically carefully answered. The power of a subpoena is the ability to find out information the lawyers do not know or to see how a witness may act during a trial. An interrogatory does not provide that type of nuanced information, but it is a useful took to get specific answers to questions.[8]

As the trial approaches each side may make pretrial motions on various matters. This typically includes evidentiary motions to limit or admit some type of evidence. The attorneys prepare for trial by getting their witness lists ready, creating a theory of the case, preparing their opening and closing statements, and handling any last-minute details. Sometimes lawyers use consultants to help them design a case. This may include the use of jury consultants who assist lawyers with creating the profile of the ideal type of jury. For expensive, high-stakes trials, lawyers may use consultants to test the reception toward certain theories of the case, presentation styles, or effective means of communication. Consulting at trials is a lucrative business, and there are professional organizations devoted to trial consulting, such as the American Society of Trial Consultants (ASTC) founded in 1982.[9] Consultant services include focus groups, mock trials, image management, and other services. While most lawyers and litigants do not use these services because of their cost, the fact this type of work exists demonstrates the nonlegal factors that go into trial work.[10]

Pretrial practice is an important aspect of trial work, and in an era where most civil cases settle, it is pretrial work that really impacts the outcome of a case. Sometimes this pretrial work includes motions about certain aspects of the case. While appellate courts typically require a case to have a final judgment before hearing an appeal, sometimes pretrial decisions by the trial judge can be appealed. These special appeals prior to trial, technically called interlocutory appeals, take up issues that are of such major importance to the parties that the outcome of the case may hinge on that specific issue. These vary by jurisdiction, but most states have specific rules about when an interlocutory appeal can be made. Typically, these appeals deal with issues such as evidence, or some issue of procedure that is of high importance to the outcome of the trial.

The Trial

Once a trial has been set, lawyers first must select a jury. Juries are notoriously unpredictable, and for that reason many cases settle out of court before a jury trial ever occurs. Juries in the United States typically consist of 12 people, but in some state court matters, such as misdemeanors crimes and civil cases under a certain amount, the jury can be as few as 6 people. Juries are selected through a process known as voir dire, French roughly translated to mean "to speak the truth." Sometimes pretrial surveys are used to find out information about jurors. These can include basic information, but also can include information about the juror's professional background, media viewing habits, and any experiences they have with courts. During the voir dire process lawyers for both sides ask prospective jurors questions. It is during these questions that lawyers gain a better understanding of the jurors and their perceptions about the potential case. In a state trial court, that means the jurors come from the county in which the case is being tried. In federal courts, the jurors are drawn from the U.S. District in which the case is tried.[11]

Lawyers can eliminate jurors from the jury pool based on strikes for cause and preemptory strikes. A strike for cause is done when a juror indicates that they may not be impartial for the trial. For example, in a lawsuit involving a local hospital, a juror may be eliminated if he indicates his wife works at the hospital. Preemptory strikes are different. Those strikes can be used to strike jurors from the pool so long as the underlying reason is not discriminatory. Lawyers typically have a set number of preemptory strikes that can be used to eliminate a juror from the jury pool. Preemptory strikes vary depending on the type of case. For example, in federal civil cases, each side gets three preemptory strikes. In federal criminal cases, each side gets six, but when the death penalty is sought, the defense gets 20 and the prosecution gets six.[12] These preemptory strikes can be used for any reason so long as they are not connected to discrimination of jurors based on race or sex.[13]

Once the jurors are selected, the trial begins. Lawyers present their opening statements. These statements are one of two times the lawyers for each side get to speak directly to the jury. In the opening statement the lawyers for each side present what they think the evidence in the case will show. Opening statements are important as they typically frame the trial and introduce a theory of the case to the jury. However, there are limitations to what opening statements can be. Specifically, opening statements do not contain argument, that is, they cannot be used to apply facts to law as in a closing statement. Once the opening statements are concluded, the plaintiff presents their case.

It is important to note that in a civil case, the plaintiff—the person bringing the lawsuit—has the burden to prove their case by preponderance of the evidence. That is, essentially, proving more likely than not that the civil defendant is responsible for whatever the case is about. That is an important standard to understand, especially in comparison with the criminal burden of proof, beyond a reasonable doubt. The criminal standard of beyond a reasonable doubt is what most people are familiar with because of the representation of criminal law in television shows and true crime podcasts. That standard has been part of many U.S. Supreme Court cases and has been established as the constitutional requirement in all U.S. criminal cases.[14] The civil standard of preponderance of evidence has not been as developed through Supreme Court case law (although some cases have addressed it), but it is a standard largely assumed within codes of evidence and civil procedure. However, the civil burden of proof should not be considered easy, even though it is far less of a burden than the government's burden in a criminal trial.

The burden of proof is why the plaintiff in a civil case must present their case first. They must establish the elements of their case through testimonial and documentary evidence. The plaintiff will have witnesses that are called to the stand to testify under oath about pertinent information that advances the plaintiff's case. For example, in a defamation trial the plaintiff would need to show that they could prove the prima facie case of defamation. That means the plaintiff must establish through evidence that (1) defamatory statement was made, (2) to at least one person, (3) the statement caused reputational harm, and (4) the statement was made with the required degree of fault (either actual malice or negligence). Once that is established by the evidence of the plaintiff, the plaintiff will rest their case. At that point the defendant usually makes a motion for a directed verdict as a matter of course, arguing that the plaintiff did not establish their burden of proof. Typically, this is denied and then the defendant can introduce evidence.

A defendant's responsibility is important for PR practitioners to understand because it underscores one of the main tensions within the legal versus PR analysis. In a civil lawsuit, the plaintiff has the burden of proving their case. Just like with a pleading, if the defendant denies the arguments of the plaintiff, the plaintiff must prove these in court by the preponderance of the evidence standard. At trial, the plaintiff must prove their case with their evidence. The defendant has a right to cross-examine the plaintiff's witnesses, and sometimes through effective cross-examination the defendant can demonstrate the weaknesses in the plaintiff's case. However, the defendant is not required to put forth any evidence. They do not have to put on witnesses. All they must do to be successful is to point out the weaknesses of the plaintiff's case. This is why many attorneys dislike the communication tactic of admitting fault. In the context of public opinion, admitting fault may allow for some remediation for the client and expedite image repair. However, in a court of law where there are clear-cut burdens and obligations, the defendant can do nothing and still win.

There are some circumstances where the defendant may want to put on witnesses. If defense witnesses are available to disprove one the elements of the plaintiff's case, then certainly the defense will call them to testify. Take the example above about defamation. A defense witness may testify as to whether there was actual malice involved in making a defamatory statement. That would be important information for the defendant to put on because it helps disprove the plaintiff's case. There are other circumstances where the defendant may put on witnesses as well. If the defendant has an affirmative defense, that is a defense that mitigates the fact that the plaintiff's case is in fact true. For example, in a copyright infringement suit, the affirmative defense of fair use can be presented. When raising that type of defense, it is the defendant who must meet the burden of proof for the specific defense.[15]

Once the presentation of evidence is concluded, the defendant will once again make a motion for a directed verdict. Typically denied, the parties will then begin giving closing statements. The plaintiff, having the burden of proving their case, typically closes first. Then the defendant has the right to close. Then the plaintiff is given one more chance to speak to the jury in a rebuttal to the defendant. Unlike an opening statement, during a closing statement, lawyers are allowed to argue the facts of the case and apply those facts to the law. This provides the lawyers the opportunity to tell the jury how they should vote during deliberations. The length of a closing statement varies. Sometimes lawyers go on for a long time and may use evidence or even props during the closing to emphasize their main points. At the end of the closings the judge then instructs the jury on the law of the case. Judge's instructions are important because they tell the jury what the law is and how they should go about their deliberations. Lawyers make recommendations to the judge regarding the instructions at the conclusion of a trial. Once a jury goes into deliberation, the jurors may ask the judge questions about the instructions and law for clarification.

Jury deliberations are done in secret. The first issue is the election of a foreperson who assists with the management of the deliberation. The foreperson has no greater vote than a regular juror; their role is more of facilitator of the deliberation process. Juries sometimes discuss the evidence, take straw polls to see where they are in terms of unanimity, and sometimes ask the judge clarifying questions. In civil cases juries typically must be unanimous, but not always (note that criminal juries must be unanimous). Juries sometimes deliberate for a long time. The Guinness Book of World Records gives the record of longest deliberation to a 1992 case in Long Beach, California, in which the jury deliberated for four and a half months (the case took eleven and a half years to come to trial).[16] This is an extreme example, but it demonstrates the length of deliberations. Famously, the 1995 double murder trial of O. J. Simpson took 11 months, with the jury sequestered in the Hotel Inter-Continental in Los Angeles for 265 nights (the hotel later became a tourist attraction).[17] The jury deliberated for less than four hours before finding Simpson not guilty on all charges. However, a jury may be deadlocked. Sometimes called a hung jury, a deadlocked jury is one in which a unanimous verdict cannot be reached. In such cases the trial judge provides a jury an Allen charge, called that because of the 1896 case *Allen v. United States*. In that charge the judge tells the jury to go back and reconsider their votes in the case.[18] The judge must be careful in this situation to not favor one side of the case, but instructs the jury to consider the other jurors' opinions without violating their own personally held beliefs. If, after this Allen charge is given, there is no unanimous verdict, the judge will declare a mistrial and the plaintiff can bring the case again to trial with a different jury. A retrial is an expensive process, and plaintiffs and defendants may choose to settle the case out of court.

The Appeals Process

After a trial ends, the losing side can file an appeal to the appropriate appellate court. If the case is in U.S. District Court, then the appeal goes to the U.S. Court of Appeals for the circuit the District Court is in. In the federal system there are 13 U.S. Courts of Appeals, and these federal appeals courts act as intermediary courts of appeal. If the trial is in a state trial court, then the appeal would go to the intermediate state court of appeal and then to the state supreme court. While this is the way most appeals work in the United States, it is important to note that sometimes in the state system appeals from a trial court go directly to the

state supreme court. Also, in the federal system there are certain categories of cases that bypass lower federal courts altogether and originate in
the U.S. Supreme Court. These types of cases are outlined in Article III,
Section 2 of the U.S. Constitution, and list the cases where the Supreme
Court has original jurisdiction. They are disputes between states, cases
involving ambassadors and public ministers, and cases where a state is a
party. The reality of Supreme Court original jurisdiction is that disputes
between states are the most common type of case heard originally by the
Supreme Court. Cases involving ambassadors are rare, and cases where
a state is a party are frequently heard by lower federal courts and then
appealed through the federal appeals process.

The appeals process is distinct from trial courts. There are no juries,
only judges. Sometimes the appellate court will permit the parties to
give oral arguments, but many appeals decisions are made without any
hearings. Instead, the parties for each side of the appeal file a brief out-
lining the legal issues of the case. The terms plaintiff and defendant are
not used in the appeals process. Instead, the party bringing the appeal is
called the appellant, and the party responding to the appeal is known as
the appellee. The appellant's appeal cannot be based on retrying the facts.
Instead, the appeal must be for an issue of law, such as a legal error made
by the trial judge. For example, an appellant could not appeal the verdict
in a defamation case stating that the jury was in error when it found the
defendant legally responsible. Instead, an appellant could bring an appeal
on a defamation case by claiming that the standard of fault used in the
jury instructions was legally in error. Additionally, appeals sometimes
allege constitutional issues, such as the law applied in a particular case
violated the First Amendment of the Constitution. When an appellate
court decides a case and publishes its decision, that decision becomes case
law, and it is included in a collection of case laws from that court. For
example, the decisions made by the Supreme Court are case law for the
entire United States, and those decisions are included in the *U.S. Reports*,
a publication published annually that lawyers may refer to when examining the judicial interpretation of a case. It is important to note that
appeals are a protracted process, and decisions will take years to be fully
exhausted. For example, as mentioned in chapter 1, in May 2023 the

Supreme Court issued a landmark decision on fair use in copyright law in the case *Andy Warhol Foundation for the Visual Arts v. Goldsmith*.[19] That appeal took 3 years and 10 months from the time the U.S. District Court for the Southern District of New York issued a decision that was the basis of the appeal. The entire time of the lawsuit from the first initial complaint was six and a half years, and cost the plaintiff, Lynne Goldsmith, $2 million. The 75-year-old photographer had to mortgage her home to continue the case, demonstrating the personal and financial expense of such a lawsuit.[20]

The number of appellate judges hearing a case vary depending on the court. The U.S. Supreme Court has nine justices, appointed by the President of the United States, and confirmed by the Senate. That number of judges has been set since 1869.[21] Federal courts of appeals usually hear cases with three-judge panels, although if a case is of "exceptional importance" a federal appeals court can hear cases en banc, which typically means that all federal appeals judges for that circuit sit on the panel to hear the case.[22] This means there can be as many as 15 judges hearing those cases, but in federal appeals courts with more than 15 judges, such as the U.S. Court of Appeals for the Ninth Circuit, there is a system in which 11 randomly selected judges sit en banc. An appeal to the U.S. Supreme Court can come either from a state supreme court or the U.S. Court of Appeals. The Supreme Court must grant certiorari to hear a case. The Court does this by a vote of at least four justices that occurs during the certiorari process, which includes reviewing a list of summaries of certiorari petitions prepared by the justices' law clerks. Those summaries are created in what is known as the cert. pool.[23] In the 2020s the number of cases granted certiorari by the Supreme Court has been low. On average the Supreme Court receives around 8,000 certiorari petitions annually, and grants certiorari for approximately 100 cases.[24]

Alternative Dispute Resolution

Most civil cases in the United States never get this far as a trial. Most civil cases settle, and criminal cases often have a negotiated plea, prior to trial. There is a good reason for this. Trials are expensive, and plaintiffs and defendants typically do not want to go through the expense of a trial.

In a civil case, pretrial negotiations may end during the discovery process. Litigants may also use alternative dispute resolution (ADR) to handle their cases. This approach to resolving civil cases is less expensive, less formal, and a faster means to resolve cases. ADR is typically thought to include a variety of formats, but the main types of ADR are negotiation, mediation, and arbitration. Negotiation occurs between the parties in the lawsuit, plaintiff and defendant, typically through their attorneys. Once an agreement is met, then that is the end of the matter and a settlement occurs.

Mediation is a type of negotiation that uses a third party, typically a seasoned mediator or retired judge, who works with the parties to find a resolution. This mediation can be set up in several ways, including group-facilitated discussion or individual one-on-one discussions between the mediator and the parties. A type of mediation sometimes uses what is called a conciliator, which is a mediator who actively provides suggestions for the resolution of a case. These types of mediations are sometimes called conciliations because of the more active role of the mediator. Arbitration works like a mini trial. There is an arbiter designated to hear a case and render a decision based on the facts and evidence. This too can take various forms, including having a single arbiter in a quasi-trial setting, to having multiple arbiters. The arbitration can also be binding, meaning the parties must adhere to the ruling, or nonbinding, meaning the parties can choose to not follow the result of the arbitration and continue with their lawsuit. Online platforms, such as Zoom and Microsoft Teams, have made these types of ADR more accessible to litigants, and online ADR is a fast-growing industry in the United States.

WHEN I'M SORRY MEANS GUILT: ANALYSIS OF APOLOGY IN PR AND THE LAW

The legal process is protracted, and success depends on many factors including an underlying legal strategy. However, it is important to note that cases depend largely on the evidence. Having the facts on your side and being able to prove them gives anyone in litigation an advantage. Within public relations, one of the largest challenges is how to communicate during a crisis. Sometimes these communications help alleviate the crisis, but sometimes these communications can create problems for later lawsuits. The role of the organizational apology highlights this potential problem and is an excellent example of the philosophical and professional tension between lawyers and PR professionals.

Apology is so commonplace in society that we hear "I'm sorry" multiples times a day for matters ranging from important to trivial. Within public relations an apology is frequently used to resolve a crisis. Sometimes it is thought that providing a sincere apology helps organizations to move past a crisis event and make amends with its stakeholders. In the academic literature, mortification strategy is the term commonly used that includes apology. Essentially mortification embraces the idea that organizations should make amends to their publics when a transgression has occurred, and that through mortification the organization can help improve its image. For scholars and practitioners, the ability to own one's actions is part of having credibility with the public, and it is leveraging that credibility that helps organizations regain their lost status.

However, as the previous section on trials demonstrates, mortification as a legal strategy does not work always within litigation because of legal procedure. Owning responsibility and accepting fault would be unusual for an attorney to do, and the civil procedure process does not really provide advantages for that. For example, in a copyright infringement suit the plaintiff must be able to prove all elements of infringement to win. Defendants answer the complaints denying their breach, which in turn requires the plaintiff to gather evidence to prove the underlying elements of infringement. If the plaintiff cannot prove the elements, then the plaintiff loses. These denials have to do with making the plaintiff prove their burden.

The denial makes plaintiffs prove their cases by a preponderance of evidence. It makes them gather evidence during a protracted discovery process to proves their case. The defendant, the one who is sued, does not have to do anything. The defendant participates in the lawsuit, but has no burden. They do not have to find evidence absolving them (although most do). They do not have to do anything if they do not want to. In fact, during the pretrial and trial process, the defendant can make the case very difficult for the plaintiff. They can file motions for summary judgment, asking the judge to dismiss the case for various reasons. They can file motions to suppress evidence at trial. They get to cross-examine the plaintiff's witnesses using leading questions. They get to make motions for directed verdicts because the plaintiff failed to meet their burden halfway through a trial. These motions, if granted, end the trial in the defendant's favor. For these reasons, lawyers are inclined to not admit anything. The philosophy is to let the plaintiff bring the suit and prove it with evidence. Only then will a defendant pay.

How does apology fit into this scenario? Apology is a communication tactic that many organizations and PR practitioners use to mitigate negative public opinion. However, apology is a loaded form of communication because its subtextual meaning can create problems in litigation. So, what is an apology anyway? As children we are taught to say sorry and mean it. By mean it, our parents and teachers meant that we needed to atone for our actions and hold ourselves accountable. Being accountable is part of being a mature adult. It is about acknowledging that the fault of our actions is ours alone, and that sincere apology provides us the ability to redress our own failures and seek redemption. It also provides others who are wronged with the ability to feel validated. Frequently, people want apologies because they want someone to acknowledge they were wrong. Some even argue that these apologies decrease litigation, because sometimes people sue others to make them acknowledge their bad acts. However, in litigation, saying "I'm sorry" comes in the form of a check instead of a verbal statement.

Being sorry has its legal drawbacks. Part of apology is rooted in ownership of behavior. That can be interpreted as admission of fault. That has major legal implications for organizations because those admissions, either spontaneous verbal statements or carefully crafted PR news releases, can be used as evidence of wrongdoing. The Federal Rules of Evidence even provide a special hearsay exception for admissions of fault. It states that while an out-of-court statement is typically viewed as hearsay, and thus inadmissible, an admission by a party opponent is not hearsay and is therefore admissible at trial.[25] The admission by party opponent rule is the largest exception to the hearsay rule in the Federal

Rules of Evidence, and it is a standard that is present in many state rules of evidence. The rule requires that the admission:

A. was made by the party in an individual or representative capacity;

B. is one the party manifested that it adopted or believed to be true;

C. was made by a person whom the party authorized to make a statement on the subject;

D. was made by the party's agent or employee on a matter within the scope of that relationship and while it existed; or

E. was made by the party's coconspirator during and in furtherance of the conspiracy.[26]

This means that a statement of admission through an apology, however contextualized, can constitute an admission by party opponent. The party does not need to testify to have this evidence introduced, and it has produced some concerning developments in medical malpractice litigation. In those cases, doctors' apologies when telling a patient that their family member has died, for example, "I'm so sorry, she didn't make it," have been turned into evidence at malpractice trials indicated legal malpractice on the part of the doctor. States have even created legislation that makes a special exception to the admission by party opponent that excludes these types of emotionally driven apologies that are not reflective of responsibility.[27]

For PR practitioners, apology serves as a cautionary litigation tale, but it also raises ethical questions. What does it mean to technically not admit fault in order to succeed at potential litigation? If a practitioner is operating from an ethical standpoint that dictates their work must reflect well on their profession and serve the benefit of society, not admitting fault raises the concern of whether the lack of admission is, in fact, a lie. The other issue is that sometimes the apology phase of a crisis starts in the early moments of transgression. Admitting fault sometimes has the consequence of mitigating damages, for example, a product recall. Additionally, it may create an environment where plaintiffs are less likely to sue because they feel that the organization has heard them and has their best interests in mind. This ultimately is an issue that must be resolved through a discussion between the PR counselors and lawyers. It presents the age-old question of winning in a court of law versus winning in the court of public opinion.

PR PRACTITIONER–CLIENT PRIVILEGE: HOW CONFIDENTIAL CAN A PR PRACTITIONER BE?

Safeguarding client confidences is one the most sacred parts of being a professional. Journalists have long been known for safeguarding the confidences of their sources. In fact, there have been high-profile cases where journalists, such as *New York Times* journalist Judith Miller, who have even gone to jail to protect their sources.[28] The U.S. Supreme Court has never fully recognized the right of a journalist to not reveal their sources, but there are some who argue that the right is part of the First Amendment and has been acknowledged, at least tacitly, in the case *Branzburg v. Hayes*.[29] States sometime provide shield laws for journalists as well, and the U.S. Justice Department has recognized the importance of journalist confidentiality in their own processes to obtaining confidential source information as something done as a last resort.[30]

PR practitioners, however, do not have a rich legal history of client confidentiality protection. Almost any standard of PR ethics, whether it be the Public Relations Society of America (PRSA) or the International Public Relations Association (IPRA), has some acknowledgement that PR practitioners have a fiduciary duty of professionalism to clients. That professionalism means keeping their confidences. This is important as a professional, because for a PR practitioner to effectively do their job they must be able to have candid conversations with clients and know the truth of a situation. Horror stories of PR backfiring frequently involve the practitioner communicating without all the facts. That creates a snowball effect for bad public relations and media attention, worsening a crisis.

However, from a legal standpoint, PR practitioners do not have legally recognized confidentiality with clients. It is an industry standard, and one that can be upended by a lawsuit with a subpoena. Consider the following situation. Suppose an organization gets embroiled in a crisis involving paying subcontractors money to bribe local officials to look the other way on manufacturing violations. This information becomes public, and the company hires a PR firm to help them with their crisis response. During the representation, the CEO of the company reveals to the PR firm that it was widely known that the company was providing these extra funds for bribes and that the company chose to do nothing to stop it. The PR practitioner in that situation knows the truth about the situation and has information that could be potentially useful to parties, including the government, who may wish to sue the company for their transgressions. Can the PR practitioner be forced to testify? Can they retain their client confidences? Suppose they refuse. Could the PR practitioner end up in jail for contempt of court?

The answer to those situations is complex, and it turns on whether the PR practitioner is an information consultant who is essential for providing legal advice, such as an accountant providing tax advice for an IRS case, or the functional equivalent to an organizational employee. As mentioned above, lawyers regularly hire consultants who work with them on cases. In those situations, the attorney–client privilege, something that is well recognized and is a sacrosanct aspect of U.S. law, can attach to nonlawyers working on a case. There have been mixed decisions regarding when nonlawyer consultants enjoy attorney–client privilege.

Consultants frequently help attorneys with preparing a case, especially in the complex world of twenty-first-century litigation. This includes attorney staff members, but also specialized consultants, such as PR practitioners. The extension of attorney–client privilege to them stems from accounting services used during tax litigation. In 1961, the U.S. Court of Appeals for the Second Circuit held that nonlawyers could have attorney–client privilege extended to them because of the complexities of modern legal practice. However, the extension was not automatic. Certain facts had to exist for the privilege to attach. Specifically, the court held, "What is vital to the privilege is that the communication be made in confidence for the purpose of obtaining legal advice from the lawyer."[31] The court likened these non-attorney services to having a consultant help the attorney with a foreign language. However, the foreign language in this case was accounting and, in other circumstances, could be public relations. These types of situations have resulted in PR practitioners becoming a necessity to the legal representation. Therefore, the privilege attaches to the PR practitioner or firm under what is sometimes called the necessity test of privilege.

The other way attorney–client privilege can exist for the PR practitioner is when the consultant becomes a functional equivalent of an organization's employee. In one case from the U.S. District Court in the Southern District of New York, a Japanese-based commodities firm hired a PR firm to handle media relations because the company had limited experiences working with Western media.[32] While the company had an internal communications team, they only dealt with the Japanese press. All U.S. press was handled exclusively by the American PR firm. The District Court held that this sort of relationship made the PR firm effectively an in-house communications division. However, there is no bright line rule about functional employee status, which attaches attorney–client privilege. New York is reluctant to extend attorney–client privilege to PR practitioners. For the privilege to attach, the PR firm or practitioner must be working directly within the litigation, not just handling the media fallout from litigation.[33] In some situations, even the attorney–client privilege can cease if the attorneys are speaking with the communications team. For example, attorney–client privilege was waived when general counsel discussed an FDA filing with the client's outside marketing team.[34] The U.S. District Court for the Northern District of California describes the legal status of PR and law as, "the dispositive question is the consultant's relationship to the company and whether by virtue of that relationship [s]he possesses information about the company that would assist the company's attorneys in rendering legal advice."[35] The U.S. District Court for the Western District of Washington held that a consultant on a trademark infringement suit did not qualify as a functional employee where attorney–client privilege attaches because the conversation between the consultant and organization were of a business, not legal, nature.[36]

What about work product, and its role within attorney–client privilege? This has been an issue, especially when a consultant receives shared information. In 2019 the Supreme Court of Pennsylvania analyzed whether attorney–client privilege ceased when a healthcare company forwarded an email from general counsel to an outside PR consultant. The court held that this was not a violation of attorney–client privilege, using a standard that attorney work product is "is waived when the work product is shared with an adversary, or disclosed in a manner which significantly increases the likelihood that an adversary or anticipated adversary will obtain it."[37] This is based on a case-by-case analysis of the situation, but the standard is not the same as when attorney–client privilege is breached. The standard for keeping work product confidential is lower.[38]

All of this presents issues for attorneys, especially when dealing with outside PR firms as counsel. The more distant the relationship, the more likely it is that the privilege between the lawyer and PR firm will be discoverable, especially if the PR firm is hired prior to a lawsuit being filed. Conversely, the closer the PR firm or practitioner is to the attorney or in-house counsel, the more likely privilege will extend through either the necessity test or functional equivalency. However, the issue of attorney–client privilege and confidentiality brings into question perhaps the starkest example of law and ethics not mirroring each other. Without the attorney dimension to the relationship, a PR practitioner has only ethical industry norms to dictate their confidentiality with clients. This means that individual practitioners must make their own decisions as to how and when confidentiality works. This is complicated by situations in which the client may reveal a confidence that the PR practitioner feels the public has a right to know. Further complicating the practitioner confidentiality issue is the use of nondisclosure agreements (NDAs) in which forbids a PR practitioner from revealing information. These contractual obligations create a legal enforcement of confidentiality and, perhaps in some situations, these NDAs work to legally effectuate a confidentiality protection. However, such contracts are not absolute, and a PR practitioner should be aware of the limits NDAs have. The issue of confidentiality, however, is one that will continue to evolve, and likely will not have a concrete set of legal parameters in the coming decades. It is an issue that the PR industry, rather than the law, will have to sort out.

PR PRACTICE AND LAW: PHILOSOPHICALLY DISTINCT, EQUALLY NECESSARY

This chapter examines the philosophical differences between public relations and the law, showing how each profession approaches the role of communication. While some may view the law as a profession that is adversarial in nature—after all it is an adversarial legal system—the truth is that legal counsel is risk avoidant. Communications professionals also have distinct views of problem solving that is based on engagement and relationship building. It is no surprise that communicators view communication as a primary means for solving issues. There are few, if any, scenarios where a PR professional would adopt a stance that encourages nonengagement with key publics.

Understanding the philosophical perspectives of lawyers and PR practitioners is important when examining strategy, especially in a crisis. A lawyer's craft teaches them to focus on the potential for litigation, and if a lawsuit occurs, the civil procedure in a case requires them to deny their responsibility to counter an initial case from a plaintiff. Additionally, lawyers look at communication, including public relations, as potential evidence. The discussion on admissions by party opponents is an important part of how lawyers examine what a PR practitioner says. Admissions, or statements that can be interpreted as admissions, are a major factor in any type of liability. It is an area where PR practitioners and lawyers can work together to craft legally sound public statements that serve the best interests of an organization in the courts of public opinion and law.[39]

Finally, the way lawyers and PR practitioners work together matters both in terms of legal strategy and organizational security. Safeguarding client confidences is a major aspect of PR ethics. In fact, the PRSA Code of Ethics states that the confidentiality between a PR practitioner and a client is a core part of client trust.[40] The issue of confidentiality within the law is further evidence of why there is an important and crucial relationship between legal and PR counsel. That close relationship for client work is the only way that a PR practitioner can ensure they have legal protection for an ethical industry standard.[41]

DISCUSSION QUESTIONS

1. Why are lawsuits so expensive? What does the fact that many suits settle out of court mean for justice?

2. Discuss the pros and cons of apologizing during an organizational crisis. When should an organization apologize despite legal fallout?

3. Practitioner–client confidentiality is an area that pits law against ethics. If you were confronted with having to reveal a client confidence or go to jail, what would you do?

4. If a PR practitioner revealed a client confidence, what does that do to their professional reputation?

5. Which is more important for a client, a lawyer or PR counsel? How can they work together to solve the client's problems?

CASE SCENARIO

You are a PR practitioner working on an account for a restaurant chain. The chain serves hamburgers made from frozen patties that it buys from a vendor that supplies frozen meat for the restaurant industry. Recently at one of your locations, a shipment of meat was delivered that contained small bits of plastic in the hamburger patties. The plastic was the result of a manufacturing process, and the manufacturer was unaware of what was happening. No warning was issued to any restaurant. Your restaurant serves the hamburgers to customers. Some of the customers get sick from consuming the meat with small bits of melted plastic. Some of them go to the hospital because of their reactions, and several of them must stay home from work to recover from their reaction to eating the tainted hamburgers. The issue of the tainted meat is covered in the news, and the story becomes viral on social media as #plastichamburgers. The meat vendor is totally responsible for the plastic in the meat. In some ways, the restaurants are victims of this crisis. You want the restaurant to release a statement stating the following "We recently learned that some of our hamburgers contained plastic bits that caused some of our customers to become sick. At our restaurants we pride ourselves on serving the best hamburgers with the best ingredients. We know we have let you down.

We promise to do better." Are there any legal problems with this statement? Can it be construed as an admission of fault in future litigation? Is there a better way to craft this statement to avoid legal liability?

Transparency in Digital Public Relations

OVERVIEW: This chapter examines the legal issues around public relations transparency. Specifically, the chapter discusses how regulation of paid content impacts the PR profession, and how in digital communication transparency is a legal requirement rooted in concerns over consumer trust. Laws concerning brand influencers, substantiation, and puffery are discussed as well as laws and regulations affecting financial public relations. The chapter ends with a discussion on how ethical PR practices focus on transparency leads to a higher reputation for the profession, and how legal mandates of transparency are establishing a baseline for open and honest communications.

OBJECTIVES:

- Detail the laws affecting brand influencers.
- Define and analyze the laws affecting paid content, especially substantiation and puffery.
- Explain the laws affecting financial PR and how they impact communication transparency.
- Discuss the role of ethical transparency in relation to legally mandated disclosures.

Transparency is one of the biggest buzzwords in communication. Being transparent in your communications offers great rewards to clients and the public alike. It builds trust and confidence in the profession of public relations, and helps practitioners achieve two-way communication. This rule of transparency goes beyond academic literature and is present in numerous industry and professional codes of ethics (to what extent it is followed is murkier).[1] Those entities that lack transparency frequently pay the price with public backlash.[2] In fact, the role of transparency within public relations has a long history going back to the development of the railroad and corporate entities of the late nineteenth century. The expansion of corporations during this time, especially public utilities, created environments in which organizations had to be transparent to earn public trust. This expectation of transparency, in turn, led to the development of laws and regulations that mandated transparent communications and honest relationship management between corporations and stakeholders.[3]

However, transparency brings forth several questions from a practice standpoint. What level of transparency is required of PR practice? Does everything have to be transparent? What, if anything, can remain private? Can transparency be harmful? While "transparency" is a word that is popularized across PR practice (try to find a PR textbook that doesn't mention it), the practice of transparency is much more complex. Within professional codes, transparency is frequently viewed as coexisting in the realm of honesty. The International Public Relations Association (IPRA) mandates transparency as part of their Code of Conduct.[4] For IPRA, transparency means practitioners must clearly articulate their interests and point of view when communicating. Other professional PR organizations do not explicitly endorse transparency, but suggest it as a core value. For example, Public Relations Society of America (PRSA) lists honesty as one of its professional values and that mandated honesty includes "accuracy" and "truth" in communications; something that is synonymous with transparent communication.[5] Within the larger philosophical discussion of ethics, transparency is sometimes viewed as part of virtue ethics as it relates to the character traits of an organization.[6] The continued process of transparency, known as habituation, makes this approach part of the core identity and practice of an organization.

In the twenty-first century, PR practitioners are faced with a complex set of questions regarding transparency because of digital communication and social media. This is made even more complex by the proliferation of generative artificial intelligence. These platforms and systems allow for the widespread dissemination of content and, in the case of generative AI, the fast creation of content. That presents certain challenges for transparency.

This chapter approaches transparency by looking at four major legal issues. The first is FTC regulations on paid promotions and advertisements. Second, the regulations on brand influencers are analyzed. This includes analysis of noninfluencer endorsement regulation, and how federal agencies, notably the FTC, have instructed brands to monitor and self-regulate promotional content made by third parties. Third, the chapter discusses financial transparency and how disclosures for publicly traded companies must be made. The chapter concludes with looking at transparency in the new age of artificial intelligence, and how regulations may require disclosure of AI-generated content. This area is particularly important because AI operates in a legal vacuum in which practitioners and organizations must use their own ethical guidance to determine how they will utilize and disclose AI.

Paid Communication: What Can a PR Practitioner Legally Say?

In the past, public relations and advertising were distinct areas of communication. PR dealt mainly with earned media and, because of that, media relations was a large part of the job. However, with the introduction of digital and social media, the blurring of the communication boundaries has caused public relations to merge with other types of communication, namely marketing and advertising. While debate on these silos and the supremacy of each type of communication remain, the practical effect of the convergence of communication is that PR is a much more multidimensional form of communication than it was 30 years ago. Because of that, PR practitioners need to know how advertising regulation affects content. As mentioned in chapter 2, the commercial speech designation of public relations is something that is important because most PR content falls within that speech category. Judges and laws typically do not make a distinction between public relations and advertising and therefore

PR practitioners need to be aware of how "advertising," broadly defined, is regulated. In that discussion are three major issues: false advertising, substantiation, and puffery. Because the law of paid communication typically uses advertising in its broad legal sense, this chapter considers advertising throughout this section in the same way. Readers should consider the term advertising as a tool used in public relations, marketing, or strategic communication.

False Advertising

Suppose you are put in charge of a new campaign for a brand of shampoo. The shampoo is targeted toward women, ages 18 to 35, who have color-treated hair. The shampoo is supposed to allow for the coloring to last longer and to prevent split ends and other damage that comes with hair care. Part of the communication strategy is to use paid social content to promote user experiences with the hair product. You have a list of users who have endorsed the product, but one user has an experience that is exceptional. While using the product the user claims her hair, which was thinning at the time, grew back. Her hair is thicker, shinier, and fuller than ever before, and she believes there is an ingredient in the shampoo that activated her hair growth. She would like to give her testimonial in a video that could be incorporated into this social media campaign. Now, the shampoo company never intended these types of results, and they are as excited and baffled by the results as the woman. Can you use her story in the advertising campaign? Can you make a claim that the shampoo can cause hair growth without tests? Is the woman's experience enough to support a major claim like this? These types of issues are typical questions within paid content creation, and the federal government has laws and regulations that provide an answer.

Advertising is largely regulated by federal agencies, but advertising works somewhat differently than many other industries. Within advertising is a large industry of self-regulation especially in false advertising. The reasons for this are rooted in the rationale that self-regulation takes the onus off the government, notably the FTC. Self-regulation in advertising is done by certain organizations such as the National Advertising Division (NAD) of the Better Business Bureau. Created as a partnership in 1971 by the American Advertising Federation (AAF), the National Association of Advertisers, and the Council of Better Business Bureaus, NAD has become a recognized force in the self-regulation of advertising. Although it is purely voluntary, NAD is a respected entity within the advertising profession, and false claims made in advertising can be brought to NAD for a disposition (approximately 150 cases a year).[7] The creators of NAD also created the Children's Advertising Review Unit (CARU) and the National Advertising Review Board (NARB), which functions as an appeals panel for NAD. Of course, the NAD process does not have the same effect as the federal government. NAD receives approximately 75 percent of its cases from referrals, frequently from competitors, but 25 percent are initiated by NAD's own monitoring. This monitoring looks for serious advertising issues with a focus on ads targeting vulnerable populations (e.g., children or elderly), leverages consumer fear as a strategy, presents unique issues that the FTC has not addressed, involves claims by ads that an ordinary consumer cannot evaluate, or deals with diversity within participating self-regulatory industries.[8]

Some advertisers may choose to not participate in that system and may refer the case to the FTC for a final disposition. An advertiser has the right to not participate in NAD hearings. If an advertiser does not comply with a NAD hearing, the case is referred to the FTC. However, after referral, the party refusing to submit to the NAD hearing typically agrees to the NAD process and modifies the ad. The FTC supports dispositions by organizations like NAD because of efficiency and because it takes the burden off the FTC to be the sole arbiter of false advertising. Many who work in advertising choose to comply with NAD decisions to maintain industry credibility, and many in the advertising field think that going through the NAD process is better than being subjected to an FTC review.[9]

The prohibition against false advertising has several sources of law. Typically, false advertising lawsuits are brought under federal law, although state laws on false advertising do exist.[10] In fact, in chapter 2, the discussion of PR's exposure to false advertising laws in *Nike v. Kasky* in was a lawsuit brought under California state law.[11] The Lanham Act, a federal law that mainly addresses trademark, has a provision that permits false advertising claims.[12] The law provides that anyone, real or corporate, can be liable for false advertising when their content either: (1) is likely to cause confusion, or cause mistakes, or deceive as to the affiliation, connection, or association of such person with another person, or as to the origin, sponsorship, or approval of his or her goods, services, or commercial activities by another person; or (2) in commercial advertising or promotion, misrepresents the nature, characteristics, qualities, or geographic origin of his or her or another person's goods, services, or commercial activities.[13]

The FTC also has federal laws that enable it to regulate false advertising. The Federal Trade Commission Act (FTCA) allows the FTC to specifically address false and misleading advertising.[14] The FTC describes its role under the FTCA as ensuring the following:

A. Prevent unfair methods of competition and unfair or deceptive acts or practices in or affecting commerce;

B. Seek monetary redress and other relief for conduct injurious to consumers;

C. Prescribe rules defining with specificity acts or practices that are unfair or deceptive, and establish requirements designed to prevent such acts or practices;

D. Gather and compile information and conduct investigations relating to the organization, business, practices, and management of entities engaged in commerce; and

E. Make reports and legislative recommendations to Congress and the public. A number of other statutes listed here are enforced under the FTC Act.[15]

The FTC's enforcement of "truth in advertising" laws includes all platforms, digital and traditional. The FTC's particular interest is in healthcare products and consumer protection during purchasing. This includes large areas of law such as fraud and deception targeting consumers, environmental claims made in ads, endorsement guidelines, gift card promotions and content, and health claims. The FTC not only receives complaints but actively monitors the content within advertising. Sometimes the agency sends warning letters to organizations because of deceptive advertising practices. For instance, during the COVID-19 pandemic, the FTC became very active in monitoring health and medicine sites that claimed their products helped with or cured COVID-19.[16]

The FTC's purpose is consumer protection, and in that role the agency looks at how to protect consumers from various scams. The agency provides a list of potential scams that affect consumers. Among them are auto warranty scams, charity scams, disaster relief scams, free trial scams, gift card scams, and grant scams. The FTC even monitors what is called a grandparent scam, in which a caller calls an elderly person pretending to be a relative asking for money because of an emergency, such as for bail or a hospital bill.[17]

The FTC also regulates types of advertising to eliminate and mitigate the potential for false advertising. For example, native advertising is a highly effective type of advertisement that can lead to consumer deception because the ad appears alongside editorial content as earned media. The FTC defines native advertising as "content that bears a similarity to the news, feature articles, product reviews, entertainment, and other material that surrounds it online."[18] Native advertising is big business in advertising because it is highly effective at engaging consumers. Native ads have higher click-through rates, increased brand recognition, and increased visual stimulation. However, there are risks. Consumers looking at content with native ads are more likely to view that content as deceptive.[19] However, the FTC wants consumers to be able to recognize this deception based on the "net impression" of the advertisement.[20] The FTC described its own enforcement policy statements as three rules:

1. From the FTC's perspective, the watchword is transparency. An advertisement or promotional message shouldn't suggest or imply to consumers that it's anything other than an ad.

2. Some native ads may be so clearly commercial in nature that they are unlikely to mislead consumers even without a specific disclosure.

In other instances, a disclosure may be necessary to ensure that consumers understand that the content is advertising.

3. If a disclosure is necessary to prevent deception, the disclosure must be clear and prominent.[21]

Part of the FTC's overall philosophy of advertising is rooted in the ability of consumers to recognize when something is an ad and when it is not. For example, in 1967 and 1968, the FTC addressed the issue of advertising deception when a restaurant formatted an ad to look like a newspaper column. This early native advertisement, although it was not called that at the time, was thought to be inherently deceptive to ordinary readers.[22] Decades later, when the Federal Communications Commission allowed infomercials on broadcast outlets, the FTC brought several cases about formatting that did not explicitly mention that the infomercial was a paid advertisement. In 1989, the FTC brought a case against an infomercial, resulting in the words "PAID ADVERTISEMENT" to appear at the beginning of the program and when the program switched to the sales portion of its content.[23] Similarly, the FTC requires that search engine results that appear at the top of a web page contain a disclosure that they are paid to be placed there, because consumers could otherwise think those are legitimately ranked results not based on paid placement.[24]

Native advertising regulation is no different in that the FTC requires disclosure that the content is a paid promotion or advertisement and that consumers can clearly see and understand that this content is not "regular" media coverage. The FTC likens native advertisements to a "door opener," that is, content that opens the door to a consumer by disguising its true intent. This type of "door opening" is prohibited, especially in spam emails, and has been outlawed by federal law, such as the CAN-SPAM Act of 2003.[25] The FTC identified specific factors that they look at when evaluating whether a native advertisement is properly identified. In their "Native Advertising: A Guide for Businesses," published in 2015, the FTC wrote, "Factors to weigh include an ad's overall appearance; the similarity of its written, spoken, or visual style or subject matter to nonadvertising content on the publisher site on which it appears; and the degree to which it is distinguishable from other content on the publisher site."[26]

The main issue regarding native advertising is not whether a disclosure is explicit (most are) but when a disclosure is required. In effect, the issue is when does an advertisement become native? The answer to this question, according to the FTC, is when the content of the ad is like the content in the outlet and formatting of other content. In some instances, this integration of content and format is technologically complex. For example, the FTC provides an example where billboards integrated into a virtual reality experience would need to be disclosed as paid advertising because the virtual reality user would not necessarily know those billboards contained sponsored content. Another example includes integration of certain products into a video game character's image, such as a sunglass brand, which is a paid advertisement that is not easily identified as sponsored by players. These disclosures are required because the "ordinary expectations" of the consumer would not necessarily include subtle paid promotions throughout a virtual experience or video game. Borrowing from its 2013 guidance ".com Disclosures,"[27] the FTC states that proper native advertising disclosures are

- in clear and unambiguous language;
- as close as possible to the native ads to which they relate;
- in a font and color that is easy to read;
- in a shade that stands out against the background;
- for video ads, on the screen long enough to be noticed, read, and understood; and
- for audio disclosures, read at a cadence that's easy for consumers to follow and in words consumers will understand.[28]

This creates some prescriptive guidance for content creators, particularly PR practitioners creating paid content, on how to avoid a violation of the law.

CHAPTER 4

Substantiation and Puffery in Promotional Content
Saying what you mean and being able to back it up is a cornerstone of good communication. Going back to the scenario about the shampoo, the content that is used to promote the product cannot be false or misleading. Making a claim that is extraordinary, even if supported by one incidence, is not permissible without proper evidence. What advertising regulation does is mandate truth and transparency to ensure the consumer is protected.

False advertising can take two basic forms. The first is statements that are patently false. The second is statements made without a reasonable basis.[29] The latter issue in advertising involves what is known as substantiation. Like the disclosures in advertising for native ads, there are requirements on what an ad can claim about a product or service. This is especially important when an advertisement makes an express statement, such as "9 out of 10 doctors recommend," "studies show that," or "tests show . . . ," among others. Those types of statements must have support—that is, substantiation. This substantiation requirement not only applies to statements but includes any type of implied result from a product. While an express claim makes a verifiable statement, such as "this spray kills 99 percent of all household germs," an implied claim is more nuanced. An implied statement may be customer testimonial that suggests a certain outcome for a consumer (like the shampoo's hair-growth claim). Another example of implied outcomes is seen in ads for sports equipment where it could be implied that users become better at that specific sport because of the product. The advertiser, regardless of express or implied statements, are liable for all reasonable interpretations of the advertisement. Even if there is a misunderstanding regarding the advertisement's message, the advertiser can be held liable for false advertising if a reasonable person could perceive the misleading information as true.[30] It is also important to note that a good-faith belief that a claim has been adequately substantiated is not a defense.[31]

This means those engaged in promotional content are at risk of liability based on consumer perception. Enacted in 1972 by the FTC, the substantiation requirements for advertising have remained largely unchanged in their approach since the 1980s.[32] The requirement of substantiation is rooted in what consumers can expect from a claim based on a reasonable basis. The standard of reasonable basis at its core means some type of evidence must support the claim. That may take various forms, but the more substantial the basis, the stronger the substantiation will be. The FTC states that the level of reasonable basis required is predicated on several factors: "the type of claim, the product, the consequences of a false claim, the benefits of a truthful claim, the cost of developing substantiation for the claim, and the amount of substantiation experts in the field believe is reasonable."[33] The FTC states that advertisements imply all of the reasonable interpretations that can be made by a significant minority of consumers.[34] That means that advertisers must consider a broad audience with multiple interpretations, even interpretations that are not based in fact. One of the biggest, and most expensive, questions is how much substantiation is enough. The FTC allows for extrinsic evidence, such as consumer surveys, to determine how much evidence an advertiser needs to prove a specific statement. At a minimum the substantiation provided must meet the express statements made. For example, if a promotion says that 9 out of 10 doctors recommend a medicine, the advertiser needs a study that shows that fact.[35] If a significant minority of consumers could interpret that an advertisement has made an express or implied statement, the advertiser had two choices: (1) substantiate the claim or (2) change the advertisement to remove the express or implied statement. When the statement made is health related, the substantiation requirement increases. The level of substantiation of medical- and health-related statements typically requires a scientific study, and the substantiation cannot be based on anecdotal evidence or popular press articles.[36]

This does not mean that all statements in an advertisement or paid promotion must be substantiated. Puffery, a statement made about subjective taste, requires no substantiation because it is assumed to be an opinion, not fact. Puffery has its roots in nineteenth-century English law, when an advertisement claiming the manufacturer would pay customers £100 if anyone contracted the flu after using a device known as the Carbolic Smoke Ball (a rubber ball with a tube with which individuals could inhale carbolic acid, thus preventing disease). A customer eventually sued after using the device and later contracting the flu. The company said that the advertisement was not meant to be taken seriously, but was "mere puff," thus creating the term and legal convention known today as puffery.[37] By the early twentieth century, courts in the United States were also recognizing puffery as a standard within promotional communication. In 1918, the U.S. Court of Appeals for the Second Circuit found that puffery was a legally valid defense against false advertising.[38] In the current legal reality, puffery is something that has no standardized definition within the courts. In an analysis of puffery in U.S. law, puffery is generally defined as statements that are outlandish or superlative in nature. The closer the puff gets to a quantifiable statement, the less likely it is going to be puff.[39] For example, Papa John's slogan, "Better Pizza, Better Ingredients," was the subject of lawsuit brought by Pizza Hut, which alleged the slogan constituted false advertising under the Lanham Act. Although Papa John's lost at the trial court, the judgement was reversed by the U.S. Court of Appeals for the Fifth Circuit based on puffery. The court characterized puffery as an "exaggerated advertising, blustering, and boasting upon which no reasonable buyer would rely," or "a general claim of superiority over a comparative product that is so vague, it would be understood as a mere expression of opinion."[40]

The Fifth Circuit went on to quote the classic treatise Prosser and Keeton on Torts' definition of puffery, stating: "*Prosser and Keeton on the Law of Torts* defines 'puffing' as 'a seller's privilege to lie his head off, so long as he says nothing specific, on the theory that no reasonable man would believe him, or that no reasonable man would be influenced by such talk.'"[41] Despite the broad umbrella definition of puffery, an advertiser can mis-puff and end up with a false advertising lawsuit and judgment. According to lawyers looking at puffery and false advertising, false advertising is a strict liability offense. There is no defense of poor puffing resulting in mitigated damages. When creating exaggerated content, the content creators should be careful that they are merely puffing and not making an express claim.[42]

So, going back to the shampoo example, an advertisement that claims, "I love using my new shampoo, my hair has never looked so good!" is permissible. It is based on an actual experience of an individual user. Another claim, "You'll love using our new shampoo, your hair never looked so good!" is puffery. Take another iteration of the promotion, "You'll love using our new shampoo. Your hair will grow back thicker and lusher than ever before!" Now there is a claim in need of substantiation. If that substantiation is one unusual user experience, it's not enough to make the claim.

BRAND INFLUENCERS

Social media personalities have made a big business out of being brand influencers. Popular on social media outlets such as Instagram and TikTok, brand influencers, or influencers for short, are people, usually on social media, who have high levels of influence within a particular market segment and can generate interest and purchases of products and services. Sometimes these influencers are celebrities, such as Kylie Jenner, who promotes lifestyle brands, and others are noncelebrity influencers who have reputations in niche markets, such as Alexa Chung, who uses Instagram to promote health and beauty products. The influencer market is a big business within communications. In 2022, the influencer market was a $16.4 billion industry, with 75 percent of brands having budget allocation for influencer marketing.[43]

The strategy of influencers targeting is also a sophisticated communication practice in which communicators must engage with the right type of influencer to gain the right amount of market share. The role of the influencer within the market economy has been disruptive. Influencers have replaced more traditional approaches to promotion, and many have become wealthy and famous within their niche sphere of influence. Essentially, an influencer's business model relies on them creating content within a specific market segment, for example shoes, and then creating engaging content that attracts followers. Once the influencer gets to a certain level of popularity, brands may engage with them to create sponsored content that resonates with consumers. These relationships are essentially like those of endorsers, except that the influencer's power comes from their dedicated following in a particular sphere. Because of that, the branding does not include media purchases, such as advertising spots on television, and instead includes having a paid relationship with the influencer. Influencers can become quite wealthy in the process.

According to *Forbes*, in 2022 influencers made collectively $1.9 billion with content on Instagram, TikTok, and YouTube. In 2021, the top influencer MrBeast, aka Jimmy Donaldson, made $54 million a year having 162 million followers on social media.[44]

The influence of influence marketing has gotten the attention of policymakers. Increasingly, lawmakers' concerns focus on how influencer marketing can be deceptive and ultimately confuse consumers. Like native advertising, the power of influencers rests in their ability to be authentic in their communication. Agencies, particularly the FTC, have become highly active in this area and have placed regulations on how influencer content should be packaged for consumers for maximum transparency of the relationship between brands and influencers. In 2023, the FTC updated its endorsement guides that specifically impacts reviewers and influencers.[45]

Endorsements for the FTC regulation is a broad category that is "any advertising, marketing, or promotional message for a product that consumers are likely to believe reflects the opinions, beliefs, findings, or experiences of a party other than the sponsoring advertiser."[46] Endorsement or testimonial content is treated the same under the FTC guidelines, and the regulation of testimonial content includes any product or service. This means these regulations include influencers, but not exclusively. Content that is merely a paid review of content on a website also is regulated under the same rules.

Like substantiation, an endorsement, whether paid or not, must be authentic to be used in an advertisement. It must be a genuinely held belief and cannot be used in a way that is out of context (although it does not have to be the exact words of the endorser).[47] Influencers, like any endorser, must disclose their material connection with the advertiser if the relationship is not "reasonably expected by the audience."[48] This connection is a broad category, and the FTC defines this as including familial relationships between the endorser and the organization being endorsed, paid endorsements, or endorsers who receive free products or discounts on the products they endorse. In addition, the exchange of goods, including free goods, is broadly defined. It includes disclosing any product, whether it is included in the endorsement or not. It also does not matter if the free product or discount was given in exchange for an endorsement. Even if the organization provides a free product or discount and does not expect an endorsement in exchange, that relationship must be disclosed to the audience.[49] The FTC provides an example of this with a hypothetical woodworker who uses a lathe, a machine used for rotating wood, in a series of online videos. If the lathe was provided to the woodworker by the manufacturer, and the woodworker praises the quality and ability of the machine in a way where a "significant minority" of viewers would not know the woodworker received the lathe for free, then the woodworker influencer must disclose his relationship with the manufacturer. The FTC states that "the woodworker should clearly and conspicuously disclose receiving it for free, a fact that could affect the credibility that viewers attach to the endorsements."[50]

It is important to note that liability for nondisclosure can fall to both the entity paying for the endorsement (i.e., the advertiser) as well as the endorser. Sometimes there is even a scenario where the liability will only extend to the advertiser. The FTC states that when considering how to disclose, there are three guiding factors. Advertisers should:

1. provide guidance to their endorsers on the need to ensure that their statements are not misleading and to disclose unexpected material connections;

2. monitor their endorsers' compliance; and

3. take action sufficient to remedy noncompliance and prevent future noncompliance. While not a safe harbor, good faith and effective guidance, monitoring, and remedial action should reduce the incidence of deceptive claims and reduce an advertiser's odds of facing an FTC enforcement action.[51]

The philosophy behind the FTC's approach to endorsements and influencers is based on the idea that some consumers do not know that there is a relationship between an endorser and a product. While there is a general societal awareness that there may be a relationship, that is not always the case, and the FTC's guidelines reflect this reality.[52]

The FTC created guidance for social media influencers entitled "Disclosures 101 for Social Media Influencers" in 2019. That document details what influencers should consider when they are creating content and maintaining a relationship with an organization. Chief among these guidelines is recalibrating what an influencer thinks of as a paid relationship. Payment does not just include money, but also goods, services, or anything of value, including "perks" from the organization. There is also a warning about assumptions, especially consumer knowledge of a sponsored relationship. When in doubt, the FTC advises influencers to disclose and assume their followers are unaware of the underlying relationship between the brand and themselves. The endorsement also doesn't have to be explicit to qualify for disclosure. The FTC notes that pinning, liking, and sharing content on social media can qualify as an endorsement that requires disclosure. The agency also suggests that the disclosure itself follow certain guidelines, specifically that the disclosure is explicit, easy to understand, and appropriate within the platform it appears on.[53]

Going Beyond Influencers: Ordinary User Endorsements

Many businesses rely on testimonials and endorsements from everyday customers. If a customer wants to provide an online review without any compensation or pay, they are free to do so. In that situation there is nothing to disclose, because there is no relationship between the organization and the endorser. That type of endorsement is a true and authentic endorsement, the type that most other customers look at to determine if they want to make a purchase. Review sites online are particularly important in this area of endorsement. Online review sites are a way for customers to make decisions about what products they will purchase, particularly in the hospitality industry. However, what are rules for what an organization can do to solicit one of these endorsements? Can those endorsements be incentivized? Can they be controlled? What, if anything, can an organization require of its customers? The FTC and Congress have entered this space as well, recognizing that this presents important questions about consumer rights and free speech.

One thing endorsers should know is that they do not have carte blanche to say anything they want. The FTC's guidelines for endorsements provides the following rules on what cannot be said in an endorsement, regardless of compensation:

- You can't talk about your experience with a product if you haven't tried it.
- If you've only tried a product once, you can't suggest you use it regularly.
- If you thought it was terrible or mediocre, you can't say it's good or terrific.
- You can't otherwise misrepresent your experience with or opinions about a product.[54]

There are also rules about what an endorser can say about a product or service. Any statement that would require substantiation cannot be made absent that substantiation, or any statement that goes beyond the endorser's actual experience. In these cases, the endorser, not the advertiser, is legally responsible for what is said.

Organizations seeking endorsements must also be careful in making it clear that even ordinary noninfluencers are receiving some type of compensation. For example, in a social media sweepstakes asking users to provide an engaging hashtag that is complimentary of a company requires the disclosure that the sweepstakes is a game with some type of reward. The FTC provides guidance that, in this situation, the sweepstakes campaign should contain an explicit disclosure, such as "#XYZ_Contest." That disclosure also must have proximity to the content provided. For example, in the sweepstakes example it is not enough to have the word "contest" or "sweepstakes" in a post. The closer these words are to the actual contest content, such as the hashtag, the better.[55]

Those organizations providing free materials to reviewers, even in situations where the reviews can be negative, must be disclosed because that relationship can matter to consumers who are seeking authentic reviews. Technology also cannot be used to solicit reviews from groups or areas that a company believes may generate a high rate of good reviews. Moreover, software that allows for negative review suppression is disallowed under the FTC guides.[56]

There are also issues surrounding the authenticity of reviews, with many consumers being skeptical of perfect review scores on businesses. Reviews follow the same rules as any type of endorsement, but some laws do create some protection for reviewers. For example, organizations cannot contractually force customers to give good reviews or ban them from giving bad ones. In one case, the FTC found that Fashion Nova, a fast fashion retailer, did not publish hundreds of thousands of negative, or less-than-glowingly positive, reviews from 2012 until 2019. The company had a software package that allowed for immediate publication of four- and five-star reviews. Fashion Nova eventually entered a settlement agreement with the FTC for $4.2 million in 2023.[57] After the settlement, the FTC also sent out standing letters to other companies who provide review management services stating that removing negative reviews is illegal under FTC regulations. Part of that letter states:

> One of our [FTC] concerns is when companies take improper steps to avoid collecting or publishing negative reviews. Examples may include asking for reviews only from those likely to leave positive ones, preventing or discouraging submission of negative reviews, subjecting negative reviews to greater scrutiny, refusing to publish negative reviews, or otherwise not treating positive and negative reviews equally.[58]

However, it is important to note that reaching out to customers to make their experiences better after a negative review is allowed.

What about contractually making consumers only provide positive comments about an organization? That is a violation of federal law. Companies cannot contractually mandate customers provide only good reviews. The Consumer Review Fairness Act of 2016 (CRFA) expressly prohibits organizations from barring customers from providing negative or critical reviews.[59] The CFRA barred any contract that banned a customer from providing a review of a product or service, had a penalty levied against a consumer for a negative review, or required customers to release their intellectual property rights held in their reviews (i.e., copyright). A violation of the CFRA works the same as a violation of a FTC regulation, and a company can be fined and a court order can be entered to stop the effects of the contract. This does not mean there is no recourse for any type of review, however. Reviews of organizations that include defamatory content, sexual harassment, content unrelated to the organization, misleading, false, racist, or inappropriate can be removed.[60]

The FTC's approach to these endorsements also places the liability back onto the organization or business that is being endorsed. They advise that part of the endorsement strategy of any organization should include certain considerations. According to the FTC, an organization should regularly monitor its endorsers, influencers, and reviews to make sure proper disclosures are made. The FTC suggests the following be considered in all endorsement strategies:

1. Given an advertiser's responsibility for substantiating objective product claims, explain to members of your network what they can (and can't) say about the products—for example, a list of the health claims they can make for your products, along with instructions not to go beyond those claims.

2. Instruct members of the network on their responsibilities for clearly and conspicuously disclosing their connections to you, including exactly how you want them to make the disclosures.

3. Periodically search for what members of your network are saying.

4. Take appropriate action if you find questionable practices.[61]

The FTC stops short of providing precise guidelines of how often these audits should take place. However, within the PR industry, it is commonplace to engage in environmental scanning of online reputation. These environmental scans could include this type of review of disclosures and endorsements as well. In fact, the FTC acknowledges that the scanning of online disclosures frequently falls to the PR team within a company. Training materials provided to endorsers and influencers

CHAPTER 4

may be a good start in making their endorsed content FTC compliant. However, this is not enough. The FTC states that active environmental scanning of endorser content is necessary to ensure compliance with regulations.

FINANCIAL TRANSPARENCY

For PR practitioners working in the financial sector, transparency is important, not only because it is legally required, but because the lack of transparency can have major economic implications. For example, Enron, once one of the world's leading energy companies, collapsed in December 2001, creating a ripple effect in the U.S. economy. Once a company that was hailed by Wall Street investors, Enron plunged many of its investors into poverty by losing its $63.4 billion in assets.[62] Investors brought a $40 billion lawsuit, and the company's CEO and CFO went to prison. Part of the reason Enron was able to carry on as it did was the lack of accountability for the executives who worked there. Communications that were provided were in effect disinformation, and Enron's lies caused many people, including smart investors, to fall victim to the company's inexcusable greed and malevolence. The residual effect of Enron on the stock market was also significant. Prior to Enron, investors had much more confidence in U.S. companies and had not seen large-scale implosion of a company based on fraud. The collateral effect of Enron spurred Congress to ensure greater levels of transparency in the way companies report and communicate about their financial health.[63] PR practitioners were now in an important role of having to verify the content they gave to stakeholders and shareholders. However, this was nothing new to PR professionals, as they had been dealing with financial transparency issues since the 1930s.

U.S. financial regulations began in response to market excess. During the late nineteenth century when the stock market was becoming a force within the U.S. economy, market speculators were able to drive stocks up and down using a variety of nefarious tactics. During that era, market speculation led to turbulent markets with a market panic that lasted from 1893 to 1897. Many of these problems were created by the market speculation that was part of the railroad and manufacturing expansion in the late nineteenth century. It was in this environment that corporate public relations first emerged as a stand-alone profession in the United States. Those practitioners were tasked with speaking on behalf of organizations to an increasingly skeptical and demanding press.[64]

The federal government responded to these market forces with laws that addressed financial transparency. By the 1929 stock market crash, there was a political movement to address the factors that affected trading, including communication. Investigations into Wall Street revealed that the health of corporations was frequently exaggerated, and that the truth was that trading practices that led to the 1929 crash frequently included corporate disinformation and insider trading. Ferdinand Pecora, the counsel to the U.S. Senate Committee on Banking and Currency, revealed this information during his 1933 investigation into Wall Street trading, and the result was that Congress passed multiple laws addressing trading, including the Glass-Steagall Banking Act of 1933, the Securities Act of 1933, and the Securities Act of 1934.[65]

Federal laws in the 1930s were meant to send a message to the public that the federal government was taking the factors that led to the 1929 market crash seriously. Glass-Steagall, formally the Banking Act of 1933, separated investment and commercial banking, and served as a benchmark for banking regulation globally (it was repealed in 1999). The Securities Act of 1933 and 1934 had a more direct impact on communication. The 1933 Securities Act, sometimes called the Truth in Securities Act, mandated greater disclosure about a security sold to individuals through a financial prospectus that contains information about a company.[66] At its core, the Securities Act of 1933 required:

- a description of the company's properties and business;
- a description of the security to be offered for sale;
- information about the management of the company; and
- financial statements certified by independent accountants.[67]

By 1982, the Securities and Exchange Commission (SEC) created the form S-K, which outlines what information must be provided to the public such as a description of the business, property owned, material legal proceedings, and risk factors facing the company.[68] While S-K filings are more qualitative in nature, financial statements, found in form S-X, contain quantitative information about a publicly traded company.[69]

Perhaps one of the best-known provisions of the Securities Act of 1933, section 5 was the introduction of the quiet period.[70] That rule prohibits any communication between the registration of a security and its initial public offering (IPO). For a private company going public this begins when a registration statement (S-1) is made to the SEC. What occurs is a quiet period, between 10 and 25 days, which allows the stock to trade without any new information. There is also a second quiet period that exists, though it is less defined as the IPO quiet period. In this second quiet period, a company limits its communication with investors and analysts during the end of a quarter. The length of this period begins at the end of the quarter until the earnings call reporting out the quarterly result. The rationale behind the IPO quiet period is that it prevents companies from issuing statements that may influence analysts from issuing positive reports about a new stock. In an IPO quiet period, managers must be extremely careful about interviews and other communication with the media and potential investors.[71] In 2004, Salesforce.com, which sells software produces, got into trouble with the SEC because its CEO, Marc Benioff, gave a quote in a *New York Times* article about the company.[72] As a result, Salesforce.com had to delay its IPO to provide a cooling-off period. These types of inadvertent violations are why many companies practice an overly cautious communications strategy before an IPO. Quarterly quiet periods exist to comply with Regulation FD, which prohibits companies from making statements that are based on known, but unreleased, quarterly report information. Compliance with quiet periods vary from strict silence to communications only about information that is currently publicly available. The risk of not going totally silent during these periods is inadvertent disclosure, which is a violation of the law.[73]

The Securities Act of 1934 was much more robust than its predecessor in that it established the SEC.[74] The SEC has the power to regulate the securities exchanges, such as the New York Stock Exchange,

NASDAQ Stock Market, and Chicago Board of Options Exchange. Companies with more than $10 million in assets whose securities are held by more than 500 owners are subject to the reporting rules of the SEC and their annual reports are available to the public (now through the SEC EDGAR database). Other information must be disclosed to the SEC including materials for proxy solicitations and market participants, for example, brokers, exchanges, and transfer agents, must register with the SEC. The 1934 Act also banned insider trading and gave the SEC power to enforce these laws.[75]

After the establishment of the SEC, other laws were enacted to control markets. These include the Trust Indenture Act of 1940 (regulating bonds and notes), the Investment Company Act of 1940 (regulation of mutual funds), and the Investors Advisor Act of 1940 (mandating advisor registration). These laws passed in 1940 along with the SEC regulations governed securities for the next 60 years. The next major change occurred in 2002 with the passage of the Sarbanes-Oxley Act (SOX), which was passed because of high-profile market failures such as Enron.[76] The provisions of SOX created new provisions for corporate transparency and accountability. This included the CEO and CFO certifying the accuracy of financial reports and making CEOs and CFOs subject to criminal penalties for financial misinformation from those reports.[77] Other provisions made off-the-books transactions subject to greater reporting requirements, and mandated faster reporting of financial changes.[78] The net result of this law has changed corporate structure, some say for the better. The SOX requirements mean there must be greater transparency internally and externally as well as a higher level of documentation of work.[79] However, some in the PR field have expressed less than optimal experiences post-SOX in terms of workplace collaboration and corporate transparency.[80]

Investor relations and corporate communications are some of the most lucrative careers in the PR industry. Understanding the nuances of these requirements can help practitioners make a promising career for themselves. Being able to take complex financial information and making it understandable to the public is important, but being able to do this while also complying with federal regulations is a unique skill that requires both PR expertise and more formal training in the financial industry.

ETHICS IN PUBLIC RELATIONS: WHEN THE LAW IS NOT ENOUGH

Legally mandated transparency is something that is implemented because lawmakers thought disclosure benefitted society. That is evident in advertising content, influencer regulations, and financial disclosures. All that transparency was created to benefit consumers and investors because informed people make better decisions. In communication ethics, transparency is thought to be a good thing because it builds trust with publics and ensures credibility with stakeholders. However, the law should not be thought of as the ceiling, but as the floor of transparency. Ethical communications can always go beyond what is legally mandated by the government. In fact, there are benefits to this approach. Organizations that build trust with stakeholders have better reputations, and sometimes have a competitive advantage in image repair when a crisis emerges.

There is also a moral obligation that PR practitioners should consider. Inherent in transparency is respect for individuals, publics, and society. Providing information reduces the risk of misinterpretation, and that disclosure sometimes saves lives, for example, product recalls. There is also an increased sense of accountability when an organization goes beyond the minimum of disclosure. PR practitioners frequently act as wise counsel and as the conscience of an organization. Transparent actions increase both the stature of the organization, but also the profession of public relations. It echoes many of the ethical maxims of the profession: truth, honesty, duty to publics, and duty to the profession. As communicators, public relations provides the information that helps in society's decision making. The ability to make those decisions, fully informed of all benefits and risks, is one of the cornerstones of a democratic society. It is why mis- and disinformation are so insidious. Public relations as a profession and practice has a unique position in this larger issue. By facilitating transparency, PR benefits not only organizations and clients, but also the commercial and intellectual marketplace.

The technological revolution in AI presents new ethical questions. These questions are made more important because of the lack of substantive law in the AI field. Currently self-regulated with a few subject-specific laws, such as copyright, AI use has proliferated and potentially transformed PR practice.[81] However, issues of transparency abound. One of the biggest is whether PR practitioners should disclose the use of AI to clients. Part of the concern is rooted in the fact that generative AI can do so much, very quickly. It seems in some instances that PR practitioners' jobs may be replaced by this new platform, but practitioners also recognize that much of the work of AI frees them to do other, more important work. Disclosure remains a subject that has no clear-cut industry requirement. Some practitioners say disclosure should be required because it maintains honesty with the client. Others say disclosure is not required because the use of AI is no different than other forms of technology. For example, would a PR practitioner disclose that she used the internet to do research or editing software, such as Grammarly, to review written content? Probably not. While an industry answer to this question remains up for debate, what is not a matter of debate is the fact that discussion about transparency in public relations only increases with platforms like AI. The profession stands at a precipice that presents new technological challenges, but more opportunities than ever to be thought leaders in the ethics of communication. Because the legal solutions to AI's problems are still under development and likely to be slow to enact, especially given the polarization of U.S. politics, it will be up to PR practitioners to establish an ethical solution to the issue of technological transparency in the age of AI.

DISCUSSION QUESTIONS

1. Why is PR practice so focused on transparency?

2. Write a legally sound definition of PR transparency. Include in the definition what is legally mandated transparency and what is ethically mandated. Is there a difference?

3. What is the value of disclosing brand influencers' relationship with organizations? Does that make a difference in consumer decision making?

4. What is the difference between substantiation and puffery? Why is substantiation required for certain claims?

5. Does ethical transparency in public relations exceed legal requirements of transparency? Why or why not?

CASE SCENARIO

You are a PR practitioner working for a shoe company where you are tasked with all social media posts. Part of your duty is to post blogs and other content on behalf of the company's CEO. The CEO reviews the posts and occasionally makes changes to them. However, the posts are written by you. In many of the posts, both on social media and the corporation's website, you post the endorsement of certain shoes worn by the CEO. These posts read like a brand endorsement from the CEO, much like a consumer review. The blogs and posts clearly identify the CEO in his role in the company. Should the blogs contain a disclosure that you are writing these on his behalf? What legal issues are there, if any? What ethical issues are there, if any?

CHAPTER 5

Reputation Management in a Digital World

OVERVIEW: REPUTATION MANAGEMENT IS A SUBCATEGORY OF PR PRAC-
tice that involves a complex set of laws and regulations. This chapter examines those in context with content creation by PR practitioners.
Specifically, the chapter examines the role of defamation as a means to
ameliorate reputational harm. Particular attention is paid to the actual
malice standard in relation to the media for these categories: public official, public figure, limited purpose public figure, and business plaintiffs.
The chapter also analyzes online review sites, and the legal approaches
to removing false and inaccurate reviews. The chapter concludes with an
analysis of social media policy writing for employees, and how public
employee criticisms of employers are largely protected by federal law.

OBJECTIVES:

- Detail the elements of defamation and the standards of fault for
  specific plaintiffs.

- Analyze the actual malice standard for defamation for media
  defendants.

- Discuss online review sites and the protection given to those sites
  by the 1996 Communications Decency Act, Section 230.

- Analyze social media policies considering National Labor Relations Board regulations.

- Provide ethical considerations for reputation management, specifically how communications solutions may provide better results than litigation.

Reputation management has become an important aspect of communications practice. In this era of digital media, where internet rumors and a bad review can tank a business overnight, PR practitioners must be aware of the legal avenues available to them to protect their clients.

Reputation management, however, is not a new phenomenon. The practice of managing a reputation, whether individual or business, has roots in the growth of the press and the public's opinion. Within public relations, reputation management intersects with many areas of practice, such as credibility, which is important in staving off reputational challenges, including disinformation. Crisis communication is also affected by reputational issues, particularly an organization's record of responsiveness to public concerns. The better the history, the better the chances that an organization will recover from a crisis.

Reputation is also related to stakeholder engagement and an organization's ability to engage in honest two-way communication with various publics. Trust in an organization, which is fostered by reputation management, helps PR practitioners achieve their goal of attitudinal and behavioral change. Financial reputation also brings organizational value. A business's goodwill, the intrinsic value of the business itself including its brand, is predicated on its reputation.

So, what does the law have to do with reputation? A lot. Reputational attacks are frequent in digital communications today. Disinformation, fake reviews, and internet rumors can all lead to reputational problems. In the United States, defamation has a long history rooted in English law. The legal protection of one's reputation developed during the nineteenth century with states enacting laws to hold speakers accountable for untrue statements that caused reputational harm. However, reputational protection under the law has a much longer history. Going back to ancient Roman law, reputation itself was the basis for defamation. Privacy laws such as false light serve as a basis for managing an individual's reputation. Interestingly, legal systems outside the United States, notably the

European Union, provide other legal rights that protect reputation, such as the right of erasure, sometimes called the right to be forgotten.

Despite these protections, there are also limits to what the law can do to protect an individual or organization's reputation. Certain types of individuals, particularly the celebrity and the public official, must endure more harmful disinformation about themselves compared with the average citizen. The platforms that host reputationally damaging content also have certain protections that immunize them from litigation.

Reputation management also introduces tough questions for PR practitioners. To what lengths is a PR practitioner willing to go to protect a client's reputation? In today's world of disinformation, there are many cases where an organization uses disinformation deliberately to protect their reputation. This ranges from parsing words to create "spin" to outright lies about an organization. For example, in chapter 4, the issue of transparency in an organization's relationship with influencers is an example of the complex legal and ethical issues that have now arisen in reputation management. Concealing these relationships can increase reputation because of the perception of endorsement, until the relationship is uncovered. The practice of "astroturfing," the use of fake accounts that endorse or even promote an organization's stance or products, is a devious communication practice that, left uncovered, can enhance reputation, at least temporarily. The deletion of negative reviews online, another issue addressed in chapter 4, is another practice of reputation management that violates the norms of ethical communications practice.

In this chapter, the legal issues of reputation management are examined. The chapter begins by looking at defamation law by delving deeply into the standard of fault for actual malice with particular attention paid to media reporting standards. Next, the chapter looks at the issues of review sites and their power to determine online reputation for businesses. Specific attention is paid to fake or activist reviews that negatively portray an organization and what the organization can do to redress this problem. The section also examines the immunity of online host platforms allowed under the 1996 Communications Decency Act (CDA), Section 230.[1] This immunity is discussed considering new cases facing practitioners in which AI has created defamatory content, and how CDA

Section 230 may immunize platforms from lawsuits. The chapter then examines social media speech rights. As a group, employees frequently have access to sensitive and damaging information that organizations may attempt to control with social media policies. The parameters of these policies considering employee speech rights is discussed along with regulations on social media policies set by the National Labor Relations Board (NLRB). Ethical issues within reputation management close the chapter by looking at how communication, rather that legal actions, can improve reputation.

DEFAMATION LAW

Public relations practitioners are in the business of reputation. What happens when someone makes a statement that harms a client's reputation? What should a PR practitioner do?

While communication professionals may want to dispel this untruthful statement with better communication, state law also provides a legal option—a defamation lawsuit. Consider the following hypothetical situation. A PR practitioner is representing a new restaurant in a major metropolitan city. The restaurant has been reviewed positively by food critics. The chef has been featured in the newspaper, and the social media account of the business has a strong following. Most of the reviews are five stars, with the occasional nasty review about service and wait times. Overall, the restaurant is positively reviewed with an average of a 4.7 on a 5-star scale with over 400 reviews.

However, one day you notice a particularly nasty one-star review. The review criticizes the chef, making claims that he has been in prison and has been dealing drugs out of the kitchen of the restaurant. The review even goes so far to say the restaurant is a front for a group of notorious drug dealers and that patrons should stay away if they value their safety. The catch is, that review is 100 percent false. It is made up out of revenge, likely by a competitor or fired employee. What are the chef's options legally? Whom can he sue? What can he recover? How does he restore his reputation?

This scenario is a textbook example of defamation, that is, an untrue statement made about a party that brings reputational harm. In the

United States, defamation is largely governed by state civil law and, because of this, there are subtle nuances to how defamation works from state to state. However, U.S. defamation law has some constitutional boundaries in how it can be used in civil litigation. Defamation receives no First Amendment protection and, as such, states can pass laws that allow parties to sue for defamation. Typically, these laws require the plaintiff, the person bringing the lawsuit, to prove the following:

- Statement: A defamatory statement is made.
- Identification: The statement identifies the plaintiff (directly or indirectly).
- Publication: The statement is published or spoken to at least one other person.
- Harm: The statement causes reputational harm.
- Fault: The person making the statement did so with the required degree of fault. If the plaintiff is an ordinary person, then the fault is typically negligence. If the plaintiff is a public figure, public official, or limited purpose public figure, then the standard is actual malice.

In some, but not all, jurisdictions, a plaintiff may have to prove the falsity of a statement, but typically that is not required. Defendants, those who are sued, also have affirmative defenses to defamation. Those defenses vary by jurisdiction, but traditionally they are truth (a defamatory statement cannot be true), privilege (the location where the speaker is speaking immunizes them from defamation law, e.g., Congress or courts), and fair comment (opinions are not facts and therefore cannot be defamation).

To understand how the contemporary legal concepts of defamation developed, it is helpful to understand the evolution of defamation law. The idea of being able to sue another person for reputational damages has deep roots. In ancient Rome, the Twelve Tables posted in the Forum listed laws that addressed reputational harm through the spoken word. As Roman society grew and developed, there was a greater awareness of the impact of reputational harm within society. Around 60 BCE, the Roman philosopher Cicero wrote that the Twelve Tables mandated the death penalty for anyone, usually singers and authors, who produced slanderous or libelous content. Although this claim is subject to some debate among classical historians, the recognition that reputation was something that could be legally protected is important for the development of defamation law.

By medieval times, English Year Books, the law journals of the era, contained cases that discussed lawsuits concerning dishonor. These laws were inherited from Norman times, when cases involving spoken dishonor were created to discourage feuds and other violent means of redressing insults.[2] In that era, disputes regarding defamation were adjudicated in a combination of ecclesiastical and secular courts. By the sixteenth century, defamation would be absorbed into the King's Bench exclusively, and libel, that is, written defamation, was a type of lawsuit that had limited legal remedies. The mid-1400s invention of the printing press would change this dramatically. Until the proliferation of printing, defamation cases largely involved slander, or spoken defamation. With the advent of the printing press and the proliferation of books and pamphlets, courts began having an increased number of libel, or written defamation, cases. As such, a differentiation between libel and slander requirements developed in English courts, making a sharp distinction between the two during the sixteenth and seventeenth centuries.[3]

While the history of defamation may strike some twenty-first-century PR professionals as interesting, but inapplicable to modern issues, it is important to point out that the development of current defamation law is largely predicated on how these historical standards changed over time. Events in English legal history influenced the development of U.S. law. These events included the Star Chamber, an English court that was known for suppressing dissent for political reasons; the English licensing of printing presses during the reign of Henry VIII; and the suppression of dissent during the Interregnum era of Oliver Cromwell. These legal approaches ultimately shaped colonial American sentiment toward the development of defamation.

In colonial America, the trial of Peter Zenger in 1735 served as a flashpoint for development of U.S. legal attitudes toward prior restraint and defamation. Zenger, the publisher of the *New-York Weekly Journal*, was accused of seditious libel, or criminal libel, by the Crown for his criticism of colonial Governor William Crosby. He was held in jail for 10 months awaiting trial, and he was ultimately acquitted based on the concept that truth was an absolute defense to libel. This trial became a turning point in U.S. defamation law development, and it served as a historical basis for why the framers enshrined freedom of the press in the First Amendment of the U.S. Constitution.[4]

The English common law tradition of libel and slander was imported to the United States with most cases in the eighteenth century mirroring that of Zenger, with government officials suing individuals. Defamation had two components. First, the statement was false. Second, the statement caused reputational harm. Libel per se, a statement that is automatically presumed to be detrimental to a person's reputation, such as criminal conduct, professional misdeeds, and loathsome diseases, was distinguished from libel per quod, a statement that was libelous because of its context.[5] In the United States defamation was and still is a largely civil action (lawsuit for money damages), although criminal libel did and still does exist in some states.

By the nineteenth century, U.S. defamation law had been largely codified in state statutes. A person suing for defamation did not have to prove falsity of the statement, nor did they have to prove actual reputational harm. All that was required was proving a statement was said that could have caused reputational harm. Moreover, these laws varied in their approach to defamation, with some jurisdictions having laws that made defamation a strict liability offense. That is, a plaintiff only had to show that a defamatory statement was made. A defendant's intent or knowledge of the statement's falsity was of no consequence. This made defamation lawsuits easier for plaintiffs to win.

The affirmative defense of truth existed in most states, but again the burden of proving truth was placed on the defendant. Damages in this era were largely presumed, meaning that the plaintiff did not have to show any actual harm done reputationally. Moreover, the status of the plaintiff did not matter. Celebrities, politicians, and ordinary people all had the same standard of fault to prove, which in many jurisdictions was strict liability or negligence. It is important to note that during this era, First Amendment analysis of defamation was not viewed as a legal issue. Instead, the issue of defamation was viewed through the lens of societal preservation and police power. The idea that a person could be held legally responsible for defaming another was an important part of law and order.[6]

Journalism has always been heavily intertwined with the creation and application of defamation law. The American newspaper industry proliferated from the partisan press in the early nineteenth century to the penny press of the 1830s to the sensational "yellow journalism" of the 1890s. This historical arc of journalism was driven by greater accessibility to an increasingly literate society and greater sensationalism of stories. At the time defamation was a common problem because of the inaccuracy of newspaper reports. This was compounded by wire service stories containing libelous content that ran in multiple newspapers. Chain libel or wire service libel was a form of defamation that had disastrous consequences for newspapers because of the compounded defamation that was republished in multiple outlets. These lawsuits proliferated as well because of the changes in the way legal fees were collected. By the late nineteenth century, attorneys began working in contingency fee arrangements with clients, where lawyers would receive no money upfront but would collect a percentage of what the client collected from the lawsuit. This is a practice still commonplace today among lawyers practicing tort law, such as premises liability cases and automobile accident litigation.[7]

This system of defamation law existed until the mid-1960s when the U.S. Supreme Court fundamentally changed the nature of defamation law with their 1964 decision in *New York Times v. Sullivan* and later in the 1974 decision in *Gertz v. Welch*.[8] In *New York Times v. Sullivan*, the Supreme Court had to decide how defamation law should apply to a public official. In that case the Montgomery, Alabama, police commissioner J. L. Sullivan sued the *New York Times* over an advertisement that ran in the paper entitled "Heed Their Rising Voices," which was critical of the Montgomery police department. Although not specifically mentioned in the ad, Sullivan felt that he was a target of the ad's criticism. As a result, he sued the *New York Times* under Alabama defamation law and was awarded $500,000 in damages. The advertisement did contain some factual errors, including the number of times civil rights leader Dr. Martin Luther King Jr. was arrested and inaccurate portrayals of events at Alabama State College, a historically black university in Montgomery.

The Supreme Court agreed to hear the case and held in a unanimous decision that the *New York Times* was not responsible for defamation. In the case, the Court established a different defamation standard of fault for public officials. That standard of fault would mean that a plaintiff who was a public official would have to prove their case of defamation, showing that the defendant made the defamatory statements with actual malice. This means that the defendant either knew the statements were false or made them with reckless disregard for the truth.[9]

Writing the unanimous opinion of the court, Justice Brennan justified this heightened actual malice standard by asserting that having a regular negligence standard for defamation for public officials would lead the press to self-censor their criticism of politicians and others in public positions. Brennan wrote:

> A rule compelling the critic of official conduct to guarantee the truth of all his factual assertions—and to do so on pain of libel judgments virtually unlimited in amount—leads to a comparable "self-censorship." Allowance of the defense of truth, with the burden of proving it on the defendant, does not mean that only false speech will be deterred. Even courts accepting this defense as an adequate safeguard have recognized the difficulties of adducing legal proofs that the alleged libel was true in all its factual particulars.[10]

The practical result of this holding was that U.S. defamation law changed. Essentially, a public official had a much harder time proving the prima facie case of defamation because of the actual malice standard.

The actual malice standard was expanded by the Supreme Court to include other types of plaintiffs as well. In the 1967 case of *Curtis Publishing v. Butts*, the Supreme Court held that public figures were also subject to proving defamation under the actual malice standard.[11] In 1974, the Supreme Court held that for an ordinary person, the standard of fault in a defamation case had to at least be negligence, removing the strict liability standard as an option for state statutes. This meant that for a defendant to legally commit defamation, the defendant had to at least be acting with negligence, that is, lacking ordinary care.

What if the plaintiff is an organization and not an individual? That presents an interesting scenario in defamation law. Corporations are subject to the same defamation laws as individuals. Like individuals, they can be required to prove actual malice in defamation suits when they are the plaintiff. An example of this is in the 2021 lawsuit between Dominion Voting and Fox News. Both the plaintiff and defendant were corporations, and while individuals were at issue in the lawsuit, the plaintiff, Dominion Voting, was a corporate plaintiff that was also a public figure. The 1974 Supreme Court decision regarding *Gertz v. Welch* addressed the issue of corporate plaintiffs in defamation suits but did not provide clear guidance. However, many interpretations of *Gertz v. Welch* favor the idea that corporate plaintiff status is determined much like public figure status. That is, it is based on the fame of the plaintiff.

This presents many questions about determining the threshold for corporate fame. Courts have a variety of approaches that range from advertising to a rule that corporations are automatically public figures because of the nature of their status as businesses.[12] There is an extra layer of complexity to corporate defamation plaintiffs. Some businesses use lawsuits to suppress criticism. This sometimes silences critics by using the legal system as a force to intimidate a defendant who may be making truthful claims.

To combat this weaponizing of the legal system, states have crafted what are known as anti-SLAPP statutes, which bans this type of frivolous lawsuit. SLAPP is an acronym that means "Strategic Lawsuit Against Public Participation." In the context of defamation, these lawsuits are meant to protect defendants. The law typically allows defendants to make a motion striking a lawsuit based on the grounds that the lawsuit involves speech on a matter of public concern. These statutes typically mandate that plaintiffs need to show that they would prevail on the lawsuit if it were to go to trial. If a plaintiff cannot meet this burden, then the lawsuit is dismissed, frequently with defendants receiving attorney's fees from the plaintiff.[13]

Another form of defamation that is related to businesses is trade libel, or the disparagement of products made by a business. This type of lawsuit is distinct from defamation in that defamation is about the reputational harm of an individual or business. Trade libel, by contrast, covers the disparagement of a specific good or product. These types of lawsuits typically arise from product comparisons made by competitors. These lawsuits work differently than defamation, although these cases have the same core elements of defamation and the same terminology. The issue in a product disparagement case is not reputation, but loss of sales. It is important to note that trade libel or product disparagement is also related to trademark law (covered in chapter 7) in that sometimes it involves using similar trademarks of a product to produce disparaging content.

Product disparagement cases typically require a plaintiff to prove actual malice. Although the Supreme Court has not directly ruled on this element of disparagement cases, lawyers point to the 1984 decision, *Bose v. Consumers Union*, which involved the product disparagement of Bose loudspeakers by *Consumer Reports*.[14] Other courts have not established a bright line rule on disparagement claims. These cases are difficult, because frequently at issue is the balance between normal business competition and disparaging remarks. Complicating the issue of trade libel is its intersection with false advertising (see chapter 4), and regulations related to product comparisons. However, product disparagement and trade libel are something of a cottage industry. An internet search of lawyers specializing in this area are plentiful, especially in the era of online reviews.

Actual Malice and Media Relations
The actual malice standard is important because it is so uniquely applicable to U.S. media outlets. It requires one of two possible actions, either reckless disregard of the truth or knowing falsity. For PR practitioners in media relations, this is important. Whether a practitioner is dealing with untrue statements about an individual client who is a person or a client that is an organization, actual malice may apply as the standard.

Typically, these cases will involve a news outlet as a defendant, and the key issue of the case will be whether the plaintiff can prove the actual malice standard at trial.

Even though the standard of reckless disregard for the truth or knowing falsity may seem straightforward, the evidence needed to prove these fault levels can be difficult. It is one of the reasons why many public figure/public official plaintiffs do not even bring defamation suits. However, that does not mean actual malice cannot ever be proved. It can, and the ability of parties to prove actual malice may be a motivator for the settlement of cases before they go to trial. For example, in 2023 the lawsuit between Dominion Voting and Fox News was settled out of court for $767.5 million (down from the initial request of $1.6 billion) before the case was to go to trial over whether Fox News and its employees acted with actual malice.[15]

For PR practitioners, it is important to understand that knowing falsity and reckless disregard for the truth in defamation cases is not a matter of choice for the plaintiff. The choice of the two standards is based on what the plaintiff can prove with evidence. Frequently, this evidence involves newsroom practices and journalistic ethics. In defamation cases, reckless disregard for the truth is by far the more popular of the two standards.[16] This is because publishers, which constitute a large amount of defamation defendants, rarely publish information with knowing falsity. Additionally, the evidence needed for knowing falsity is difficult to obtain because it turns on a defendant's mental state at the time the content was created.

That does not mean knowing falsity cannot be legally proved. There are some high-profile examples, including a case where then Senator and 1964 presidential candidate Barry Goldwater sued *Fact* magazine over an article called *Goldwater: The Man and the Menace,* and a second article titled *What Psychiatrists Say About Goldwater,* over a claim that psychiatrists thought he was mentally unstable.[17] In that case, the knowing falsity was proven by the magazine's sloppy reporting and use of a scientifically invalid method to achieve a predetermined outcome for a critical piece on Goldwater.[18] In fact, the psychological evaluation aspect of the article was a survey that was sent to 12,356 psychiatrists, most of whom did not respond.[19]

Knowing falsity can also be proved by inconsistent statements that a publication contains. The Supreme Court held that materially altering quotes can be evidence of knowing falsity.[20] After all, writing down verbal statements includes certain decisions about grammar and punctuation, which can change the meaning of a quote. Writing for the majority in *Masson v. New Yorker Magazine*, a defamation case about misquotes and knowing falsity, Justice Anthony Kennedy wrote:

> In some sense, any alteration of a verbatim quotation is false. But writers and reporters by necessity alter what people say, at the very least to eliminate grammatical and syntactical infelicities. If every alteration constituted the falsity required to prove actual malice, the practice of journalism, which the First Amendment standard is designed to protect, would require a radical change, one inconsistent with our precedents and First Amendment principles.[21]

The court went on to say that during an interview, a subject should not expect total accuracy in the reporting of statements because of the nature of communication during these interviews. Justice Kennedy addressed how misstatements during an interview that were later corrected constitute typical practice in journalistic writing:

> Even if a journalist has tape-recorded the spoken statement of a public figure, the full and exact statement will be reported in only rare circumstances. The existence of both a speaker and a reporter; the translation between two media, speech and the printed word; the addition of punctuation; and the practical necessity to edit and make intelligible a speaker's perhaps rambling comments, all make it misleading to suggest that a quotation will be reconstructed with complete accuracy.[22]

This interpretation of journalistic convention is important for PR practitioners to note, especially those involved in media relations. A reporter's job is such that there is no expectation, at least from a defamation standpoint, that everything said will be reported verbatim. Moreover, that lack of precise accuracy does not necessarily constitute the actual malice required in certain defamation suits. Reckless disregard for the truth follows a similar rationale, looking at journalistic conventions.

Reckless disregard for the truth is the more common actual malice standard proven at trial, and when dealing with a news organization, this frequently is proven by examining journalistic and industry standards. The reckless disregard standard, unlike falsity, is about actions. Frequently these actions are predicated on what the person making the statements believed about the underlying truth of the claim.[23] In a news context, this standard is met when adequate reporting is not done or when the organization, or reporter, in exploring a subject, fails to do research that would meet industry standards.

These standards for reporting may be internal to the organization or may be part of an ethical standard set out for reporters by a professional organization. For example, the Society of Professional Journalists' Code of Ethics exhorts its members to "[t]ake responsibility for the accuracy of their work. Verify information before releasing it. Use original sources whenever possible."[24] Of course, this verification depends on what is being reported and the nature of the claim being made. Alleging that an organization or individual committed fraud requires a different level of fact checking than, say, the spelling of someone's name. In addition, the type of source of the verification of content may be part of the analysis that courts use to determine what constitutes reckless disregard for the truth, for example, single sources or sources on deep background.

The Supreme Court described reckless disregard for the truth as when an individual knows of the "probably falsity" of the statement or writing.[25] It is important to note that this standard of recklessness is more technical than what the legal standard is in cases that require negligence. Recklessness in this context is not what an ordinary person would do or understand given the situation or evidence. Instead, the Supreme Court said that reckless disregard for the truth is something more, and that the defendant accused of defamation must have "entertained serious doubts as to the truth of his publication."[26]

Negligence is the minimum standard of fault for proving defamation when the plaintiff is a nonpublic plaintiff. Negligence is a term that is pervasive in U.S. tort law, and it typically hinges on what the ordinary or reasonably prudent person would do in a particular situation. *Black's Law Dictionary*, the definitive legal dictionary in the United States, defines reckless disregard as "serious indifference to truth or accuracy of a publication."[27] In the context of defamation, negligence has been generally defined by state courts as conduct lacking ordinary care, with some states defining that term more professionally as lacking the standard expectations of journalists.

However, negligence is not automatically journalistic malpractice; it is more about failing to take ordinary care. The Court of Appeals of Texas defined journalistic malpractice as it relates to actual malice this way:

> A lack of care or an injurious motive in making a statement is not alone proof of actual malice, but care and motive are factors to be considered. An understandable misinterpretation of ambiguous facts does not show actual malice, but inherently improbable assertions and statements made on information that is obviously dubious may show actual malice. A failure to investigate fully is not evidence of actual malice; a purposeful avoidance of the truth is.[28]

The actual malice versus negligence standard in defamation cases is not as absolute as it may appear to be. While public figures, public officials, and limited purpose public figures must prove actual malice, nonpublic plaintiffs do prevail at trial by just proving negligence. Sometimes cases require even nonpublic plaintiffs to prove actual malice. For example, for plaintiffs seeking punitive damages, those damages that are meant to punish the wrongdoer, actual malice is required regardless of the plaintiff's status.[29]

Other standards may exist as well that make for more complex analysis of cases. For example, the Supreme Court held in the 1986 case *Philadelphia Newspapers v. Hepps* that a nonpublic plaintiff suing a newspaper that published a story about a matter of public concern must prove falsity to recover damages.[30] In this case, the plaintiff, who owned a franchise business of convenience stores, had ties to organized crime and used those connections to influence state government officials. The court in an opinion written by Justice Sandra Day O'Connor held that the balancing of the free speech rights of the newspaper compared with those of the private figure plaintiff required courts to favor free speech rights. She wrote:

> In a case presenting a configuration of speech and plaintiff like the one we face here, and where the scales are in such an uncertain balance, we believe that the Constitution requires us to tip them in favor of protecting true speech. To ensure that true speech on matters of public concern is not deterred, we hold that the common-law presumption that defamatory speech is false cannot stand when a plaintiff seeks damages against a media defendant for speech of public concern.[31]

However, the tipped scales do not mean the media has no accountability to verify what they write. In 1990, the U.S. Supreme Court held that even if a story is an opinion, a type of speech that is typically exempt from defamation lawsuits, the publisher can still be held liable for defamation if the opinion is predicated on defamatory content.[32] The Court also addressed other nuances of defamation under the *Sullivan* standard. Misquotes, even if deliberate, do not automatically constitute defamation unless the changes result in a materially different interpretation of what was originally said.[33]

There are also defenses to defamation that defendants may assert. For example, truth is a defense to defamation because truthful content is not defamation. This is a principle that was first established in the colonial era during the Zenger trial, and remains central to American defamation law. The importance of protecting truthful information, particularly in context of the press, is seen in the Supreme Court's decision in *Philadelphia Newspapers v. Hepps*, requiring plaintiffs to prove falsity in cases where the issue is a matter of public concern.

Another affirmative defense is opinion. Opinions are not facts, and their expression is protected under the First Amendment of the U.S. Constitution. Consider the following scenario. A negative review appears on an online review site about a restaurant. The statement says, "I hated this restaurant. This was the worst food I've ever eaten. Never again!" That is a statement of opinion based on the reviewer's negative experience. Compare that with "I hated this restaurant. This was the worst food I've ever eaten. No wonder, I later found out that several people have gotten food poisoning there and one almost died. Never again!" Suppose that last statement is a lie made up by the reviewer to get attention on the review site. That lie in the second review constitutes defamation. The first review does not.

Finally, there is a rare category of plaintiffs whose reputations are not damaged by any degree of defamation. Known as the libel-proof plaintiff doctrine, these peoples' reputations are so bad that defamatory statements about them causes no change in their reputations. The U.S. Court of Appeals for the Second Circuit describes the libel-proof doctrine as, "plaintiff may have had his reputation so badly damaged by true statements in a particular publication that minor false accusations within the same publication cannot result in further meaningful injury."[34] Specifically, when this occurs, the plaintiff cannot bring suit if the defamation causes only incremental amounts of reputational harm when compared with other, true statements about that person. For example, the Supreme Court of New York, the state's trial court, dismissed a defamation case brought by a well-known professional baseball player because the court determined the player was libel proof. In that case a book described the player as making racist statements and taunts against other players during the World Series. However, the court said that the player's well-publicized out-of-court behavior of outrageous conduct was abusive toward others. The court held that because both the player's autobiography and public record contained numerous examples of racist, misogynistic, homophobic, and criminal behavior, including bribing umpires, his reputation could not be further damaged by an allegation that he made racist remarks to players during a World Series game. This libel-proof status was further established by the fact that teammates had recounted this exact same behavior to the press without being sued.[35] The status of libel proof is predicated on the idea that the plaintiff cannot sustain further defamation damages. What would be the damage to a murderer's reputation who is also accused wrongfully of assault? Really not much. This status of libel proof is known as incremental harm. It is a standard that is not universal, but the Supreme Court has held that it can be something that states can use as part of their defamation law.[36]

REVIEW SITES AND CRITICISM: WHO IS ACCOUNTABLE?

Online review sites have proliferated in the twenty-first century, and frequently customers make decisions based on what ordinary people say about a business. Having a five-star review is important, and studies have been done to show that those using review sites have a system for processing what is said about businesses. Sometimes this includes not believing a business that has all perfect scores on the basis that those types of reviews have been created by friends, family, or employees of a business. Review users also tend to make up their own minds about what to believe in the individual reviews, even if they suspect some of the content may be less than accurate. However, managing reputation in the 2020s requires PR practitioners to consider what is on these review sites, and sometimes whether what is there constitutes defamation.

Consider this scenario. Suppose a restaurant makes a political statement that angers some people. Those who are offended take to the internet, go to a review site, and give the restaurant nothing but one-star reviews. They post incredibly negative information on the site, with the goal of putting the restaurant out of business. None of these reviewers ever ate at the restaurant, and the one-star reviewers are based on political beliefs, not customer experiences. This is an example of what has been termed "cancel culture." It exists along both poles of the political spectrum, and it is a reputation management nightmare. As a PR practitioner, what can be done? Can the business be saved? Can the reviews be taken down?

The first reaction to this type of scenario is to try to get the reviews removed. However, the process for this depends on the policies of the review site. Sometimes those policies allow for reviews to be flagged and removed, but certain conditions must be met. Moreover, review sites' reputations are predicated on the authenticity of the reviews. So, if a business can request that negative reviews be removed, the review site's credibility becomes imperiled. For PR practitioners, this presents a unique problem of trying to save a reputation by getting defamatory reviews removed while negotiating that process with another business whose reputation is based on providing unfiltered reviews.

This hypothetical above is based on a real incident. A well-known example is an activist review of a small restaurant in Lexington, Virginia, where wait staff asked then White House Press Secretary Sarah Huckabee Sanders to leave. The restaurant's Yelp site was later flooded with poor reviews from individuals who had never been customers, and the restaurant's rating nosedived in the following weeks.[37] The issue with this type of case is that CDA Section 230 immunizes platforms such as Yelp from lawsuits.[38] So, in cases like these, the person or organization that has been defamed must sue individual posters, not the underlying platform, to be compensated for their loss of reputation. This proves highly difficult, perhaps impossible, given the fact that those users may have little money to pay for a judgment or may be hard to locate. The host website retains the right to remove content. In fact, part of the CDA protects those companies with a so-called "good Samaritan provision" that gives them power to remove content. The issue, however, is that review sites are typically reluctant to remove negative comments because they want to appear authentic.

What if the organization wants to proceed with a defamation suit? There are practical problems to overcome. The first is how to identify who posted the fake reviews. Usually reviews are made anonymously or through online pseudonyms. Knowing the identity of whom to sue is essential for plaintiffs, and in this situation the plaintiff must get that information from the review site. These situations come up frequently in litigation with online defendants, and while there is no universal approach, the typical process involves issuing a subpoena to the website, internet service provider, or search engine to uncover the legal identification of an alleged defamer. This presents some constitutional questions as well, given that anonymous speech is protected under the First Amendment. Moreover, these websites have an interest in protecting the online identity of anonymous users. In fact, ISPs are subject to the Electronic Communications Privacy Act (ECPA), which places limits on what private information can provide.[39] In all, the big issue with anonymous speakers involved in online defamation is that the plaintiffs in those cases have an exceedingly hard time uncovering the identities of the speakers. Though jurisdictions may vary in their approaches, the most common approach is for the plaintiff to present in their motion the basic outline of the defamation case and demonstrate that the case is a viable one that could go to trial.[40]

A compounding issue in online defamation is the immunity that third-party host sites receive under the Communications Decency Act, Section 230.[41] Section 230 was part of the Telecommunications Act of 1996, which was a major reform to the telecommunications industry.[42] Part of the issue at that time was the regulation of the internet, which was then in its infancy. The concern at the time was that lawmakers did not want the internet to fail because of lawsuits filed by multiple plaintiffs seeking damages for online defamation posted by third parties. As a result, CDA Section 230 barred interactive computer services from being sued for content posted by third-party users. The specific provision of the law stated:

No provider or user of an interactive computer service shall be held liable on account of—

A. any action voluntarily taken in good faith to restrict access to or availability of material that the provider or user considers to be obscene, lewd, lascivious, filthy, excessively violent, harassing, or otherwise objectionable, whether or not such material is constitutionally protected; or

B. any action taken to enable or make available to information content providers or others the technical means to restrict access to material described in paragraph (1).[43]

While these organizations may create community standards and terms of use that allow them to manage content online, those rules are not laws. Those rules can also change, such as is the case with the purchase of Twitter, renamed X by its new owner, Elon Musk.[44]

CDA Section 230 has been challenged in courts several times, all unsuccessfully.[45] These cases involve individuals violating the law online through their online content. Some of the issues involved in Section 230 illustrate the power that online defamation has in ruining the reputations of others. The first challenge to CDA Section 230 occurred in *Zaran v. AOL*, a 1997 case decided by the U.S. Court of Appeals for the Fourth Circuit. In that case, a man's phone number was published online and linked to the Oklahoma City bombing, a 1995 attack on a federal office building that is still the deadliest act of domestic terrorism in U.S history.[46] The court held that under CDA Section 230, AOL was immune to lawsuits. Other cases have discussed the application of Section 230 protection to various businesses. In a major case demonstrating the limits of Section 230 immunity, the U.S. Court of Appeals for the Ninth Circuit held that immunity did not apply to a website, Roomates. com, when the website used a questionnaire of roommate preferences and demographics. That approach to content made Roomates.com an information content provider, a status not protected under Section 230.[47] However, that ruling is narrow and predicated on the specific choices the site made about processing information from users.

Politically, CDA Section 230 has been criticized by both Republicans and Democrats. During the Trump administration, Section 230 became a political slogan with President Trump tweeting "revoke 230" in response to what he alleged were abuses by social media platforms in screening conversative content using platform community standards.[48] He issued an Executive Order in May 2020 asking for the Federal Communications Commission (FCC) to examine the application of the immunity and sought to have the Federal Trade Commission (FTC) empowered to report political bias on the platforms.[49] Being issued in 2020, the executive orders were not continued in the next administration. However, criticism of CDA Section 230 continued. Democrats have attempted to reform Section 230 with various bills, none of which have become law.

It seemed that CDA Section 230 may have been finally coming to an end in 2022 when the U.S. Supreme Court took up the issue of the statute in two cases: *Gonzales v. Google LLC* and *Twitter v. Taamneh*.[50] These cases involved international terrorism and the roles Google and Twitter played in providing platforms that were used to post and curate terrorist content, which was in violation of Antiterrorism and Effective Death

Penalty Act of 1996 (AEDPA).[51] The Supreme Court unanimously decided that Twitter had no legal liability under the AEDPA, and it remanded the Google case to the U.S. District Court.[52]

This means the fate of CDA Section 230 lies with Congress to change the law on this issue. PR practitioners should expect the immunity of online platforms, such as a social media platform, to continue. Therefore, the reputation management aspects of online review sites will continue to be solved by working with the review platforms to provide countervailing information. Frequently, the solution to these types of reputational problems lies not in a court of law but in the ability of PR practitioners to deliver an effective communications effort to dispel disinformation.

With the proliferation of generative artificial intelligence (AI) platforms, such as ChatGPT, there are new questions about the liability of platforms that are providing defamatory content. As of the writing of this chapter, this remains an unresolved issue, but it is likely that liability lies with the user. However, there are some scenarios in which the platform could be held liable. Moreover, CDA Section 230 likely would not allow for the platform to be immunized because it is producing, not hosting, the information. In 2023, a Georgia journalist sued ChatGPT for producing what the journalist alleged were defamatory comments about him.[53] That case is ongoing, but it may present an opportunity for courts to consider whether Section 230 immunity will extend to generative AI platforms.[54] The outcome of this and likely other lawsuits will have a major impact on the liability of defamation in the AI era. It serves as a cautionary tale for PR practitioners who use AI to produce content and demonstrates the need to verify facts produced by AI. This has major implications for defamation, especially for those who are sued for defaming plaintiffs who must prove actual malice. Not verifying AI content may now be evidence of reckless disregard of the truth.

SOCIAL MEDIA AND EMPLOYEE SPEECH: MANAGING INTERNAL COMMUNICATION

One of the most difficult aspects of reputation management concerns internal communication about an organization. No group has the potential to harm an organization more than employees who divulge information about an organization online. While some of that communication, such as trade secrets (discussed in chapter 7), can be limited through contracts and even the law, other types of communication are protected under the First Amendment and workplace speech rights. Understanding how these rights are protected by federal law and agencies such as the National Labor Relations Board (NLRB), a federal agency that regulates union and nonunion workplace policies, is important for PR practitioners who may be asked to craft workplace social media policies. These policies are frequently crafted in ways to deliberately or inadvertently limit workplace speech that may be legally protected. Understanding the contours of what is allowable within policies is important, especially for PR practitioners who are involved in establishing workplace communication policies.

The issue of social media policy writing has become a particular focus of the NLRB since the 2010s. Established in 1935 to regulate workplace issues involving unions, the NRLB also regulates workplace policies and speech, including social media policies. The National Labor Relations Act (NRLA) established the structure of the NLRB and enables the investigatory wing of the agency. The NLRA protects the rights of workers "to engage in other concerted activities for the purpose of collective bargaining or other mutual aid or protection."[55] Concerted activities under the NLRB means that two or more employees "take action for the mutual aid or protection regarding terms and conditions of employment."[56] The NLRB gives examples of concerted activity, including:

- Two or more employees addressing their employer about improving their pay.
- Two or more employees discussing work-related issues beyond pay, such as safety concerns, with each other.
- An employee speaking to an employer on behalf of one or more coworkers about improving workplace conditions.[57]

In 2011, the NLRB began issuing decisions on social media policies and whether those policies violated concerted workplace activity protections under the NLRA. Part of the issue in many social media policies is an overly broad ban on specific types of speech that could include protected concerted activity. For example, a ban on "unprofessional" speech can be interpreted onto concerted workplace activity speech that is protected under the NLRA. There is also the inverse issue of firing employees based on what they say on personal social media. In those cases, the content on the personal sites may also be protected.

The NLRB has provided some examples of workplace speech policies that violate the NLRA. Examining social media policies, the NLRB has found that overly broad policies, policies that use vague terminology, and policies that mandate speaking with managers prior to posting comments all violate the NLRA. Moreover, a savings clause that mandates social media policies follow secondary workplace environment policies also can invalidate a policy because the social media policy must be able to be understood as a stand-alone document. There is also an intersection between these social media policies and intellectual property (discussed in chapter 7). A social media policy cannot ban an employee from using the trademark logo of a business outright because that speech can be part of concerted workplace activity, such as in a protest post about the company's policies.[58] One social media post that was struck down as unlawful stated:

> Respect all copyright and other intellectual property laws. For [Employer's] protection as well as your own, it is critical that you show proper respect for the laws governing copyright, fair use of copyrighted material owned by others, trademarks and other intellectual property, including [Employer's] own copyrights, trademarks and brands. Get permission before reusing others' content or images.[59]

In social media policy writing, it is very important that employers not create policies that are overly broad or can be interpreted in ways that violate NLRA protections. Here are some policies that the NLRB has found unlawful as they relate to concerted workplace activity:

If you enjoy blogging or using online social networking sites such as Facebook and YouTube (otherwise known as Consumer Generated Media, or CGM) please note that there are guidelines to follow if you plan to mention [Employer] or your employment with [Employer] in these online vehicles. . . . Don't release confidential guest, team member or company information.[60]

This was considered unlawful because the broad statement of releasing workplace or customer information could be interpreted as banning employees from discussing legitimate workplace grievances that are concerted activity.[61]

Another problematic workplace social media policy included the following provision:

TREAT EVERYONE WITH RESPECT. Offensive, demeaning, abusive or inappropriate remarks are as out of place online as they are offline, even if they are unintentional. We expect you to abide by the same standards of behavior both in the workplace and in your social media communications.[62]

This policy was considered problematic because the word "everyone" could be interpreted as a ban on legitimate criticism of an employer's behavior toward employees. This same policy had a provision about "friending" that was deemed unlawful; it read:

Think carefully about "friending" co-workers . . . on external social media sites. Communications with co-workers on such sites that would be inappropriate in the workplace are also inappropriate online, and what you say in your personal social media channels could become a concern in the workplace.[63]

This was deemed to be unlawful and a violation of Section 7 of the NLRA, which prohibits actions that can be interpreted as inhibiting collective bargaining, unionization, and mutual aid or protection.[64] Other provisions have been struck down because they potentially restrict employee commentary on claims about employers. For example, an employee policy on legal matters stating "Don't comment on any legal matters, including pending litigation or disputes" was found unlawful because legal matters may include employee-based lawsuits against an organization or management.[65]

The NLRA has identified several instances of illegal firings for social media content, including firing employees criticizing coworkers for poor work product, employee criticism of the structure of a business's promotional sales event, and social media communication about withholding tax policies at a business.[66] Social media policies also must keep in mind that workplace behavior mandates cannot run afoul of NRLA. Consider this social media policy about workplace behavior that involves online conduct:

> Adopt a friendly tone when engaging online. Don't pick fights. Social media is about conversations. When engaging with others online, adopt a warm and friendly tone that will encourage others to respond to your postings and join your conversation. Remember to communicate in a professional tone. . . . This includes not only the obvious (no ethnic slurs, personal insults, obscenity, etc.) but also proper consideration of privacy and topics that may be considered objectionable or inflammatory—such as politics and religion. Don't make any comments about [Employer's] customers, suppliers or competitors that might be considered defamatory.[67]

The NLRB interpreted these communication restrictions as based on a general desire to minimize conversations that could be problematic or cause discord within a workplace, which could be interpreted as banning protected workplace discussions. It is also important for writers of social media policies to not include any language that makes it mandatory for employees to directly engage with management prior to posting. Here is an example of an unlawful social media policy rooted in preapproval and prescreening of content:

> You are encouraged to resolve concerns about work by speaking with co-workers, supervisors, or managers. [Employer] believes that individuals are more likely to resolve concerns about work by speaking directly

with co-workers, supervisors or other management-level personnel than by posting complaints on the Internet. [Employer] encourages employees and other contingent resources to consider using available internal resources, rather than social media or other online forums, to resolve these types of concerns.[68]

These applications and interpretations from the NLRB may lead PR practitioners to wonder if a social media policy is even possible within the workplace. The answer is that it is possible, but it must have certain characteristics. It must be written in a way that is expansive enough so that it does not imply or outright ban concerted workplace activity. It also must be written in a way such that workers of all backgrounds and literacy levels can understand the policy. Moreover, this social media policy creation illustrates the relationship between PR practitioners and lawyers. This is a professional relationship becomes highly valuable when documents must be both legally compliant and understandable to a mass public. Only then will the true purpose of social media policies be realized.[69]

ETHICAL SOLUTIONS TO REPUTATIONAL PROBLEMS

While this chapter focuses on the legal aspects of defamation, there are ethical considerations as well. Truth and honesty are cornerstones of good PR practice. Almost every ethical code in the PR industry has that principle enshrined in its guidance for PR practitioners. Liars and lying should be universally reviled in the public relations and communication industry, and because of that using defamation as a type of strategy to gain leverage for clients is an unethical, unprofessional form of PR practice.

However, the ethics of defamation presents another interesting question. Is it ethical to use litigation to maintain reputation? This is an important issue to consider because there are factors that go beyond outcome or law but look to the underlying philosophy of PR professionals. For example, the use of litigation to suppress free speech is clearly an ethical violation, and sometimes illegal. It is a form of censorship of speech, which can make an organization appear to be interested in stifling criticism rather than engaging with it. That is why we see anti-SLAPP statutes that prohibit this practice. However, PR practitioners may be forced to have difficult conversations with clients about whether an alleged defamation has a kernel of truth in it. In that case, is litigation a better strategy than engagement? Moreover, does the litigation itself amplify the criticism, making it a larger and messier reputational issue? Sometimes the case may be, at least from a communication perspective, that reputational harm could be increased because the awareness and knowledge of the defamation becomes more pervasive.

Another issue within online defamation is the immunity of third-party sites that host content. Their lack of culpability in defamation is unique in American law. While the purpose of their immunity in the CDA Section 230 was to help grow the internet at a time when it was new, the protection they receive now arguably provides them with an unfair advantage in how they manage their content. Weaponized reviews that are defamatory and meant to cause public backlash present a host of problems for reputation management. Those affected can only go after the individual poster, not the platform, for damages (assuming the speaker can be identified and whether they have any money to pay a judgment). This makes the communicator's role more important and complex because the only way to combat these types of disinformation campaigns is with accurate and truthful counter-information.

The issue of defamation and reputation management also underscores the importance of the communication professional within the organization. They serve an important function of conducting environmental scanning to uncover defamatory content, and practitioners also have the crucial role of serving as the ethical voice within an organization. This role may make them confront situations where a statement may be perceived as defamatory but is the truth. This role may also mean that PR practitioners have a better solution than litigation to restore a reputation damaged by defamation. And, this role may present situations where the PR practitioner works with the litigation team and the client's lawyers to combat disinformation and defamation by providing truth.

There is another ethical issue that reputation management presents—the ability to take criticism. As a profession, public relations is rooted in communicating with diverse publics, using active listening as means of two-way communication. While removing negative online reviews that are defamatory is a legitimate concern and strategy for PR, removing authentic negative reviews are not. Similarly, crafting a social media policy that overly restricts employees from speaking about their concerns is a bad strategy from both ethics and communications perspectives. Successful social media policies that are both legally defensible and ethically sound provide a level of elasticity to the employee's ability to speak freely (within certain boundaries). After all, public relations is consistently the voice at the table that speaks the truth, and having a full and comprehensive vision of the reality of a situation allows for good decision making that ultimately preserves and enhances an organization's reputation.

DISCUSSION QUESTIONS

1. Suppose a client has been defamed online. What is the best way to handle the reputational damage, a lawsuit or communication?

2. An online review site's scoring system frequently impacts reputation. How would you handle a defamatory negative review from a legal and communication perspective?

3. What are the ethical considerations for suing over a negative online review?

4. Why are social media sites so important for reputational management? If you were to write for one, what would be your primary concern?

5. Find a social media policy of a company online and analyze it. What makes it successful or unsuccessful? How does it comport to the standards of the NLRB?

CASE SCENARIO

Suppose you are working as a PR practitioner for a local coffee shop. The shop has a strong local following, and many business meetings are held in the shop. The shop has many five-star reviews on various online platforms, and the shop's business has an active presence on social media.

One day you see on the shop's Facebook page a post that says "Had my last visit to this place. The owner and staff are rude, and their coffee makes me sick. As if it weren't enough to pay $5 for stale coffee and day-old pastries, their employees have been caught numerous times stealing credit card info from customers. DO NOT GO HERE! YOU WILL GET SCAMMED!" While the statement about the taste of the coffee is a matter of opinion, the statement about the credit cards and employees is 100 percent false. However, many people start interacting with the post, and business takes a downturn. Should you delete the post from the shop's Facebook page? What if it shows up on a third-party review site? How could you get it removed? Who could you sue for defamation? What liability would a third-party review site have for this type of post?

CHAPTER 6

Privacy and Public Relations Practice

OVERVIEW: THIS CHAPTER DISCUSSES PRIVACY WITHIN PUBLIC RELA-tions, particularly examining privacy in communication technology. Specific attention is paid to privacy torts in the United States, for example, false light, appropriation, public disclosure of private facts, and seclusion. The chapter also discusses the role of privacy law in the European Union (EU), particularly the right to be forgotten. The chapter concludes with an analysis of the ethical issues of privacy, especially privacy issues that may affect PR practice with the proliferation of artificial intelligence (AI) use in the industry.

OBJECTIVES:

- Explain the privacy torts of false light, appropriation, public disclosure of privacy facts, and seclusion.

- Compare the privacy philosophies of U.S. law to those developed by the European Union.

- Examine how the right to be forgotten is a law that has helped the cottage PR industry of online reputation management.

- Analyze how privacy issues in AI will create significant ethical and legal issues for PR practice in the 2020s.

As technology has proliferated in the PR industry in the past two decades, privacy issues are more common than ever before. The advent of big data as a tool to create targeted messaging highlights the issue of privacy in PR practice. Big data is big business in communication with the analytics providing insights into publics, trend forecasting, and assisting with precise targeting of messages to stakeholders.[1] Revenue in the global market from big data is estimated to be $273.4 billion by 2026, driven largely by a lower technological entry barrier as access to analytics tools become more affordable and easier to utilize.[2] The growth of AI, particularly generative AI, is fueled by big data because the aggregate data sets populate the information in AI platforms, such as ChatGPT. AI also plays a major role in the analysis of big data, as the data sets are usually highly complex and need programs, such as AI systems, to process the information. This helps communicators use big data via AI to create personalized communications that have greater resonance with potential publics and stakeholders using the natural language processing (NLP) of AI. Forecasts using big data also become easier for organizations to produce because of the reduced barrier to entry, especially in terms of cost.

Privacy is a large part of this technological revolution within public relations. While the privacy regulations of AI are currently under development at the time of this writing, it is evident that privacy issues writ large are going to be part of any consideration of big data and AI discussion in PR practice. Privacy as a legal concept also presents unique challenges for PR practitioners operating in a global practice. Unlike copyright law, which has international treaties like the Berne Convention that establish universal standards for the law that can apply worldwide (with some exceptions), privacy standards differ even among Western democracies. For example, the European perspective on privacy law is much more robust than that of the United States, in part because of European legal history and because of the U.S. Constitution's First Amendment. These differences are seen in how the laws are configured, enforced, and interpreted. While this chapter does not provide a comprehensive analysis of the differences between the two types of law, it is important for PR practitioners to know that their work in a global practice may operate in a space that is subject to a different understanding about privacy, and that understanding may be counter to U.S. legal principles and history.

This chapter provides an overview of U.S. privacy law development beginning with an analysis of the privacy torts that are common in most

U.S. states and federal regulation of privacy by sector, such as healthcare and higher education. Next, the chapter examines the role of privacy within data, specifically big data and AI focusing on the EU approach to data protection and how those protections create a globalized standard for data storage and use. The chapter concludes by looking beyond the law to examine the ethical issues of privacy within PR practice; namely, what PR practitioners should do when confront with privacy issues, and how ethical values, such as transparency, can assist them in making ethically, legally, and morally sound decisions in contemporary PR practice.

PRIVACY LAW IN THE UNITED STATES

Privacy as a legal concept is rooted in technological change. Just as AI has transformed contemporary understandings of personal and public, the nineteenth-century growth of camera use created new questions about what was personal, private, and public. Like today, European law led the way on this issue. France, for example, had laws about appropriation of images and how cameras could invade privacy, and capture moments that were not meant to be public. There was also a greater awareness that privacy issues would proliferate with the growth of the press. In 1890, an article in the *Harvard Law Review* by Samuel Warren and Louis Brandeis addressed this issue of privacy in the United States, arguing that inherent within the U.S. Constitution existed privacy rights. Recognizing the power of the press, they wrote:

> The press is overstepping in every direction the obvious bounds of propriety and of decency. Gossip is no longer the resource of the idle and of the vicious, but has become a trade, which is pursued with industry as well as effrontery. To satisfy a prurient taste the details of sexual relations are spread broadcast in the columns of the daily papers. To occupy the indolent, column upon column is filled with idle gossip, which can only be procured by intrusion upon the domestic circle.[3]

Warren and Brandeis were influential lawyers during the late nineteenth century. Both were Harvard educated; Warren was highly interested in protecting personal privacy, especially with the growth of photography

in the late nineteenth century, and Brandeis, who would later join the
U.S. Supreme Court in 1916 as the first Jewish member of the court,
was Warren's law partner. Their work had a profound impact on the
development of privacy law in a way no other scholarly work has ever
done.[4] Their work on privacy gained the attention of states with the New
York Court of Appeals, which recognized appropriation as a privacy
right in 1902 in *Roberson v. Rochester Folding Box Company*, and later the
Georgia Supreme Court recognized privacy in a 1905 case, *Pavesich v.
New England Life Insurance Company*.[5]

State and Federal Laws Concerning Privacy by Sector

By the mid-twentieth century privacy rights were increasingly recognized by states, and their enforcement came in the form of what is called
torts. That is, plaintiffs could sue defendants for violations of privacy for
money damages based on privacy breaches. In 1960, University of California Berkeley School of Law Professor William Prosser expanded on
Warren and Brandeis's work on privacy in an influential *California Law
Review* article entitled "Privacy."[6] In the article he presented four privacy
torts: intrusion, public disclosure of private facts, false light in the public
eye, and appropriation. Prosser also noted that within the nexus of privacy is a discussion of what is expected by public figures, who give up a
certain level of privacy for fame; and private citizens, who have a greater
expectation of privacy because they are not seeking fame. He thought the
boundaries of the public figure's privacy were difficult to establish because
the nature of public figures' desire for attention and their desire for privacy, at times, were at odds. Prosser wrote, "The famous motion picture
actress who 'vants to be alone' unquestionably has as much right as any
one else [*sic*] to be free from intrusion into her home or her bank account;
and so, has the individual whose divorce is the sensation of the day."[7] The
idea of fame is one that is part of legal analysis in defamation cases as
well. It is worth noting that for Warren, Brandeis and, later, Prosser that
defamation law was noted as being tangentially related to privacy, but as a
tort did not remedy what privacy issues presented. At its core defamation
is about untruthful statements that harm another. Conversely, privacy is
about information and control of self, and having the ability to control

one's image, name, likeness, and privacy facts in a world where information is more available because of technological progress.

Privacy torts are driven by state law, and because of that there is no universal privacy law in the United States. However, most states' privacy laws are very similar, so it is possible to have a general sense of how state privacy works holistically. These laws typically include the traditional privacy torts first articulated by Prosser, but recently they have included new privacy laws concerning data protection. For example, the California Privacy Rights Act (CPRA), which went into effect in 2023, established the California Privacy Protection Agency and details new consumer rights including the right for consumers to correct information online.[8] This new law, which is an addendum to the California Consumer Privacy Act (CCPA) established in 2020, represents the cutting edge of state privacy law and demonstrates how states are taking the lead on privacy issues, particularly in the sphere of data.[9] The CPRA limits how businesses can use sensitive consumer information for commercial purposes. This is a logical extension of the CCPA, which permitted consumers to demand businesses not sell their information to other third-party organizations. Virginia and Colorado have similar laws focusing on consumer data protection and giving consumers the right to correct false information.[10]

Children's data protection is another major area for which states have regulation. Again, California has been a leader in this area, passing the California's Privacy Rights for California Minors in the Digital World Act, known as the eraser bill, which gives children the right to demand the removal of content about themselves online. Additionally, the law bans online marketers from steering children to sites where the purchase of items is illegal for minors, such as alcohol, and it bans the advertising or marketing of certain products to minors.[11] States also have robust privacy laws surrounding online access to social media accounts for current and prospective employees. As of 2022, there are 27 states that have laws that address when employers can access employees' personal social media accounts by demanding usernames and passwords, and 16 states have similar laws that apply to educational institutions.[12] In essence, state privacy laws vary according to a variety of state-specific rules, and three states—California, Colorado, and Virginia—have comprehensive privacy laws. Other states address a variety of privacy issues within specific privacy contexts.

Federal statutes have also addressed privacy issues by sector. Depending on the PR practitioner's specific practice area, these laws may affect what type of communications a practitioner can provide. What follows is a list of several federal privacy laws that may affect PR practitioners, and a description of how they apply to communication.

- *Fair Credit Reporting Act (FCRA):* This law, passed in 1970 and enforced by the FTC and the Consumer Financial Protection Bureau, protects the consumer information stored by consumer-protecting recording agencies. Communicators working in consumer credit must take certain precautions with this privacy information.[13]

- *Privacy Act of 1974:* This is a federal statute that regulates the private information held by the federal agencies and provides a set of exemptions for when private information may be disclosed without consent of the individual.[14] These exemptions impact communicators working within federal agencies that may gather and share information, and how record transparency is communicated and facilitated to the public. This law also works in context with the Freedom of Information Act (FOIA), which gives greater access to records than the Privacy Act of 1974.[15]

- *Family Educational Rights and Privacy Act of 1974 (FERPA):* This law regulates the privacy of student records both in K–12 settings as well as institutions that receive federal funding.[16] The rules governing these records are important for anyone in educational public relations. There are also nuances to FERPA, such as allowing student directory information unless the student or parent opts out. FERPA also has different requirements based on secondary versus postsecondary institutions, with postsecondary students having greater control over records.

- *Electronic Communications Privacy Act of 1986 (ECPA):* This federal statute bans wiretapping of phones, absent a warrant, and the storage of electronically recorded communications.[17] The ECPA has three parts: the Wiretap Act, the Stored Communication Act, and a pen register trap and trace statute. These work together to protect information from being intercepted.

- *Children's Online Privacy Protection Act of 1998 (COPPA):* This federal law is designed to protect the privacy of children under the age of 13 and includes provisions about obtaining parental consent prior to collecting data on children, and regulating the circumstances in which children's data could be obtained.[18] COPA has application in the era of big data analytics in which communicators may gather information for targeted communication and marketing.

- **Health Insurance Portability and Accountability** *Act of 1996* **(HIPPA):** This federal law protects patient records in hospitals, medical facilities, and insurance companies. Specifically, the law regulates how personally identifying information must be maintained, and when that information can be legally released.[19] This is a major law that affects PR practitioners in healthcare communication. Specific precautions must be taken in the realm of AI and communication for healthcare communicators. A closed system AI program has certain technological aspects that may violate HIPPA.

- **Financial Services Modernization** *Act of 1999* **(Gramm-Leach-Bliley Act):** This law addresses consumer privacy and information in financial institutions, and was a major shift in the deregulation of the financial industry as it repealed the Glass-Steagall Act of 1933.[20] However, it contains privacy protections such as notifications to consumers on the sharing of financial information, and mandatory safeguards for consumer privacy data.[21]

These laws offer a cross-section of federal regulations that impact privacy, and it is important to note that unlike in the European Union, there is no comprehensive privacy law at the federal level in the United States. While some states have entered that legal space, most have not.

These laws are applicable not only to the content produced by communicators, but also the tools they use. Big data, a major tool used to create targeted messaging to segmented audiences, must comply with these regulations at both the state and the federal level. There is a growing concern that data compilation creates privacy problems and even facilitates discriminatory practices, such as using data for decision making that results in illegal discrimination. When looking at privacy, specifically in the context of communication platforms, it is important to note that platform guardrails, not laws, play one of the most important roles in preserving user privacy. It is those community principles and terms of use that PR practitioners should be most familiar with when crafting content for diverse publics.

PRIVACY TORTS

Suppose a PR practitioner represents a celebrity client who makes his living through commercial endorsements. The client has a catchphrase, "You betcha!" that he uses regularly to distinguish his endorsement of various products. One day you see a billboard for a car dealership with a picture of a look-alike of your celebrity client. On the billboard, the car dealership states "Best Prices in Town! You Bet!" What can your client do, if anything, to prevent this use of his likeness and catchphrase? Can the look-alike endorse products using the likeness of the celebrity? Suppose the celebrity suddenly dies. Can his family bring a lawsuit on his behalf for using his image and a variation of the catchphrase? All these issues are related to privacy, specifically the privacy tort of appropriation. Privacy torts are important to understand for PR practice in that they frequently involve professional communicators or the media as parties. Moreover, privacy tort law is not a universal application in the United States. Some states have torts that others do not. For example, in Virginia, false light is not recognized as a cause of action for a lawsuit because, the thought goes, defamation statutes provide the same opportunity for a plaintiff.[22] While the following torts have certain idiosyncrasies depending upon the state statute, this section is a general overview of traditional privacy laws, as articulated by Prosser in 1960.[23]

False Light

False light is a privacy tort that occurs when false information is presented and places a person in what would be considered an unfavorable light by an ordinary person. This is like defamation, but differs in a major way. Where defamation is about the reputational harm done to a person, false light is a claim rooted in the emotional distress of an individual. For example, an untrue statement that a person is a convicted criminal could be the root of both false light and defamation claims. The difference is in defamation, the issue would rest on the reputational harm, such that the person cannot be employed or earn a living, where false light would focus on the emotional toll the false information had on the person psychologically. Because false light and defamation are so intertwined, there are some states that only recognize false light as a claim. The prima facie case of false light requires two criteria: (1) the false light in which the other was placed would be highly offensive to a reasonable person, and (2) the actor had knowledge of or acted in reckless disregard as to the falsity of the publicized matter and the false light in which the other would be placed.[24] These elements for false light were first articulated in the Restatement (Second) of Torts, which is a model statute for states to follow. The second element is parallel to the actual malice standard of defamation law, but it is not conditional on the status of the plaintiff in a false light case. The U.S. Supreme Court in *Time v. Hill* held that actual malice was the standard in a false light case where the content at issue was a matter of public concern. Negligence invasions of privacy by the media where the issue is a matter of public concern cannot be the basis of a false light lawsuit.[25] Later, the Supreme Court further distinguished false light from defamation, holding in the 1974 case *Cantrell v. Forest City Publishing Company* that false light content does not necessarily have to be defamatory.[26] In that case, the false light came from a newspaper story about a family whose father was killed in a bridge collapse. The coverage of the incident insinuated that the reporter had spoken to the man's widow when he had not, and that because of the accident, the family lived in abject poverty.[27] Not all states recognize false light because of its closeness to defamation. However, some states recognize the distinction between false light and defamation, highlighting that the emotional distress caused by false light is legally distinct.[28] That does not mean states are uniform in their approach. The Supreme Court holding in *Gertz v. Welch*, a defamation case discussed in chapter 5, has been interpreted to apply to false light's level of fault. So long as a state does not impose strict liability for false light, states are free to establish negligence or actual malice as the burden of proof for the plaintiff.

For PR practitioners, false light is an area of law that works well to combat disinformation that is not related to reputational harm. Its elasticity also allows for lawsuits about false information that is not necessarily defamatory at all, but a misrepresentation of information. The problem for practitioners is that false light is not uniform, nor is it the type of case for which it is easy to prove damages. Emotional distress as a damage is controversial as it is rooted in mental health, a subject that is still taboo in many circles of U.S. society. Compounding the problem is when false light is applied to celebrity clients who are regularly subjected to disinformation about their lives.

Appropriation

Appropriation is another privacy tort that has major implications for PR clients. It occurs when a person's name, likeness, or image is used without prior authorization for commercial or noncommercial purposes. It is an important invasion of privacy tort, especially for celebrities who use their image and name for endorsement work. This tort is extremely important to the image and reputation management of an individual, and it serves as a mechanism to protect celebrities and other well-known individuals from having their name utilized in a way that they do not endorse. The tort of appropriation is distinct from other areas of image control, such as trademark or copyright infringement. Those areas of law have technical requirements to exist; for example, copyright must be original and fixed in a tangible medium. Appropriation is a privacy right rooted in the idea that individuals have the right to control the use of their own image and name and is a right that is rooted in the older concept of the right to publicity.

Although some scholars make a distinction between the two, generally the terms "publicity rights" and "appropriation" are interchangeable.

The first privacy cases in the United States involved appropriation, and by 1953 the right of publicity was first used as a legal term by the U.S. Court of Appeals for the Second Circuit.[29] The Restatement (Second) of Torts defines appropriation as the unauthorized use a name or likeness for personal benefit in commercial and noncommercial contexts.[30] However, there are limits to the appropriation of a name or likeness. Incidental use of person's name or likeness is not appropriation, nor is it appropriation when a name or likeness is used for newsworthy content or parody, as those areas create a conflict between publicity rights and the First Amendment.[31] However, there are limits to this rule. The U.S. Supreme Court held that appropriation could exist for the news media and that the media does not enjoy a special status exempting them from appropriation law. In *Zacchini v. Scripps-Howard Broadcasting Company* the court held 5–4 that a broadcaster can be held responsible for appropriation when they broadcast an entertainer's entire act without authorization, therefore taking away the entertainer's ability to earn money from his act.[32]

For PR practitioners, the right of appropriation is one that is important for image control. It is comparative to copyright and trademark infringement in that the appropriation takes away the ability of an individual to earn money from their image and name. However, unlike copyright and trademark, publicity rights typically lasts only as long as the person is alive. There are exceptions to this rule, notably in California where a person's estate can control their publicity rights for 70 years after the person's death.[33] This law is having some interest at the federal level considering the growth of artificial intelligence and deepfake technology. At the time of this writing, there is a bill introduced in the U.S. Senate entitled the NO FAKES Act, short for Nurture Originals, Foster Art, and Keep Entertainment Safe Act of 2023. The bill, which has bipartisan support, would create federal protection of image and likeness for 70 years. The 70-year mark is parallel to the current duration of copyright, which is life of the author plus 70 years. However, the bill is yet to become law, and critics argue the law may be too severe a reaction to the appropriation power of AI technology.[34]

Public Disclosure of Private Facts

Imagine a reporter who writes a personal interest story about a person involved in a local charity. As part of the story, the newspaper reporter provides background information about one of the volunteers. The volunteer is a dedicated worker and has been involved with the charity for years. As part of the background the reporter reveals that the volunteer has a rare disease, and that this disease inhibits the volunteer's work. No one at the charity knows about this, and the volunteer has never discussed this publicity with anyone. Can the reporter be sued? Is it the fault of the volunteer for revealing this information? Is this type of story protected under the First Amendment, making a lawsuit unconstitutional? These are all factors that involve the privacy tort public disclosure of private facts.

Public disclosure of private (embarrassing) facts is a lawsuit rooted in telling the truth about someone, but the information is such that there is a reasonable expectation of privacy. The Restatement (Second) of Torts states the public disclosure of private facts as follows:

> One who gives publicity to a matter concerning the private life of another is subject to liability to the other for invasion of his privacy, if the matter publicized is of a kind that (a) would be highly offensive to a reasonable person, and (b) is not of legitimate concern to the public.[35]

States recognizing this tort typically follow these elements of public disclosure of private facts: evidence that must be present for a successful claim, the facts must be privately held, facts cannot be private if they are somewhat well known, amplifying or highlighting public information does not qualify, and the facts must be true. Unlike false light, the public disclosure of private facts is not defamation, nor can it contain defamatory information. There is also no test to determine public knowledge. The reasonableness of offensiveness is also highly subjective. There is no bright line test for this, and it must be determined on a case-by-case basis. The Supreme Court of Indiana describes offensiveness as something that "offends society's accepted, communal norms and social mores."[36] Finally, the public interest standard is a balance between the First Amendment freedom of the press and the privacy rights of the individual. What constitutes newsworthy information depends largely on the status of the plaintiff. The U.S. Court of Appeals for the 10th Circuit described this element this way:

> In our view, this standard properly restricts liability for public disclosure of private facts to the extreme case, thereby providing the breathing space needed by the press to exercise effective editorial judgment. This standard provides a privilege for truthful publications that ceases to operate only when an editor abuses his broad discretion to matters that are of legitimate public interest.[37]

This tort frequently hinges on the reasonableness of the offensiveness and the legitimacy of the public concern. The United States has a long history of this type of case, with a famous case occurring in 1940 in the U.S. Court of Appeals in the Second Circuit. That case hinged on whether a former celebrity, who was a child prodigy, was still considered newsworthy after he had ceased being part of the public eye. The *New Yorker* magazine featured William James Sidis, a child prodigy well known 30 years earlier, in a "Where Are They Now" piece. Sidis had long been out of the public eye and had fallen on hard times after his childhood celebrity, living in a small rooming house and working a menial job despite having graduated from Harvard University with a mathematics degree when he was only 16 years old. The Second Circuit held that Sidis's previous celebrity did not qualify as legitimate public concern, writing that the article's violated his right to privacy. The court held that

> the article is merciless in its dissection of intimate details of its subject's personal life, and this in company with elaborate accounts of Sidis' passion for privacy and the pitiable lengths to which he has gone in order to avoid public scrutiny. The work possesses great reader interest, for it is both amusing and instructive; but it may be fairly described as a ruthless exposure of a once public character, who has since sought and has now been deprived of the seclusion of private life.[38]

This type of tort has applicability to celebrity versus noncelebrity figures. Celebrity facts tend to be newsworthy and therefore do not qualify as private, such as a football player's bullying behavior, or the sexual orientation of a private citizen made temporarily famous by a newsworthy event.[39] For example, Oliver Sipple was a gay man who had protected President Gerald Ford from an assassination attempt in 1975. Sipple, a former Marine and political organizer for Harvey Milk, grabbed the arm of the assassin while she held the gun. The *San Francisco Chronicle* revealed Sipple's sexual orientation as a high-profile member of the San Francisco gay community. Sipple sued the *Chronicle* and other newspapers for invasion of privacy but lost because the appellate court held that his sexual orientation had become a legitimate newsworthy event in the story.[40] However, with private individuals, courts have been much more willing to find public disclosure of private facts when the plaintiff is a private person. For example, courts have found invasions of privacy with private facts when the plaintiff's health status was revealed to coworkers.[41]

PR practitioners should note that this tort has applicability in the practice of risk management, reputation management, and media relations. Like defamation, the more famous a person is, the less they can easily avail themselves of this law. PR practitioners and publicists should note that celebrity clients will have a difficult time recovering under this type of lawsuit, and that the lawsuit itself can serve to amplify the private facts, garnering even more publicity. However, for private citizens this law is an opportunity to protect from invasions of privacy in the purest sense. However, social media and open systems AI provides for many more opportunities to disclose private information. These disclosures provide defendants a great opportunity to rebut claims of public disclosure of private facts by proving the facts were not private.

Intrusion upon Seclusion

A paparazzi taking a photo of a celebrity in their backyard, the use of a secret recording device in an office, or a long-range lens looking into someone's home are all examples of intrusion upon seclusion. A classic privacy tort, the Restatements Second defines intrusion as follows:

One who intentionally intrudes, physically or otherwise, upon the solitude or seclusion of another or his private affairs or concerns, is subject to liability to the other for invasion of his privacy, if the intrusion would be highly offensive to a reasonable person.[42]

The issue in an intrusion case is the placement of the plaintiff. The tort hinges on solitude and expectations of physical privacy. The Restatement provides several examples of intrusion, such as a reporter interviewing a sick woman in a hospital room even after she refused to meet him; wiretapped recordings; or providing false credentials and evidence to obtain access to private documents, such as bank accounts. Public spaces and records cannot have intrusion because there is no expectation of privacy, such as a public street. However, even then there are some expectations of privacy depending upon the context; for example, a woman on a public street would have an expectation that her underwear would not be photographed if the wind blew her skirt up.[43] Courts have found intrusion in a variety of contexts, particularly with the media. For example, a television station's broadcast of a woman receiving medical treatment at the scene of a wreck was considered intrusion.[44] A magazine's use of hidden recording equipment for a story of a doctor practicing without a license was intrusion.[45] In 1970, General Motors (GM) was found to invade the privacy of consumer advocate and GM critic Ralph Nader when it allegedly hired a private investigator to investigate Nader though a series of personal interviews about him, the use of wiretaps, and even entrapment.[46]

This tort has applicability to PR practice, which frequently uses background information to better inform practitioners about specific publics or contacts. As the next section shows, this intrusion is amplified using technology and sophisticated gathering techniques. There are unique state laws that specifically address intrusion within the context of technology. Telephone recording, for instance, is governed by state laws that require various parties to consent to recording, ranging from one party to all participants in the phone conversation.[47]

Privacy in European Union: Exporting New Standards and Expectations
In global PR work, it is important to note that U.S. privacy law is not
necessarily the norm. Outside of the United States, individual nations
have their own historical backgrounds that inform their view of privacy.
For other Western democracies, particularly those in the EU, privacy
laws are much more robust in protecting information. Since the European Convention of Human Rights was promulgated in 1950, there has
been a focus on privacy law within EU. In fact, some of the EU privacy
laws likely would be struck down in the United States for violating
the First Amendment and other constitutional provisions. Unlike the
United States, which has privacy laws largely governed by states with
a few subject-specific laws, the European Union has a comprehensive
privacy law under the General Data Privacy Regulation (GDPR). The
enforcement of EU privacy also uses Data Protection Authority (DPA)
to enforce the GDPR in their member states.[48] Penalties are also significant in the EU for privacy breaches with up to €20 million fines or
4 percent of an organization's worldwide annual revenue, whichever is
higher, for major breaches of the GDPR.[49] Why is the EU so important
for PR practitioners? Not only is the EU a major part of the global marketplace, but it also has a high degree of influence on how other countries
craft their privacy laws. Moreover, the compliance aspects of the EU and
the GDPR make global companies comply with their stringent privacy
laws, which, in effect, imports EU law into many non-EU countries,
including the United States. The phenomenon of the global impact of
EU laws and regulations on non-EU countries is known as the "Brussels
effect," a phrase credited to Anu Bradford, who argues that the EU's
business regulation has made it a global superpower within commerce
and trade.[50] This phenomenon is not the result of the EU's active impo-
sition of legal or regulatory standards, but of corporations deciding that
they will comply with heightened standards to compete in a global marketplace, thus making EU law writ large, including privacy, the de facto
global standard for compliance. A comprehensive explanation of EU privacy and its power within the global communication sphere is beyond the
scope of this book, but it is important for PR practitioners and readers to

have a general sense of how these regulations work to create the global norms of privacy for communication in the 2020s.

The GDPR has become a major force within privacy law internationally since going into effect in May 2018. Its primary concern is the data privacy of EU citizens and, because the law deals with citizen privacy, it has applications that go outside of the borders of EU member states.[51] Hailed as the "toughest privacy and security law in the world," the GDPR focuses on key areas of privacy such as data protection, GDPR compliance, data security, data security designs, data processing, consumer content when providing private information, and when a data protection officer (DPO) must be appointed.[52] The GDPR also provides for specific privacy rights for data subjects:

- The right to be informed
- The right of access
- The right to rectification
- The right to erasure
- The right to restrict processing
- The right to data portability
- The right to object
- Rights in relation to automated decision making and profiling.[53]

Among these rights, the right to erasure, also known as the right to be forgotten, presents one of the most striking differences between privacy law in Europe and that in the United States. For PR practitioners, it is also a law that potentially provides an effective mechanism for online reputation management, although not without ethical considerations. The right to be forgotten has also had a profound impact on the cottage industry of online image management where boutique services can provide erasure of otherwise true content about a client on a third-party website.

The right to be forgotten is part of EU statutes in Article 17 of the GDPR and Recitals 65 and 66. The GDPR states the following:

The data subject shall have the right to obtain from the controller the erasure of personal data concerning him or her without undue delay and the controller shall have the obligation to erase personal data without undue delay where one of the following grounds applies:

1. the personal data are no longer necessary in relation to the purposes for which they were collected or otherwise processed;

2. the data subject withdraws consent on which the processing is based according to point (a) of Article 6(1), or point (a) of Article 9(2), and where there is no other legal ground for the processing;

3. the data subject objects to the processing pursuant to Article 21(1) and there are no overriding legitimate grounds for the processing, or the data subject objects to the processing pursuant to Article 21(2);

4. the personal data have been unlawfully processed;

5. the personal data have to be erased for compliance with a legal obligation in Union or Member State law to which the controller is subject;

6. the personal data have been collected in relation to the offer of information society services referred to in Article 8(1).[54]

While Article 17's description of the right to be forgotten is detailed and rooted in the technological realities of the digital world, the concept of erasure rights is rooted in a much longer history. French law recognizes the "*le droit à l'oubli*," which is rooted in the concept that once criminal sentences are completed, the person previously incarcerated has the right to move forward without having the criminal conviction negatively impact their life. This philosophy is seen in the laws of other countries, such as the United Kingdom's Rehabilitation Offenders Act of 1974, which eliminated requirements that criminal convictions be disclosed on certain applications, such as job, insurance, or even lawsuits.[55] Over time, this right of erasure has expanded to include other noncriminal facts. In 2014, the EU Court of Justice set the foundation for right of erasure in the GDPR, and the right has existed within EU member states since 2018.

The practical implications of the right to be forgotten on the communication field is in press content. News sources, online platforms, and search engines may receive requests by individuals to remove content. This creates practical issues surrounding data storage and archival information of news content, for which there may be requests for deletion. There are also myriad transnational legal issues with the right to be forgotten, especially within the United States where there is no right to be forgotten (such a law likely would violate the First Amendment).[56] However, the right to be forgotten is not carte blanche for anyone to request removal of content. The GDPR provides exceptions to removal requests such as "exercising the right of expression or information," where the information is posted because of legal requirements, public health, archiving for historical, public interest, or scientific purposes, or for legal claims.[57] For those working in the global PR industry, especially in a European market, the right to be forgotten continues to be an important aspect of privacy that practitioners should fully understand, both in terms of client services as well as in the context of ethical transparency.

Big Data and Regulation

One area where EU law has a major impact is in big data. Big data has become a buzzword within the public relations profession since the late 2010s. Its allure is rooted in how targeted communication can reach publics in a way where the message will be precisely delivered and consumed. Coupled with the power of AI, big data has tremendous potential for PR practice. It lowers the barrier to audiences and provides a mechanism to increase audience segmentation, predictive analysis, sentiment analysis, optimized content and distribution, and message evaluation. While there is no uniform definition of big data, it can best be described as the use of structured and unstructured data sets to make valuable insights into different aspects of society. For example, public relations uses big data for audience segmentation and targeting allows communicators to speak directly to publics in a way that audiences would be most receptive to the message. Big data is big business because there is a science and art to obtaining and effectively using this information. The ability of PR practitioners to use big data to create sentiment analysis also provides for real-time evaluation of message effectiveness, allowing practitioners to tailor messages for maximized effect.

In the United States, there is no comprehensive big data law that regulates the industry. U.S. privacy laws, such as HIPPA, FERPA, and COPPA as well as state laws like the CCPA, all affect how transparent the storage of data must be and how data can be gathered. The FTC has become more involved in how big data should be regulated, focusing on issues of privacy and transparency. In 2023 one of the biggest concerns in big data was discrimination; the FTC has issued a statement about condemning the use of data programs that couple with AI to produce discriminatory outputs, which would violate the FTC Act, the Fair Credit Reporting Act, and Equal Opportunity Laws.[58]

However, U.S.–EU data transfers presents unique challenges. Big data's power comes in the aggregate information of individuals. However, the GDPR mandates minimalization of this data gathering. Moreover, there is an increased interest in the antitrust component of big data, and how data gathering, especially those organization with large amounts of data, can create an anticompetitive environment by having advantages within paid promotional communication. Compounding this issue are mergers with companies that in aggregate have large amounts of consumer data that can be leveraged for market dominance and creating barriers to new companies. Because big data has such value, some mergers even occur because of the acquisition for commercial purposes. As PR practice continues to utilize big data to create targeted messaging, practitioners should be aware that there likely will be growing regulation of acquiring private information. This may change from mere transparent closure of data gathering, but will monetize acquiring data from individuals. Moreover, business models based on data acquisition will continue but may be shaped by regulatory forces, particularly in Europe. In short, the Brussels effect will continue to be a major force within global communication and business.

Ethical Issues in Privacy: How Privacy May Change in the 2020s

Privacy is an area of the law that presents some of the most unique ethical issues. Privacy is rooted in the concept that personal, private information must be protected, and that individuals have the right to a level of integrity. A lot of the ethical issues around privacy relate to respect for the individual, something that is a well-established maxim in PR practice. After all, public relations is rooted in the concept of relationship management and two-way communication. Within privacy it is important to acknowledge that the law establishes a baseline for behavior, not a ceiling. Because of that, PR practitioners can always make decisions that surpass the privacy protections required by law.

In the 2020s, ethical issues in privacy will become more complex because of technology's ability to gather, use, and disseminate personal information. Data analytics also provides immense power to influence audiences and publics, and given the way AI and big data work symbiotically, the power of communication will likely grow in the coming decade. This presents a variety of ethical dilemmas involving disinformation, disclosure, and transparency. The overcollection and overuse of data also presents unique challenges in the PR profession, because of the power data has in crafting and disseminating content. Creating mechanisms for opting in or out of data collection, and the transparency in how data are used, are two of the major issues facing PR today. Having a communication practice rooted in ethics means that PR can take a professional lead in these areas.

It is often said that law is the floor of what must be done. That is, the law provides the minimum basis for compliance. As shown in chapter 1, an organization can always go beyond what the law requires and exceed legal requirements. Privacy provides one of the areas where this is most true. An organization that values and protects their publics' privacy will build its reputation and goodwill. This can translate into higher value of the organization and establishes an organizational history that can be used to offset any unexpected crisis that may occur.

The proliferation of AI in the PR profession is presenting numerous issues surrounding privacy. Generative AI platforms, such as ChatGPT, present novel issues of privacy because of the materials that are input into their systems. Part of this analysis must consider the open or closed system of the generative AI platform. Open systems in AI can store data and use that within the AI platform to generate new content. This can create a host of issues for those working in highly regulated businesses like healthcare, but it also poses problems for those who regularly utilize the platforms to generate content of any type. For example, suppose a communicator uses an open generative AI platform to create a list of employees with addresses, dates of birth, and Social Security numbers. That information can be absorbed into the generative AI platform and then potentially could be reproduced for another user. Proprietary information, such as trade secrets (discussed in chapter 7) could be inadvertently disclosed using open systems AI. What this means for PR practitioners is that they must consider how these technologies are going to be used within their content creation, but must also lean into the ethical conversation when their organizations are creating standards of operation for these platforms.

So far, the pace of AI regulation has been slow compared to the technological development and industry adoption of platforms. In 2023, the Biden administration put forward a Blueprint for an AI Bill of Rights that discusses, among other things, the issue of privacy within these platforms. The privacy section begins with this statement: "You should be protected from abusive data practices via built-in protections, and you should have agency over how data about you is used."[59] Within this discussion is the idea that individuals should have their sensitive material protected, and that surveillance should be minimized. This has real consequences for PR work that may involve big data that is used to target publics for specific content. It also demonstrates that, from a legal perspective, privacy presents new concerns. Given the protracted process in which a bill becomes law in the United States, it is likely that many privacy regulations in AI will not come from the law, but from industry guardrails put in place by AI platforms and the organizations that use them. The potential for discrimination within AI is a big part of the analysis of the new platforms, and this discrimination is intertwined with potential privacy violations. A joint statement by the Department of

Justice, Consumer Financial Protection Bureau, and the Equal Employment Opportunity Commission focused on how AI can be a force that generates bad results for the public. They wrote:

> We already see how AI tools can turbocharge fraud and automate discrimination, and we won't hesitate to use the full scope of our legal authorities to protect Americans from these threats. . . . Technological advances can deliver critical innovation—but claims of innovation must not be cover for lawbreaking. There is no AI exemption to the laws on the books, and the FTC will vigorously enforce the law to combat unfair or deceptive practices or unfair methods of competition.[60]

The Biden administration in October 2023 issued an Executive Order reiterating much of the concerns about AI and privacy. The order specifically deals with the "safety and security" of AI platforms and requires transparency between the platforms and the U.S. government, mandating that these platforms notify the government when they are training AI models that have significant security risks. This includes the creation of an AI Safety and Security Board established by the Department of Homeland Security and mandatory AI labelling to assist with fraud. Part of the order also mandates that the government will provide federal support for "privacy preserving techniques," establish a Research Coordination Network for cryptographic measures to ensure privacy, and increase measures to monitor how commercial data is gathered by agencies.[61] Additionally, the U.S. government has launched AI.gov, a website dedicated to the Biden administration's measures to address AI concerns by providing information about regulations, potential AI job opportunities in the federal government, and serve as a feedback loop for those concerned about the technology.[62] However, it is important to note that executive orders and websites do not replace actual federal legislation on the topic. A comprehensive AI regulation has yet to be passed by Congress and, given the political polarization of the twenty-first century, it likely will take a long time to establish all the laws necessary to ensure privacy within AI.

There should be no greater steward and advocate for privacy than PR professionals. Rooted in the importance of privacy is inherent respect for publics. As a profession, public relations has always advocated for engagement and relationship management with publics to earn trust and goodwill. Having that dialogue allows PR practitioners to communicate effectively with publics to achieve attitudinal and behavioral change. Transgressions of privacy have resulted in some of the greatest institutional crises in the twenty-first century. Because of that, PR practitioners, especially those working in the era of AI, should look at industry ethics and personal morals to make privacy that benefits the profession, clients, and stakeholders. Given the technological revolution happening in the content creation field, public relations is poised to be a thought leader in AI ethics in content creation and communication. It seems likely that the transparency and disclosure-driven nature of PR means that AI use within the field will follow a similar path of responsible use focused on informing publics.

DISCUSSION QUESTIONS

1. What is the most important privacy tort for PR practitioners to know?

2. What is the largest privacy issue facing PR practice in AI? How should the law address it?

3. Is big data a force for good or bad in society? Can it be ethically used responsibly in public relations?

4. Deepfake technology has rapidly outpaced viewers' ability to discern deepfake and real video content. In May 2023, for example, a fake photo of an explosion at the Pentagon caused the U.S. stock market to drop briefly. What type of legal consequences are there for producers of deepfake images? How could those individuals be legally held accountable when they are anonymous? How can PR practice combat disinformation with communication?

5. Why is access to employee social media accounts important? Are there other privacy access issues that PR practitioners should think about in the age of AI?

CASE SCENARIO

You are a strategic communicator working in a position that does both PR and advertising for a client who manufactures allergy medicine. Recently the FDA made one of your client's allergy medicines over the counter, which should increase sales of the medicine. Your job to raise awareness of the medicine through social media, specifically to seasonal allergy sufferers who live in an area of the United States where ragweed, a plant that causes allergies, flourishes. You want to use data from social media sites to reach the targeted demographic for this medicine. Your research shows that not only do people in areas where ragweed grows buy more allergy medicine, but that women ages 30 to 45, college educated, and with children buy more allergy medicine. That demographic is also more likely to try pharmaceutical products. You want to use big data to target messaging to this demographic. What are the ethical issues of using big data to target this group? Are there any disclosures that should be made? Suppose the data includes self-disclosed medical issues with allergies? Does that change your answer? Does that information matter?

CHAPTER 7

Public Relations and Intellectual Property

OVERVIEW: INTELLECTUAL PROPERTY (IP) IS ONE THE MOST IMPORTANT areas of law for those in communication and content creation. This chapter provides an overview of copyright, trademark, and trade secrets and how those laws apply to PR practice. In addition to the overview of these areas of law, this chapter also discusses how IP ownership provides for message control, and how the lack of ownership can create image and reputational issues for organizations. The chapter also addresses the contemporary issue of artificial intelligence and copyright, and how copyright protections are not attached to purely AI-generated content. The chapter concludes with a discussion of how PR practitioners should consider content access, copyright fair use, plagiarism, and international laws related to IP.

OBJECTIVES:

- Provide a foundation of copyright, trademark, and trade secret requirements.
- Discuss the elements of copyright infringement and the application of the fair use defense.
- Analyze the important of trademark protection and issues of genericity and abandonment.
- Explain the relationship between trade secrets and client lists.
- Explore the relationship of U.S. intellectual property laws and AI-generated content.

Imagine a PR practitioner uses an AI platform to create a generative image for a client. The image is then reformulated by the platform into a logo, and that logo is then incorporated into the branding of the organization. Later, the PR practitioner sees a very similar logo on a competitor's website. What can the PR practitioner or her client do? Is this infringement? If so, what type: trademark or copyright? What would the damages be? Could the organization get the infringer to stop using the mark? And does any of this matter, considering AI created the image?

All these questions are major components of IP law, but they are also part of the larger conversation about organizational reputation and image management. Current PR practice has undergone a radical transformation, where practitioners are highly involved in multiplatform content creation that regularly involves visuals. Moreover, the use of fast-evolving AI technology places a new complexity on copyright and trademark creation, driving a legal environment where PR practitioners may not have the control they think they have over their work.

Intellectual property in the United States has its roots in the body of the U.S. Constitution. Article I, Section 8, Clause 8 states: "[The Congress shall have Power . . .] To promote the Progress of Science and useful Arts, by securing for limited Times to Authors and Inventors the exclusive Right to their respective Writings and Discoveries." This clause in the Constitution recognizes the importance of both IP creators to enjoy the fruits of their labor, while balancing that compensation against society's larger benefit of using this IP for public betterment. This is a balance between money versus access, individual ownership versus societal use, and incentivizing innovation versus using innovation.

Intellectual property law has a unique history that mirrors the technological and economic development of the United States. The first federal laws concerning IP were passed in 1790, focusing on patents and copyrights.[1] Trademark protection was also first addressed by the law in 1790 when a Massachusetts sailcloth company petitioned then Secretary of State Thomas Jefferson for a registered trademark. Jefferson thought such a law was a good idea and put forth a trademark system in which businesses could register their marks for interstate commerce with U.S. District Courts.[2] Trademarks would continue to be registered and then proliferated in the 1830s through the 1870s as corporate image became a norm in U.S. businesses. During the 1860s, there was a major attempt to have federal recognition of trademarks. This was largely unsuccessful, but states began passing their own trademark laws. The United States entered trademark treaties with France, Russia, and Belgium in the late 1860s, which spurred legislation for federal trademark law in 1870. Trademark law was challenged for its constitutionality, and in 1879 the U.S. Supreme Court heard *In re Trademark Cases*, an early case on infringement concerning a trademark on whiskey. The Court held the 1870 Trademark Act unconstitutional, stating that the copyright clause of the Constitution does not provide for Congress to regulate trademarks.[3]

Trademark law would once again be passed in the United States in 1881, in large part due to the pressures of international trademark agreements. By 1905[4] the United States had trademark law that specifically addressed domestic infringement, prompting a proliferation of registrations, from 4,000 in 1905 to 10,000 in 1906.[5] Copyright was similarly undergoing a recalibration during this era, especially in the 1890s when international copyright treaties, such as the Berne Convention, established global expectations for copyrighted works.[6] By 1909 the U.S. Congress made another overhaul of copyright law that would last until the Copyright Act of 1976. Remnants of the 1909 law are still seen today in copyright duration for works made prior to 1978.

Patent and trademark laws continue to evolve. The Lanham Act, officially named the Trademark Act of 1946, established the standards for modern U.S. trademark protection. As technology has changed, especially with digital media, IP laws have attempted to keep up with new realities. The Digital Millennium Copyright Act (DMCA) of 1998 is one example of an IP law that addressed changing technologies, specifically the internet. With the advent of AI, new issues surrounding IP have emerged, particularly in the recent cases where copyright has not been granted to generative AI content, notably visuals. It is important to note that the law almost always lags technological change. For example, the recent proliferation of AI has lawmakers struggling to keep up with the regulation of this new technology. This was the case for other technological innovations from the wireless telegraph to social media. Many times, laws and regulations created by legislatures and agencies do not anticipate changes in the technology. Because of that, courts frequently find themselves having to fill in the gaps within technology legislation.

These changes demonstrate the evolving nature of IP, but also show why PR practitioners need to have a working knowledge of this law. For any content creator, IP is the basis for property ownership. It allows the creator certain rights to modify, change, or license their work. In reputation, brand, and image management IP is at the basis of all decision making, and its existence provides the ability to have control over those valuable intangible aspects of an organization.

However, there are common misperceptions of IP. Many times, intellectual property is discussed in a general way in which terms such as copyright, trademark, patent, and trade secret are used interchangeably. Yet each of these areas of law is distinct, and it is important for practitioners to understand those distinctions. It is equally important to recognize that IP protection is determined by the content and rarely the type of protection, for example, copyright versus trademark, the choice of the creator.

This chapter provides an overview of the three main type of intellectual property that PR practitioners encounter in their practice: copyright, trademark, and trade secrets. In this analysis, the chapter lists the core requirements of each of these IP forms, how they can be infringed, and what defenses can be made during infringement suits, especially in terms of fair use defense for copyright. The chapter concludes with an analysis of how ethical use of IP affects practice, and how new technology, specifically AI, affects how the law approaches the evolving field.

COPYRIGHT

Press releases, video news releases, social media posts, brochures, pictures, infographics, flyers, and almost any other PR content are copyrighted material. This is important to PR practitioners because these are key work products of the profession. The copyright protection given to this content allows PR practitioners, or their clients, the ability to utilize and control their message. It provides property ownership of important and impactful content. It also offers the copyright holder certain rights for a definitive length of time to use this material for a variety of applications. As mentioned in the introduction, U.S. copyright law has a long history, and the development of the law mirrors the development of the United States as a producer of intellectual content. Currently U.S. copyright law reflects many of the standards articulated by global treaties, such as the Berne Convention and the World Intellectual Property Organization (WIPO).

It is important for PR practitioners to know the basics of copyright law because so much of their work product's protection comes from copyright. Moreover, the digital platforms that now underlie PR practice create both rich opportunities for content creation as well as lowered barriers to infringement. In a global context, PR practitioners also should be aware that while there is uniformity within much copyright law, there is not a global standard for all copyright protection. Because of that, some work will be infringed at higher rates in countries that lack similar copyright standards, especially in enforcement. Knowing these nuances of copyright equip practitioners with the power to make better decisions in both how to access and use copyrighted works—and how to protect their own content.

Copyright Requirements

Copyright in the United States has two requirements: originality and fixation in a tangible medium.[7] If those two requirements are met, copyright is automatically granted under U.S. law. Despite having only two requirements, originality and fixation in copyright law are complex concepts.

Consider originality. This requires a human author and some level of originality, although this can be a low threshold. Historically, originality is a concept that exists on a continuum. There are highly original works, such as novels, and very low-level original works, such as copies of paintings that use different color schemes. Both the highly original and low-level original work is copyrightable. However, not everything is original enough to be copyrightable, even if it takes a lot of work. For example, the U.S. Supreme Court held that an alphabetized phone book is not original enough to be copyrighted. The court held that "sweat of the brow" was not enough to constitute originality.[8] There had to be something more to constitute copyright. For PR practitioners this may be the case for calendar plans of campaigns, or other organizational list content such as contacts. It is important to note that items such as client lists typically will not be protected under copyright under this "sweat of the brow" doctrine.[9]

The human dimension of originality is extremely important, especially in the era of AI. Artificial intelligence is not considered human creation, sometimes even when a human provides the prompt for the generated work. This currently means that some AI content receives no copyright protection, a fact that should be of concern for PR practitioners using AI to create logos, content, and other visuals for clients. The practical result of this lack of copyright means the work is not property and, as such, can be used by anyone for any reason. There is no control over this type of content, and PR practitioners, especially those in reputation and image management, should be aware of the use of AI and its impact on clients. However, the intersection of AI and copyright is an evolving issue. The current U.S. Copyright Office (USCO) is examining AI and copyright to determine the threshold of level of human activity that could qualify as sufficient for originality.[10] A 2023 lawsuit in the U.S. District Court for the District of Columbia involved an AI-generated painting created by an AI platform named the Creativity Machine. The U.S. Copyright Office refused to grant copyright protection for the painting, and the owner of the Creativity Machine appealed to the U.S. District Court. The court held that the human requirement of originality barred the Creativity Machine from having a valid copyright, since it was driven by an AI algorithm. Explaining its rationale, the court held: "Copyright has never stretched so far, however, as to protect works generated by new forms of technology operating absent any guiding human hand, as plaintiff urges here. Human authorship is a bedrock requirement of copyright."[11]

This precedent demonstrates that although copyright law has a certain acceptance of new technological innovation in relation to copyrighted works, it does not accept that machine- produced content devoid of human input can qualify as original. That is in line with other court cases that have disallowed nonhumans from obtaining copyright protection. For example, the U.S. Court of Appeals for the Ninth Circuit held that a monkey, represented through an animal rights group, could not sue for copyright infringement against a photographer using his image, given that the monkey could not own a copyright of a picture even if the monkey took the photo.[12] Currently, the USCO has leaned into this conversation, providing for a notice and comment period for regulations on registration of AI works.[13]

Fixation is the second requirement of copyright. Federal copyright law states, "A work is 'fixed' in a tangible medium of expression when its embodiment in a copy or phonorecord, by or under the authority of the author, is sufficiently permanent or stable to permit it to be perceived, reproduced, or otherwise communicated for a period of more than transitory duration."[14] Fixation requires permanence and does not apply to a brief unrecorded visual or unrecorded concert.[15] It is important to note that fixation and perception are distinct. Just because someone needs a device to be perceived does not mean it is not fixed. For example, a work may be fixed in computer code and a computer may be required to decode the work to be seen.

Within copyright law, there are items that are included and excluded from copyright protection. Certain things cannot be copyrighted. Federal copyright law states, "In no case does copyright protection for an original work of authorship extend to any idea, procedure, process, system, method of operation, concept, principle, or discovery, regardless of the form in which it is described, explained, illustrated, or embodied in such work."[16] This includes a lot of material, and it is important to note that generally, facts are not copyrightable. Additionally, items including "*Scène à faire*," French for "scene to be done," are not copyrightable. This includes those stock characters such as a villain or hero, or stock plotlines such as car chases in films or books.[17] However, copyright protection does extend to many other areas of content. According to federal copyright law, all of the following may be copyrighted:

1. literary works;

2. musical works, including any accompanying words;

3. dramatic works, including any accompanying music;

4. pantomimes and choreographic works;

5. pictorial, graphic, and sculptural works;

6. motion pictures and other audiovisual works;

7. sound recordings; and

8. architectural works.[18]

This list is inclusive of much of the work product of PR professionals. Ownership of these copyrights is largely determined by the contracts between PR practitioners and clients. Ownership is critical when it comes to copyright because there are rights that attach to the copyrighted material. An owner of a copyright has the following rights: reproduction, derivative works, distribution, performance, display, and digital display.[19] These rights are held by the copyright owner and can be sold. For example, if an author of a book holds a copyright, she could sell the reproduction and derivative works rights to a movie studio to make a film based on the book. The rights are also inheritable by beneficiaries when the original owner of a copyright dies.

For this reason, it is important for PR practitioners to research potential copyright owners if a copyrighted work is going to be used, to ensure that the practitioner has the proper license to use the work. This has become a particularly important issue for independent contract photographers, whose photos appear for a limited time in a publication. For example, suppose a newspaper utilizes a photograph for a story, but the copyright owner of the photography retains the rights by giving a limited license to the newspaper to publish the photo in that one story. Because the photographer retained the copyright, permission for another use of the photo must be given by the photographer. The newspaper cannot give permission because it only received a limited license to use the photograph.

This issue can produce complex scenarios, particularly around digital archiving. Some archives cannot display photos in a magazine or newspaper because the photographs are not owned by the outlet but rather by the original photographer. For PR practitioners, it is important to note that mere physical ownership of a copyrighted work does not constitute copyright ownership. Owning a copy of a book does not give any copyright ownership. Using older photographs, reports, stories, or any other type of content requires the PR practitioner to do their due diligence to ensure that copyright permissions are provided by the actual owner. This is particularly true of photographs, where photographers frequently hold the copyright and only give a limited license for reproductions. This is also the case with special events photography, especially weddings. Confusion over these copyright ownership issues can be alleviated by establishing clear ownership rights in a contract. For example, without a contract, the photographer of a wedding could claim ownership of the photographs and retain all copyright rights including reproduction, making the newlyweds must pay for copies. Alternatively, there could be a contract that gives newlyweds a limited license for reproduction or assigns all the rights over to them upon payment. This is why these works for hire need to have clearly established copyright ownership so there is no confusion later.

Another copyright issue that affects PR practitioners is ownership of work product created in the process of PR pitches and campaign work. There is the all-too-often-told tale of a PR practitioner producing content in a request for proposal (RFP), only to have that material stolen by the prospective client and given to another firm that wins the account. Not only is this highly unethical both for the client and firm using the unauthorized material, but it also can constitute copyright infringement. Any PR practitioner or firm that retains the IP rights of their content can sue for infringement over this type of scenario. Sometimes prospective clients in RFPs request the pitched content be given to them as a matter of contractual agreement. If PR practitioners do this, they should be aware that they are giving away their content to be used in derivative campaigns by others. If they do not agree to sign over copyright to the prospective client during the RFP, then the PR firm that created the work retains the work as their own copyright. This is a balance of business strategy and law, but PR practitioners would be well advised to know exactly what a prospective client's expectations may be.[20]

This concept of retaining copyright is also important for PR practitioners working with current clients. Frequently clients want to own the copyright to the content their PR firm or employee makes. This presents unique situations where the practitioner or firm wants to use the content for their personal portfolio. Like the scenario of RFPs, PR practitioners should speak with clients to know exactly what the expectations are regarding retention of copyrighted work. This perhaps could be part of an agreement between the client and practitioner to allow the PR practitioner to retain copies of work that could later be used in a portfolio. Discussing these matters upfront is best to stave off potential problems later.

Duration
Knowing when a copyright falls into public domain is essential for content creators. While the Copyright Act of 1976 replaced the Copyright Act of 1909, the 1909 statute's legacy is still important in today's discussion of copyright duration. The 1909 Act had many formalities, which if not followed, eliminated copyright protection or did not grant it in the first place. Depending on whether a copyright holder followed those formalities, the 1976 Act and other copyright laws may or may not have extended the duration of older copyrights.

The 1976 Copyright Act, which went into effect in 1978, defines duration as life of the author plus 70 years for individuals. In the case of dual authors, duration ends based on who dies first. For an anonymous, pseudonymous, or for-hire works, the duration is 95 years from publication or 120 years from creation, whichever is shorter. These are simple rules for duration that apply to all works created or published after January 1, 1978. However, works published prior to January 1, 1978, do not follow these rules exactly. Instead, those copyrights follow a complex system of rules that are very fact-specific, frequently involving the 1909 Copyright Act's provisions.[21]

The 1909 Copyright Act gave shorter duration than the modern law. Under the 1909 law, copyright had two terms for a duration of 28 years followed by a renewal of 28 years. This initial copyright status and the renewal were predicated on a formal process. Failure to register the copyright initially or formally renew the copyright meant the copyright ended and the work was in public domain; that is, anyone could use the work without paying royalties. The 1976 Copyright Act changed this process of registration by making it optional. In addition, the 1976 Act also provided for a duration that did not require renewal. However, some works at the time of the 1976 Act were in their first 28-year term under the 1909 Act or were in their second renewal term. This presented a complicated issue for copyright holders, and subsequent laws of copyright, notably the Copyright Renewal Act of 1992 and the Sonny Bono Copyright Extension Act of 1998, have made the actual duration times for copyrights dependent on multiple factors.[22]

As of the time of this writing in 2024, works prior to 1929 (sound recordings before 1924) are in public domain and have no federal copyright protection (for future reference add on a year from the date of this publication to determine when public domain occurs pre-1929, for example, in 2025 it will be 1930). Works published from 1929 to 1977 without copyright notice, works published from 1929 to 1963 without valid copyright renewal, and works from 1978 until March 1, 1989, published without notice or without subsequent registration for five years, are all in the public domain. Other works that followed formalities of copyright prior to 1977 may be in public domain. Works from 1929 to 1963 published with notice and renewal and works published from 1964 until 1977 with notice are protected for 95 years following the publication date. The due diligence of PR practitioners is required to verify these facts of copyright. It is important to note that this highly technical copyright protection of pre-1978 content can be difficult to find. However, some clearinghouses of copyright do exist, such as copyright.com. More complex cases do exist where lesser-known copyrights may still be held by individuals or their heirs, or when copyright ownership is not known.

Infringement

Imagine a PR practitioner is working for a client who wants to create a 100th anniversary retrospective of their company. In the company archives, there are photos from the early 1950s through the 1990s. These photos were taken by a local photographer who has since died. There is no contract between the company and the photographer, and the photographer's son, who inherited his father's estate, has long moved away. What should the PR practitioner do? Could the use of these photos constitute infringement? Could there be a fair use defense? Can the PR practitioner use the photos and risk being sued? This type of situation is common, and it presents issues that those creating content face regularly. Knowing how to spot this issue is important, but knowing what to do rests in large part on how a potential infringement claim could be made.

The U.S. Supreme Court held that copyright infringement has two elements: (1) the plaintiff owns the copyright, and (2) the infringer (defendant) copied the original work. Despite the simplicity of these elements, it can be difficult to determine infringement. Notably, defendants may raise various defenses to infringement, including fair use, another area of the law that depends on various factors. Copyright ownership can be proven by circumstances, but registration, though not a requirement of obtaining copyright, can serve as presumption of ownership.[23] The second element of copying the copyrighted work can be easy or difficult to prove depending on the facts. If a copy is the same as the original, then infringement may be self-evident. However, if the alleged infringement is a derivative work—one based on the content of a copyrighted work— the proof of infringement depends on how similar the two works may be. The concept of "substantial similarity" hinges on the actual copyright held by the owner and is proven by various types of evidence. For example, in 1976, original Beatle George Harrison was sued for copyright infringement when his chart-topping song, "My Sweet Lord," was said to have infringed on the melody of a 1963 hit song, "He's So Fine" by the Chiffons. That case went to trial despite Harrison's attempts to settle out of court, and ultimately cost him over $1.5 million in damages. Harrison would claim that he certainly had access to the Chiffons' song but was not thinking of it when he wrote "My Sweet Lord." Harrison's general awareness of the song was enough to show access and substantial similarity. Harrison later claimed he never made any money from the song because of the copyright issues.[24]

Fair Use

Infringement suits are subject to affirmative defenses, which are defenses for which a defendant has the burden to prove at trial by a preponderance of the evidence. Among these are the statute of limitations (typically copyright infringement must be brought within three years), having a valid copyright license or agreement, and fair use. Fair use is one of the most important—and most widely misunderstood—concepts within copyright law. Many think that fair use automatically attaches when the person using the copyrighted material is doing so for a nonprofit or educational purpose.

Consider the following scenario. Suppose a PR professional is working for a unit within higher education that wants to create an updated website promoting its faculty. The PR professional wants to provide excerpts from faculty scholarship to showcase the expertise of the faculty. This scholarship is published in various journals and books which the university owns, but the school does not own the copyright to these materials. The work is placed on the website along with faculty photos and the excerpts. Is this infringement? Could this be valid fair use because this is an educational institution? Does the amount of work factor into the fair use claim? Does it matter that the PR professional attributed the work and cited it on the website? What are the potential financial impacts to the publishers who own the copyright? These questions illustrate the complexity of fair use, and how understanding its contours is important for anyone attempting to use copyrighted work under this exception.

Fair use permits the use of copyrighted work in certain circumstances without paying royalties or obtaining a license. It is essentially an exemption from following the normal legal protocols for using copyrighted work. The elements of fair use are:

1. the purpose and character of the use, including whether such use is of a commercial nature or is for nonprofit educational purposes;

2. the nature of the copyrighted work;

3. the amount and substantiality of the portion used in relation to the copyrighted work as a whole; and

4. the effect of the use upon the potential market for or value of the copyrighted work.[25]

Each of these aspects of fair use require its own distinct analysis. While none of these elements is proof positive of fair use, they are factors that are weighed both individually and holistically by courts to determine fair use. Next, we will look at each of these elements and examine the underlying factors of each.

Purpose and Character of the Use

Purpose and character examine commercial versus nonprofit/educational purposes of use. In short, the more commercial use is, the less likely it is fair use. On the other hand, noncommercial or educational use tends to favor a fair use ruling. That said, determining purpose and character is not cut and dried. Many people believe, incorrectly, that nonprofit or educational use is automatically fair use. Recently the Supreme Court held that unauthorized use of a copyright for commercial purposes strongly leans toward infringement, especially when the work is not highly transformative.

This concept of transformativeness is important to determining purpose and character, the first prong of fair use. An existing copyright that is transformed into something new or used for a different purpose lean in favor of fair use. For example, in 1989, the hip-hop group 2 Live Crew created new lyrics based on the 1964 chart-topping song "Oh, Pretty Woman" by country singer Roy Orbison. The owner of "Oh, Pretty Woman" sued, alleging 2 Live Crew's rendition of the song, even with new lyrics, constituted infringement. The Supreme Court held that in cases like this one, parody potentially could constitute fair use, but it was not dispositive. Writing for the majority, Justice David Souter wrote:

> Although such transformative use is not absolutely necessary for a finding of fair use the goal of copyright, to promote science and the arts, is generally furthered by the creation of transformative works. Such works

thus lie at the heart of the fair use doctrine's guarantee of breathing space within the confines of copyright.[26]

Fair use has its limits, according to the Supreme Court. In 2023, the court examined fair use as it applied to the transformation of a photograph into a silkscreen painting. In that case, a photographer, Lynn Goldsmith, took a series of photos of the musician Prince in 1981 on assignment from *Newsweek*. The photo was unpublished, and Goldsmith retained its copyright. Later, the magazine *Vanity Fair* licensed the image for artist Andy Warhol to create a silkscreen portrait that was to be used only once, with Goldsmith being credited as the photographer. Warhol, without permission, then created an entire series of silkscreens from the photo using various color overlays. Among these was a silkscreen titled "Orange Prince." In 2016 Condé Nast, the owner of *Vanity Fair*, used "Orange Prince" as cover art for a retrospective of Prince after his death. Goldsmith was unaware of the Warhol series and was not credited in the cover. Litigation ensued for years, and ultimately the case was heard by the Supreme Court on fair use grounds. The court held, 7–2, that Warhol's use of the photo was not fair use, noting that both the original photo and silkscreen had a similar commercial purpose, and that Warhol's use of the photo to create the portrait involved minor changes that did not rise to the level of transformativeness. Writing for the majority of the Court, Justice Sonia Sotomayor analyzed the necessity of transformativeness and its relation to fair use. She wrote:

> Not every instance will be clear cut, however. Whether a use shares the purpose or character of an original work, or instead has a further purpose or different character, is a matter of degree. Most copying has some further purpose, in the sense that copying is socially useful ex post. Many secondary works add something new. That alone does not render such uses fair. Rather, the first factor (which is just one factor in a larger analysis) asks "whether and to what extent" the use at issue has a purpose or character different from the original. The larger the difference, the more likely the first factor weighs in favor of fair use. The smaller the difference, the less likely.[27]

This decision was controversial, even among members of the Supreme Court. Critics argue that the decision overly relies on whether the transformative use was commercial in nature. Among these critics is Justice Elena Kagan, who wrote a strong dissent in the case. Citing the nature of the transformative in art, Justice Kagan wrote in a sharp criticism of the majority:

> Today's decision—all the majority's protestations notwithstanding—leaves our first-factor inquiry in shambles. The majority holds that because Warhol licensed his work to a magazine—as Goldsmith sometimes also did—the first factor goes against him. It does not matter how different the Warhol is from the original photo—how much "new expression, meaning, or message" he added. It does not matter that the silkscreen and the photo do not have the same aesthetic characteristics and do not convey the same meaning. It does not matter that because of those dissimilarities, the magazine publisher did not view the one as a substitute for the other. All that matters is that Warhol and the publisher entered into a licensing transaction, similar to one Goldsmith might have done. Because the artist had such a commercial purpose, all the creativity in the world could not save him.[28]

For PR practitioners, this case should serve as a cautionary example of over-relying on fair use. This protracted litigation would have been moot had Warhol and Condé Nast obtained copyright permission. Some legal scholars argue that the *Warhol v. Goldsmith* decision strikes a major blow against fair use and artistry, and some in the art community argue that this type of holding strikes at the heart of the artistic process, which should not have to take legal considerations into account during the creative process.[29] However, for those using copyright, this case demonstrates that context, particularly commercial, matters when identifying fair use.

Nature of the Work

Another fair use factor is the nature of the work used. When considering a copyrighted work, it is best to think of it as existing on a continuum from strong (or thick) copyright to weak (or thin) copyright.

This essentially is an analysis of the content of the work. As a rule, the more creative and less factual a work is, the more copyright protection it receives. For example, a novel or painting that is highly original will receive a greater degree of copyright protection than a biography that is based on facts that may have been published previously. That strength of copyright means that if a person uses a strong copyright, they are less likely to be able to successfully claim fair use.

Conversely, in the use of a thin copyright, particularly one that is based on facts, there is a greater chance of winning a fair use judgement. This thick versus thin copyright also involves the nature of publications. Typically, copyright protection is stronger for an unpublished work as compared to a published work.[30] That said, it is important to note that the unpublished nature of a copyrighted work is not dispositive of fair use. It is fact dependent, and the Supreme Court has held that unpublished works, while receiving greater copyright protection, can be part of fair use depending on the circumstances.[31]

Amount of Work Used

Using a large amount of copyrighted work leans more to infringement than fair use. However, this factor not just looks at quantity of work, but quality. For example, in 1989 the magazine *The Nation* received an advance unpublished copy of former U.S. President Gerald Ford's memoir titled *A Time to Heal: The Autobiography of Gerald R. Ford*.[32] This book had a high level of public interest because it would detail the behind-the-scenes decisions of President Ford's pardon of his predecessor, President Richard Nixon, who was in jeopardy of a criminal conviction. *The Nation* published an excerpt from Ford's book, which contributed to a 2,250–word article about Watergate and the Nixon pardon. Some 300–400 words were verbatim quotes from the autobiography. *The Nation*'s editor who used the material had no authorized use and had received the information from a person who had acquired an unauthorized advance copy of the book from an anonymous source. The Supreme Court held that fair use did not apply in this type of case because the substance of what was published was essential to the larger book, even though the amount used was relatively small compared to the larger work.[33]

For PR practitioners, this aspect of fair use is important, especially with regard to the wholesale use of images or other content. The greater amount of content used, the less likely it is to be fair use. However, those working in communication must pay attention to what exactly they are using as part of their work. The more substantive or meaningful the portion is, the less likely it is fair use. This is also important to note, not just in scenarios where copyright is being used, but when a PR practitioner or client's work is used. Just because a small amount of an underlying work is used by another person or business does not entitle them to the fair use defense.

Market Effect

Market effect is perhaps the most important factor of fair use analysis. Consider the following. Suppose a professor wants a class to read one chapter from a PR textbook. The professor duplicates the chapter and places it on an online class management site. Students do not have to buy the book, and the chapter is there for the duration of the semester. What is the market impact? Well, it depends. Would the students have bought the book had the professor not placed the chapter on the internet? What royalties did the book's author lose by the students not buying the book? Related to substantiality, was the chapter the main part of the book? All these questions point to the market effect portion of fair use. The major takeaway is that fair use is about weighing the ability to use a copyrighted work without paying royalties. The more the use impacts the copyright owner's ability to earn royalties, the more like the use is infringement and not fair use.

Intellectual property is a type of property. Ownership of property potentially provides income for the creators or owners of the work. Consider this scenario. A well-known novel has sold millions of copies. The original author is dead, and there is no sequel. A new author decides to write a new novel from a different perspective of some of the main characters. Is this infringement? Does it violate fair use? This was exactly the scenario in the sequel to *Gone With the Wind*, published in 1936, and Alice Randal's 2001 parody novel, *Wind Done Gone*.[34] In *Wind Done Gone* Randal did not make use of the character names from Mitchell's original work; however, Randal's publisher, Houghton Mifflin, was sued by the Mitchell estate for infringement. The U.S. Court of Appeals for the Eleventh Circuit held that this case likely did have a valid fair use claim based on transformity, but that the market impact on the original copyright for *Gone With the Wind* was minimal. The Eleventh Circuit based its decision from the U.S. Supreme Court's holding in *Campbell v. Acuff Rose*, which analyzed market effect, stating:

> It [market impact] requires courts to consider not only the extent of market harm caused by the particular actions of the alleged infringer, but also "whether unrestricted and widespread conduct of the sort engaged in by the defendant . . . would result in a substantially adverse impact on the potential market" for the original.[35]

In scenarios like this, there is some argument that the derivative work increases interest in the original. However, the Supreme Court's recent holding in *Andy Warhol Foundation v. Goldsmith* illustrates that the marketplace of a work is important. In that case, both the original photo and the Warhol silkscreen were used in the marketplace for similar purposes. For that reason, the financial impact to Goldsmith was obvious because the use of the unauthorized Warhol silkscreen did not provide Goldsmith with royalties.[36] This case was not part of a large analysis about market impact, but that was the undercurrent of the case. It demonstrated that market impact of a slightly transformative work was significant for Goldsmith, and in the Court's decision, the commercial nature and market impact to Goldsmith was the foundation for the majority's rationale for finding no fair use.

TRADEMARK

For PR practitioners working in brand management, trademark law is the one way to protect the brand itself. Its value is rooted in the fact that trademark can last forever, unlike copyright, and that no formalized process must occur for a trademark to be made. At the core of trademark law is identity. A trademark is a "word, symbol, or device" that identifies goods within commerce.[37] McDonald's golden arches, the Apple computer logo, and the Nike slogan "Just Do It" and swoosh are all highly recognized trademarks. There are several subcategories of trademark, such as a trade name or "doing business as" (DBA), and trade dress, which is the physical presence or color scheme that identifies a business.[38] However, the purpose behind all these types of trademarks is commercial identity within commerce.[39] A brand is largely built around trademarked content, and PR practitioners have to be vigilant in their protection of their client's trademark to protect the brand as well as the mark.

In U.S. law, federal protection of trademark was established under the Lanham Act, formally the Trademark Act of 1946.[40] This law established trademark protection and the elements of trademark infringement. For famous marks, the law also provided for protection against trademark dilution where a new mark diminishes an existing trademark even if there is no marketplace confusion.

Owning a trademark and registering one are two different processes. Ownership is established when the mark is created and held out in commerce. Registration is an optional process, but one that firmly establishes the trademark as owned by a specific person or entity through formal registration with the U.S. Patent and Trademark Office (USPTO). This formal registration allows trademarks to appear with the formal ® on the trademark. Even without registration, owners of trademarks can use "TM" for goods trademarks and "SM" for services trademarks to signify that there is ownership of the mark.[41]

Like copyright, there are strong and weak trademarks, and, as this continuum suggests, the stronger the trademark, the more protection it receives under the law. There are five general types of marks according to the USPTO, described below.

Fanciful: Receives strong trademark protection. The mark relates only to the good or service and has no alternative meaning. Examples: Exxon ®, Kodak ®, Clorox ®, Pepsi ®.[42]

Arbitrary: Receives strong trademark protection. The words in the mark have no association with the product. Examples: Apple computers, Coach purses. There is no association between apple, the fruit, and computer products; or between coach, the horse-drawn carriage, and a purse.

Suggestive: Receives strong trademark protection. The words of the trademark are part of a quality statement but are not directly descriptive of the product. Example: Coppertone suntan lotion, Android phone.[43]

Descriptive: Receives weaker trademark protection compared to fanciful, arbitrary, and suggestive marks. Sometimes descriptive marks receive no protection. Descriptive marks are more directly associated with the product, such as creamy ice cream, or hot coffee. A descriptive mark's secondary meaning takes some time to develop.[44] The U.S. Court of Appeals for the Fifth Circuit held there are five criteria to establish secondary meanings on descriptive marks:

1. Length and manner of use of the mark or trade dress;

2. Volume of sales;

3. Amount and manner of advertising;

4. Nature of the use of the mark or trade dress in newspapers or magazines;

5. Consumer-survey evidence;

6. Direct consumer testimony, and

7. The defendant's intent on copying the trade dress [or mark].[45]

Generic: Receives no trademark protection. These are not trademarks because they are part of the vernacular of language. For example, skateboard, bicycle, or toaster. These marks receive no protection. Actual protected trademarks can become generic through common use where the trademark loses its specific meaning. That process is called genericity or genericide. Examples of prior trademarks that have become generic include escalator, cellophane, dumpster, yo-yo, and kerosene. Fighting against genericization may seem counterintuitive to those in the PR field, who may see a brand's name becoming synonymous with the product as a good thing. However, once that occurs, the mark may cease to exist. Communicators working with brands must take precautions that their trademarked products do not become a verb, and they must aggressively litigate the misuse of their trademark names to ensure that the legal status remains. In fact, during the 1980s the proliferation of Xerox photocopiers became so prevalent that the term Xerox was poised to become a synonym for photocopying. To combat this, Xerox engaged in a campaign asking the public to stop using the name as interchangeable with photocopy to save the trademark. To date, that campaign has worked.[46]

Trademark Infringement

Trademark infringement occurs when a person or organization uses a mark without permission. To prove an infringement claim, the plaintiff must show that (1) they have a valid trademark, (2) they own the trademark, and (3) the infringer's use of the mark is likely to cause market confusion. The last element is one where there is much litigation. Consumer confusion is frequently proven through expert testimony or studies that show consumer confusion. The U.S. Court of Appeals for the Second Circuit created a six-part test to determine when market confusion exists in a trademark infringement claim:

1. strength of the trademark;

2. similarity of the marks;

3. proximity of the products and their competitiveness with one another;

4. evidence that the senior user may "bridge the gap" by developing a product for sale in the market of the alleged infringer's product;

5. evidence of actual consumer confusion;

6. respective quality of the products; and

7. sophistication of consumers in the relevant market.[47]

None of these factors is dispositive of infringement, however, and the determination of infringement of trademark is on a case-by-case basis.[48] Sometimes the likelihood of confusion can be nuanced, such as when competitor's products are offered as a substitute. In fact, the

U.S. Court of Appeals for the Ninth Circuit analyzed whether offering alternative products in an online Amazon search constituted trademark confusion. The court held that clearly identifying competitors' products is like a restaurant saying "No Coke. Pepsi" when a customer asks for a Coke.[49]

Related to trademark infringement is trademark dilution. Establishing a case for dilution requires a unique plaintiff. That is because dilution occurs when a famous trademark is diminished, regardless of the potential market confusion. The Lanham Act expressly provides for dilution to protect trademark. In the statute prohibiting dilution, there is a requirement for the trademark to have a level of fame. This is determined by:

1. The duration, extent, and geographic reach of advertising and publicity of the mark, whether advertised or publicized by the owner or third parties

2. The amount, volume, and geographic extent of sales of goods or services offered under the mark

3. The extent of actual recognition of the mark

4. Whether the mark was registered under the Act of March 3, 1881, or the Act of February 20, 1905, or on the principal register.[50]

To prove dilution the plaintiff, that is, the owner of the famous trademark, must prove the following:

1. The degree of similarity between the mark or trade name and the famous mark

2. The degree of inherent or acquired distinctiveness of the famous mark

3. The extent to which the owner of the famous mark is engaging in substantially exclusive use of the mark

4. The degree of recognition of the famous mark

5. Whether the user of the mark or trade name intended to create an association with the famous mark

6. Any actual association between the mark or trade name and the famous mark.

However, just because there is crossover between the brands does not mean there is automatic dilution. Consider the following dilution case where a small New Hampshire coffee shop called itself Charbucks, featuring a black bear logo on the cup. Sued by Starbucks for dilution, Charbucks won, with the court saying that the issue of dilution was not present because Starbucks is an international brand where Charbucks is a small, local coffee shop.[51] However, dilution can occur in scenarios where the products or services are totally different. A pornographic website entitled "adultsrus" was sued for dilution by Toys "R" Us, with the "r us" being the point of dilution. A federal court in California held that was dilution because of the similarity of the naming convention of the pornographic website.[52]

For PR practitioners, there is a real concern over online image management. The loss of control of an organization or person's online image can lead to dramatic reputational damage, including the loss of goodwill, thereby diminishing the tangible value of an organization. One way that online trademark infringement occurs is through cybersquatting, sometimes called typosquatting. This is where an infringer sets up an IP address using a slight derivation of a legitimate trademarked name. For example, a cybersquatter of a golf equipment company, Vulcan Golf, created a registered name wwwVulcanGolf.com.[53] The lack of a period after www allowed users who were potentially customers of the trademarked company to be rerouted to this fake site. Not only does the Lanham Act ban this type of unauthorized use, but there is also a specific federal law on the matter in the Anticybersquatting Consumer Protection Act (ACPA), which categorizes cybersquatting as dilution.[54] Unfortunately, cybersquatting is technologically easy to do because third parties are frequently used to register domain names. Depending on the registration system, these diluting sites can register anonymously, making it all but impossible to identify the diluting party.[55] Further, in examining cybersquatting cases it is notable that obtaining damages from potential third party infringers is difficult, considering many are hackers with little money. There is potential for trademark holders to sue the domain provider through contributory dilution. Although this is potentially one way to sue defendants who have deeper pockets to pay judgments, federal appellate courts—particularly the U.S. Court of Appeals for the Ninth Circuit—have been reluctant to allow contributory claims unless "subjective bad faith" can be shown on the part of domain providers.[56] One way to combat this problem wholesale without litigation is for an organization to buy all related domain names when they establish an online presence. This could be expensive, but more cost effective in the long run than litigating difficult-to-identify third parties.[57]

Parody accounts are another major concern of online reputation management. Trademark, among other areas of law (such as appropriation, discussed in chapter 6) may present a possible solution to the issue of brand infringement or dilution. However, using trademark infringement lawsuits have limitations. One is the sheer cost of bringing the lawsuit, as well as First Amendment protections of parody as fully protected speech. In addition, there is a PR dimension to these lawsuits. Frequently a lawsuit meant to remove a parody account actually has the inverse consequence of highlighting the parody account and making it more prominent. This is a scenario in which PR strategy may trump legal strategy. One approach that has proven quite successful on parody accounts is engagement, which mitigates the site and can draw attention to the original account.[58]

There are defenses to trademark infringement that mirror the defenses in copyright law. First and most obvious is permission with licensure. If an individual has a license to use a trademark, then there is no infringement. Another defense is abandonment. To keep a trademark from losing its legal status, the owner must defend the mark when it is diluted or infringed. Failing to defend can result in the elimination of the property right. The U.S. Code defines prima facie abandonment as non-use for three consecutive years.[59] Famous marks are subject to abandonment. For example, the Brooklyn Dodgers trademark was found to be abandoned by the U.S. District Court for the Southern District of New York after the team moved to Los Angeles and did not maintain the Brooklyn Dodger trademark from 1958 through 1981 (the appeal case was later withdrawn). In that case, a bar named the Brooklyn Dodger was found not to dilute or infringe upon the Dodger trademark.[60]

The other major defense to trademark infringement is fair use. Like copyright, the fair use defense in trademark is rooted in the idea that sometimes a transformative use of a mark does not constitute infringement. Also, like copyright, fair use in trademark is an affirmative defense. The strength of fair use in trademark is speculative unless it is presented at a trial. In a practical sense, that means that anyone thinking of using a trademark under the idea that it is fair use cannot know that it is fair use for certain. Fair use in trademark is present when an alleged infringers uses the mark in good faith to describe good and services.

There are two types of trademark fair use: classic and nominative.[61] Classic fair use is when a trademark is used to describe the users' goods or services, and nominative is when the trademark is used to describe the trademark owner's goods and services, such as a product review.[62] However, it is important to note that although infringement is based on consumer confusion, fair use defense can be valid even if confusion is present.[63]

TRADE SECRETS

Trade secrets are an interesting dimension of IP because they protect an unusual class of intellectual property that can sometimes fall into other IP. They are usually discussed as a counter to patents, a form of IP not discussed in this chapter because of their rare applicability to PR.[64] However, trade secrets can protect certain types of content that other IP cannot. Primary among these, and of great relevance for PR practitioners, is client lists. Trade secret law also differs from most IP in that trade secrets are protected by state and federal law. They are also unique in that there is no formal registration or even an option for registration because the secretiveness of trade secrets is what drives the secret's value. There are many examples of highly valuable trade secrets, notably the formula of Coca-Cola and Google's algorithm.

The law of trade secrets at the state level usually follows the Uniform Trade Secrets Act (USTA), which is a model law that was crafted by the Uniform Law Commission in 1979. USTA is the law in 48 states; Washington, D.C.; and Puerto Rico, a commonwealth of the United States.[65] The USTA defines a trade secret as:

> Information, including a formula, pattern, compilation, program, device, method, technique, or process that:
>
> Derives independent economic value, actual or potential, from not being generally known to, and not being readily ascertainable by proper means by, other persons who can obtain economic value from its disclosure or use; and
>
> Is the subject of efforts that are reasonable under the circumstances to maintain its secrecy.[66]

Unlike other forms of IP, notably patents, there is no formal requirements for registration of a trade secret. The determination of qualifying as a trade secret is the secrecy implemented to protect the property. The theft of trade secrets is a federal crime, and federal law also provides for civil lawsuits in federal court for misappropriation of trade secrets.[67] However, the access to federal courts for civil lawsuits for misappropriation does not eliminate a trade secret owner from suing in state courts. Sometimes these lawsuits are required not only for damages, but also for injunctions to stop a potential misappropriation of a trade secret from being used in commerce. Sometimes protections of trade secrets are made in nondisclosure agreements (NDAs) between employers and employees.

Within public relations, trade secret issues may arise when a previous employee has access to the business plans of another company. With the use of social media proliferating within the communications field, there are now arguments that trade secret law can protect the information on social media accounts. One case, in the U.S. District Court for the Eastern District of Pennsylvania, analyzed whether a LinkedIn account connection list constituted a trade secret. In that case, the courts looked several factors to determine if a trade secret even existed, relying on the first Restatement of Torts as a guide. The court held that when looking at whether a trade secret existed, they had to examine:

1. the extent to which the information is known outside of the owner's business;

2. the extent to which it is known by employees and others involved in the owner's business;

3. the extent of measures taken by the owner to guard the secrecy of the information;

4. the value of the information to the owner and to his competitors;

5. the amount of effort or money expended by the owner in developing the information; and

6. the ease or difficulty with which the information could be properly acquired or duplicated by others.[68]

In this case, however, there was no trade secret according to the court, as the client list was not a secret because it was posted online. A federal court in California came to a similar conclusion about a Twitter account because the followers on the account were publicly known.[69] That said, proprietary information, including systems for organizing donors, fundraising plans, business operations, and communication strategies could potentially be trade secrets. For PR practitioners, it is important to take strict care of those important aspects of business and ensure that strong steps are taken to protect that information, regardless of whether the organization is trying to establish them as trade secrets. Creating social media policies and contractually establishing ownership of these items is a good way to avoid these types of misappropriation suits. Moreover, if there is a problem with taking proprietary information, including trade secrets, a lawsuit over a breach of contract would provide for a more straightforward case of violation rather than having courts determine whether a trade secret was established by business practices.[70]

Ethical IP Issues for PR Practitioners

The ethics of IP use is important, especially given the massive technological changes occurring in the 2020s. One ethical issue goes back to the purpose behind the IP clause in the U.S. Constitution. The Constitution in the eighteenth century recognized that there is a trade-off between exclusivity of access and public utility of ideas. Creators of intellectual property create this work for monetary reward. In the modern era there is restricted access to IP, such as copyright or through subscriptions, paywalls, and other barriers that ensure royalties are paid. However, public access and public use of IP is part of the trade-off between exclusive control and public domain.

Content Access and Privilege

Choosing how to share content, and when to share it, becomes an ethical discussion that weighs individual versus collective rights. There is a growing recognition of privilege that stems from information access, such as access to expensive university library resources, that creates certain inequities regarding information in society. Virulent enforcement of copyright has given rise to so-called "copyright trolls" who seek to stifle any perceived use of copyright without royalty payment. This aggressive litigation practice has been criticized for its use of copyright law to obtain statutory damages on relatively minor cases of unauthorized copyright use. Sometimes this involves a business model where companies buy copyrights for the sole purpose of filing infringement claims to receive statutory damages, frequently from unwitting infringers who post online content.

Conversely, the taking of IP and sharing it without compensating the creator creates a different type of inequity for content creators. Without compensation, creators may be disinclined to innovate, creating a culture where those who contribute to the intellectual growth of society may choose not to contribute. Past platforms, such as the now-defunct file sharing system called Napster, were online platforms designed for infringement of copyright. The impact of those types of platforms on content creator revenue is significant, and is one reason why the impact of these types of platforms is so damaging to artists and other content creators.

Invoking Fair Use

Another ethical dilemma is how to decide when to use items without paying royalties under the premise of fair use. As this chapter notes, fair use is an affirmative defense to infringement, and an alleged infringer does not know if they have a valid fair use claim unless they raise it in court. Libraries and other content providers have struggled to create guidelines for individuals to determine when fair use exists. However, fair use is also frequently misinterpreted by individuals using copyrighted material as a justification for not paying royalties. Nowhere is this more evident than in nonprofit, particularly educational, organizations. It is important to note that fair use does not automatically attach to an individual because of the person or organization's nonprofit status. Thinking that fair use is a barrier to liability simply because of someone's status is an unethical rationalization of infringement.

Plagiarism and Copyright

Related to infringement is the ethical issue of plagiarism. Many people confuse the term plagiarism and copyright, but they are distinct. Plagiarism is using the unattributed work of another while copyright infringement is the unauthorized use of another's copyright without authorization. The distinction is based on attribution versus permission. For example, a writer can copy word-for-word a passage from a book without attribution if that book's copyright has expired. That would constitute plagiarism, but not copyright infringement. Conversely, a person could copy word-for-word from a copyrighted book and give attribution but could be committing infringement, depending on how much of the book was used, but not plagiarism.

Use of copyrighted material also presents unique ethical dilemmas when analyzing fan content. Frequently fan content uses copyrighted work to create unauthorized derivative works. Organizations must consider how they will approach this fan use of copyrighted material. Sometimes this means that an organization must tolerate a certain level of infringement to maintain a good relationship with dedicated fans. Conversely, some organizations use fan content, particularly reviews, to promote their products or services. This use of fan content is often without compensation, and arguably is an infringement on fan IP.

Global Considerations

Finally, the biggest ethical and legal issue facing PR practitioners in the twenty-first century is global communication. While international IP treaties, such as the Berne Convention, standardized IP requirements and durations for protection, there are substantive differences between U.S. IP law and that of other nations. The EU, for instance, has a much more robust system in place to protect the work of copyright owners, and gives them rights that are not recognized in the United States. Chief among these rights are moral rights, a set of rights that remain with the author indefinitely. This includes the right to attribution, the right to have works displayed in a way that does not dishonor the work (right to integrity), the right to determine where and when a work will be made public, the right to withdraw works from circulation, the right to protect a work from derogatory treatment, and the right against fake attribution. While some of these rights are not recognized in EU jurisdictions, they comprise the moral rights of copyright, something that does not exist in the United States. They demonstrate the different perceptions of IP held by the EU, and the considerations organizations should take when they use copyrighted materials in a global campaign. The application of these rights also varies by nation, with some countries recognizing a variation of moral rights.

Related to differing legal standard in IP protection is international infringement issues. There have been numerous cases where infringement is rampant in some countries, but access to the courts is limited. Frequently the expense of litigation outside one's home country presents cost and access barriers to litigation. However, those barriers have been lowered, at least in part, by some appellate rulings for U.S.-based plaintiffs. In 2022, the U.S. Court of Appeals for the Ninth Circuit held that a U.S. federal court could have personal jurisdiction over a Vietnamese corporation sued for infringement of films because of the corporation's involvement in the United States.[71] This approach to holding non-U.S. companies accountable for global copyright infringement may represent a change in the way copyright holders can get access to infringement occurring abroad and domestically. However, it is important to note that this case has a unique set of facts, which allows for personal jurisdiction in U.S. courts. Infringers who are not in the United States and whose infringement is entirely outside of the United States are much more insulated from lawsuits within U.S. courts. Copyright owners can proceed with lawsuits outside the United States against these infringers, but the defendants in those cases will likely be subject to the protection of their nation's laws.

DISCUSSION QUESTIONS

1. Why is copyright and trademark so important to PR practice? What do those rights allow practitioners to do with their content?

2. Imagine you are working on a PR campaign and your boss comes to you and wants to use a photograph he found in the company's archive. The photo was dated 1982 and it has a stamp on the back that says copyrighted not for republication. What should you do?

3. Same facts as above. Assume that the photographer retained the copyright ownership, but he has since passed away. Who would you contact for permission? Is there a fair use claim here?

4. Look at the fair use elements and describe which one you think is most important. Why?

5. What are the ethical issues surrounding copyright infringement? What is the boundary between infringement and fair use?

CASE SCENARIO

You are working on a project for a nonprofit organization that helps provide school supplies for underfunded schools. Part of your promotions include a school supply drive where people can donate unused supplies including pencils, paper, markers, crayons, and folders. As part of your promotion, you want to use a picture of name-brand supplies, such as

Crayola Crayons, in a social media post to show donors what types of supplies you would like. In addition, you want to create an internet meme from the 1973 series *School House Rock!*, which appeared on the ABC network. Part of the meme will show images of the series along with taglines to donate to the charity. What IP issues exist with this type of promotion? Is there a fair use defense? If so, what factor leans the strongest in favor of fair use? What factor leans the strongest against?

The Future of Public Relations Practice in the Age of Artificial Intelligence

OVERVIEW: THIS CHAPTER EXAMINES THE ISSUES OF ARTIFICIAL INTELLIGENCE regulation in context with PR practice in the 2020s. Specifically, the chapter focuses on the fluid nature of AI law and regulations and suggests that PR practitioners should establish and use industry ethics to determine how this technology should shape the field. Particular attention is given to the U.S. government's attempt to regulate AI, and how the topics of privacy, intellectual property (IP), and EU regulations will affect contemporary practice.

OBJECTIVES:

- Analyze contemporary state of AI regulation in the United States.
- Discuss major themes of AI regulation including privacy, intellectual property, and EU regulation.
- Examine how PR ethics can play a role in the development of industry norms of AI practice, especially when current AI laws are still under development.

The field of content creation is undergoing a massive transformation in the 2020s. The 2023 Hollywood writer's strike by the Writer's Guild of America (WGA) was a flashpoint that illustrates how those professionals producing content are impacted by technological and structural change in the industry. Part of the issues in the 2023 writers strike can be applied to PR professionals. Writers were worried about the gig economy and how being a Hollywood writer had changed from long-term secured jobs to short-duration, show-specific work for multiple companies on limited contracts. This gig economy model of writing has led to a business model of the writer's mini room, where writers work on a program from six to eight weeks. The mini room model means that many writers must write in multiple mini rooms to make ends meet (not unlike freelance work in PR).[1] In an already problematic gig economy, WGA members were also worried about AI's role in writing. Generative AI allows for writing at a fast rate, but also in specific styles that can replace or, at least, radically change writing. Nora Ephron, the famous screenwriter of such films as *When Harry Met Sally* and *Sleepless in Seattle*, has been dead since 2012. However, generative AI can write content in screenplay form that channels Ephron's punchy dialogue and lyrical prose within a few seconds with the right commands. The issue of using AI to write like others has prompted lawsuits against OpenAI by authors such as John Grisham and *Game of Thrones* creator George R.R. Martin.[2] That type of use of AI worries those who make a living as writers. The concern is not just that AI could replace their jobs, but that AI use could take their content and rework it to create derivative works or "improvements." After the 148-day writers strike, AI was addressed in the agreement, but the issue is far from over. Writers are not required to use AI, but studios can use it for content creation purposes. That agreement is also likely to change as the technology changes.[3]

PR practice finds itself in a similar situation with AI and its use in the field. While AI will change the field's work process, it is difficult to determine how exactly this will happen. From what has been observed since the launch of OpenAI in 2022, menial tasks, such as copyediting or scheduling, may be done through AI, freeing up practitioners to do other tasks. However, there is a real concern that AI can replace the role of the professional communicator. That fear is born out of the experiences of the past when technology changed the way things worked. For example, in 2017 before the proliferation of mainstream AI, McKinsey & Company, a management consulting firm, noted that "interacting with stakeholders" would likely need to be a skill to increase in the age of AI where data collection and processing would decrease because of the automated nature of AI technology.[4] This change is based on streamlined productivity that AI creates for many positions, and the concept that AI creates more time for higher-level thinking and strategy. AI also allows for a leapfrogging effect for skills. For example, digital editing and design may be a field that has greater access and more intuitive processes for people to learn, thanks to AI. That could consolidate many of the roles within content creation, making PR professionals even more multipurpose in their professional roles. Without a doubt, some professional roles will be eliminated. Think of the introduction of the automobile and its effect on the horse-and-carriage industry. The displacement of horses and carriages not only affected those in the horse business, but also the ancillary businesses such as liveries, farriers, and even sanitation workers in cities where horses had a large presence. Will AI be as transformative as the automobile? It is difficult to say, but as an industry PR professionals must lean into the conversation very deliberately. What is clear is that a PR practitioner's knowledge and experiences are important. Coupling that knowledge with the skills of AI makes these practitioners much more marketable.

In this chapter, the future of PR law is examined with a particular focus on AI's role in changing the industry. Specific attention is focused on how AI may affect PR work product, specifically how AI will transform the way content is created by PR practitioners. Next, the chapter examines the issue of AI and intellectual property law, privacy, and liability, along with some predictions on how those laws will develop over the next decade. The chapter concludes by arguing that public relations has a unique opportunity to be a leader in world of communication because of its ethical grounding as a profession, especially in an era when AI regulation and law will be slowly established.

What Role Does PR Have in Shaping the Law and Ethics of AI?

PR practice has a unique role to play in AI implementation. Because laws and industry norms are in a state of flux on this specific issue, public relations as an industry has a unique role to be a leader in this area. In this book, the issues of law and ethics of PR have been presented in a way that notes how PR practice is evolving and changing with societal, technological, communication, professional, and political norms. PR is a player in these important aspects of society and, by examining the previous chapters, several major themes emerge that are relevant to the AI and PR issue:

- PR practice requires both legal and ethical competency.
- While law and ethics are distinct, they frequently overlap.
- The expansion of the definition of public relations has created a more complex system of laws for PR practitioners to understand and practice within.
- Legal counsel and PR practitioners share different philosophical perspectives that are essential for client success.
- The PR focus on transparency is not just rooted in an ethical slogan but mandated by the law.
- The law helps PR practitioners effectively conduct reputation management for corporate, nonprofit, and individual clients.
- Privacy in PR practice is major issue, particularly with the field's embrace of big data and artificial intelligence.
- Intellectual property protection is an essential part of managing a client's reputation, image, and communication.
- Technological innovations are changing the nature of PR practice both in terms of content production and legal protection.
- The laws and regulations of PR practice have never been as international, evolving, or essential for PR practitioners.

Understanding PR law is essential to practicing good public relations, especially in an era of technological change. Laws affect the practice, identity, professional standards, expectations, and protection of the field. Knowing the law equips PR practitioners with the tools to practice the craft of public relations in a strategic, impactful, and meaningful way. Additionally, the ethical dimensions of public relations are interconnected with the law. Using the law as a baseline of behavior, PR practitioners can go beyond mandated behavior and embrace best practices of the field.

The intention when crafting this book was to write a volume that can be part of a PR practitioner's library for some time, not only because it explains the laws affecting practice, but because it explains why the practice of PR evolved in the way that it did. AI presents some challenges to that because it is a fast-growing industry in which law has struggled to keep up. Even during the writing of this book, specifically this chapter, there were revisions that had to be made to keep up with the status quo of the industry. However, looking at the law and ethics of PR from a broader perspective, there are some themes that are going to remain constant in the AI discussion.

Going back to the early, largely unregulated practice of public relations of the nineteenth century, it is evident how far PR has come both in terms of regulation, but also in terms of complexity. Knowing that the basis for practice allows PR practitioners to know the field in a deeper way and to have an easier time predicting what the future of public relations will look like. It is important to note that the laws discussed in the preceding chapters were mainly developed in the past century, many of them within the past 10 to 15 years. Looking toward the future, it's hard to imagine what the laws of the 2030s or 2040s will be. However, it is a reasonably good guess that they will be a continuation of today's legal standards modified by the technological innovations of the time. AI will be affected by issues of privacy, liability, IP, defamation, First Amendment protection, and political speech. It will also be heavily impacted by issues of diversity, equity, and inclusion as well as discrimination issues.

So, what is the role of PR practice and practitioners? The impact of law and public relations is significant because PR serves an important function within democratic society. In this era of disinformation, public relations can serve as a mechanism to combat lies in favor of the truth. With trust in news media at an all-time low, PR practice has a unique opportunity to increase its role as an ethical voice, especially given the field's presence within social media. The truthfulness of public relations is buttressed by the legal regulations it must follow. There is no other communication profession, including journalism, that is more regulated for its truth. Consider the regulations on paid content, brand influencers, social media use, IP infringement, and privacy. In addition, PR communications is fact-checked by the press and, if disinformation is found, the media will point that out publicly. On top of that, public relations must engage with diverse publics that have the constitutionally protected freedom to make whatever critiques of clients, organizations, or the PR profession they want. All public relations can do in response is listen, engage, and respond. All these realities mean that, from a legal standpoint, PR practice has certain institutional barriers that make it a truthful and ethical profession. Because of that, PR in the 2020s should take the lead on communication that is legally, ethically, and morally sound.

AI: The Legal Issue of the 2020s

What will the legal issues be in the remainder of the 2020s? While that is a difficult question to answer with great specificity, we do know there is an ongoing revolution in content creation with the proliferation of artificial intelligence. Looking at the power of this new platform, it is important for PR practitioners to lean into this new technology and know it well. AI is a tool, not a menace, and those practitioners who understand its power can utilize it to better serve their clients and the profession. It is important to note that AI does not replace PR practitioners because AI is not a substitute for the experiences, knowledge, reflectiveness, and strategic insights of the field. It is a tool just like any other, and once PR practitioners, and many other professionals, move beyond an initial fear of the technology, they can better understand its role within the future of the profession. However, this does not mean that AI is not a disrupter to the communication field. It is a new way of creating content, and it provides an opportunity for PR practitioners to eliminate more menial tasks so they can use that time for higher-level strategy. But like all innovation, for example, internet, television, radio, and telegraph, there is a new reality to the PR industry because of AI. The profession must be mindful that its use is not the only concern. As communicators, public relations has always positioned itself as engaging in two-way communication with stakeholders and focusing on relationship management. AI presents a new reality where relationship management and two-way communication may be between an organization and AI because content generated from AI may reflect on the reputation of the organization. Indeed, it's a new world for the PR profession.

However, it is also important to note that within AI regulation, we are in a state of flux. There are few concrete laws on the subject and as the previous chapters show, current laws may be ill-equipped to handle the mechanics of the technology. What is certain about the future of AI law and regulation is the competing interests among the U.S. lawmakers. This competition can be described as a tension between regulating the excesses of the technology versus leaving the technology alone to grow. It is the same question that came about in the 1990s with the internet, and it is why there are laws today such as the Communications Decency Act, section 230 that protects the web.[5] Protecting AI from overregulation may take a different course. Lawmakers and society are aware that the lack of regulation of social media has led to some disastrous results for youth. Perhaps had lawmakers been more conscious of the impact of social media when it came into existence in the early twenty-first century, we could have avoided some of its unanticipated consequences. However, that's speculation.

Looking at AI, there seems to be a movement to allow for guardrails from the platforms themselves through self-regulation. That might work to some extent, but it is likely that lawmakers, specifically federal officials, will have to step up to take the reins. That will be difficult because of the protracted polarization of U.S. politics and, according to some, the limited understanding of the power of AI by politicians. Compounding all of this is the rapid pace at which AI develops. Law always seems to be racing after technology. For example, when the internet was in the early stages of regulation, the FTC was focusing on how to regulate disclosures for online sales of goods and services. At the time that regulation was gaining traction, social media emerged as a new force within the digital sphere and online sales issues seemed to be passé in comparison. As of this writing there is a dominant AI platform for generative content, ChatGPT, but as time goes on that platform may be replaced by other systems. Compounding this issue will be the role that large corporations such as Meta, Alphabet, and Microsoft play within the AI sphere, and how that expansion into AI platforms triggers other issues such as antitrust (Microsoft has heavily invested in OpenAI yet OpenAI remains an independent division with its own CEO).

As I am writing this chapter, there have been rapid changes both in the way AI is being used and how the law is regulating it. From a personal perspective, it seems that AI is utilized by the PR profession, but it is certainly not yet ubiquitous. There continues to be fears around the replacement of practitioners by AI, and still a sorting out of norms of use, notably the disclosure of AI for client content. While it is difficult to predict what the future of AI regulation will look like, there are five key areas that likely will become focal points for regulations. These are intellectual property, privacy, liability, international law, and personhood.

AI and IP

This area of AI has already become a focal point because of the issue of copyright law not recognizing AI-generated content as protected. This has real-world implications for branding and control over image because without IP recognition, there is no legal recourse for infringement. Conversely, the AI platforms could be creating unintentional infringement with their work product. For example, a user of AI may ask the system to produce written or visual content that uses copyright-protected work as a basis for the new content. Is that infringement and, if so, who has the liability? In early 2023, there was a lawsuit filed in the U.S. District Court for the Northern District of California by a group of artists and illustrators that claimed that the algorithms within generative AI violated their copyrights by creating unauthorized derivative works.[6] In the lawsuit, the process for these derivative works is discussed at length, but the essential issue is that the basis for each new image is an existing image that is then modified. While the judge threw out many of the copyright claims, the case presents an interesting issue for copyright holders. It could serve as a cautionary tale to PR practitioners looking to use generative AI to create visuals or written content. It is likely that copyright issues with AI will continue to proliferate. In another case in the Northern District of California, a judge dismissed claims that OpenAI infringed on a group of plaintiffs' intellectual property because the plaintiffs could not show what specific output was substantially similar. However, the court permitted a claim to proceed on unfair business practices. Cases like these illustrate the difficulty courts will have on AI infringement claims in the future.[7]

President Joe Biden's Executive Order on the Safe, Secure, and Trustworthy Development of Use of Artificial Intelligence mandates that the director of the U.S. Copyright Office consult with the president about future Executive Orders about copyright AI issues in 2024.[8] Moreover, the Copyright Office has issued guidance on the non-copyrightability of AI-generated content and is taking comments on how it can approach copyright for AI-generated works. The World Intellectual Property Organization (WIPO) is also addressing the role of IP generally for AI and other frontier technologies, such as the internet of things, blockchain, and big data.[9] It predicts that these frontier technologies pose many new IP questions, including whether AI can generate new forms of IP including patents, and speculates that frontier technology will grow to a $3.2 trillion business globally by 2025.[10] Given that significant economic impact, PR practitioners should pay close attention to how the law in this area may change.

AI and Privacy

Privacy concerns with AI pose a potential issue for PR practitioners because use of the platforms may create situations where information is unintentionally shared. AI platforms operate on a continuum of open to closed systems, with each platform having its own level of absorption of content. Those PR practitioners working specific niche areas of communication, such as healthcare, will have to take extra precautions in determining what platform they use in their practice. This is an issue that has received some attention within the trade press and industry, but as of this writing the conversation about data privacy within AI is still in its infancy. The Biden administration's Executive Order on AI released in October 2023 addresses many of the privacy concerns of AI. Specifically, the Executive Order called on federal agencies to consider privacy concerns within AI, and called on Congress to fund a Research Coordination Network to create cryptographic tools that enhance privacy protections for individuals. More immediately, the order requires

AI developers to share their safety test results with the U.S. government when the platform is dealing with national security, public health, or national economic security. Of course, this is just the most recent step by the U.S. government at the time of this writing.

PR practitioners should also look abroad, particularly at the European Union, to see how privacy will be regulated. As mentioned in the chapter on privacy, the EU has an aggressive stance on privacy with the General Data Protection Regulation, and it is likely to create more robust laws protecting privacy than the United States.[11] This likely will have a major impact on U.S. communicators who work in global practice or use AI platforms that have global presence. Even back in 2021 the European Commission argued for more regulation on AI, specifically in the areas of potential risks for users. In 2022 the European Parliament produced an overview of AI's utility in the twenty-first century, focusing on the positives and negatives of the system. While the report showed that AI presented great opportunity for work productivity, with an estimate that 11 to 37 percent of labor productivity would increase by 2035 because of AI, and even could help with global greenhouse cases, it also showed serious concern for privacy. Specifically, the report was concerned that AI's use of private information could create aggregate information about a person in a way that would be unexpected and unwanted.[12]

Currently the EU's approach to AI has focused on the areas of risk, which include privacy protection. In March 2024, the EU Parliament formally adopted the AI Act, which provides for regulation by sector within certain categories of use. The act specifically examined what is termed "unacceptable risks" including:

- Cognitive behavioral manipulation of people or specific vulnerable groups: for example voice-activated toys that encourage dangerous behaviour in children
- Social scoring: classifying people based on behaviour, socio-economic status, or personal characteristics
- Real-time and remote biometric identification systems, such as facial recognition.[13]

It also requires registration for certain AI use in the EU database including:

- Biometric identification and categorisation of natural persons
- Management and operation of critical infrastructure
- Education and vocational training
- Employment, worker management, and access to self-employment
- Access to and enjoyment of essential private services and public services and benefits
- Law enforcement
- Migration, asylum, and border control management
- Assistance in legal interpretation and application of the law.[14]

Of course, this is an early approach to AI regulation, and other countries will likely have their own idiosyncratic approaches to AI law. PR practitioners should keep up with these developments and note that there is great potential for conflicts of law in this area.

AI and Liability

One question AI presents is who is responsible for AI's work. Under U.S. law liability has always been given to the person who causes the harm. In tort law that is known as proximate causation, which generally means actions cause consequences. For example, in defamation, the person who speaks the defamation is ultimately responsible under the law. In copyright infringement the infringer is responsible for infringing the work. There can be mitigating circumstances, such as unintentional infringement, but that has more to do with minimizing damages than excusing the underlying behavior.

AI presents a new question about liability because legal issues, such as defamation or infringement, is caused by the platform, sometimes without the users' knowledge or intent. As of this writing the concept of AI liability for users mostly follows a traditional approach. There is the idea that a user who uses generative AI for content production is going to be responsible for the consequences of the use of that content, for example, posting defamatory AI-generated content. However, there is some suggestion that the platform itself may have some legal responsibility as well. The algorithms of AI produce the content, and ultimately it is responsible for what is generated. While there is no legal recognition for AI personhood (yet), there is the idea that platforms could be held legally responsible. There is the argument that CDA 230 does not apply to generative AI platforms; at least, that is the opinion of one of its drafters, Senator Ron Wyden (D-OR). There is particular concern over the liability for hallucinations, a term referring to fake content that AI creates such as made-up quotes and content. If those hallucinations create injury, there is potential for the platform to have legal liability.[15] There may be some insight into this area of law from AI-powered products, such as cars, but the ultimate decision on liability, intentional or not, remains an area likely to be sorted out by future litigation.

Moving Forward: Why PR Practitioners Should Lead the Regulatory and Ethical Issues of the 2020s

PR practitioners have a unique role to play in the ethical and legal considerations of AI. Because the law is still developing, PR practitioners must create their own industry ethics concerning AI use. Even though there are multiple issues of AI from inaccurate ranging to disinformation, defamation, infringement, hallucinated content, privacy issues, and discrimination, the one major issue that faces PR practitioners is AI accountability. Using a tool and relying on its expertise is not unethical. However, PR practice has the potential to erode its own credibility by having an overreliance on AI. Practitioners must use AI responsibly and do their due diligence as professionals to maintain professional credibility and honor the responsibilities they have to publics, stakeholders, media, and the profession. In fact, overreliance of AI platforms creates a situation where PR practitioners not only expose themselves and clients to liability, but risk confirming their greatest fear—that they can be replaced by machines.

Looking at the ethical and legal issues of the 2020s, PR practitioners will have to work in more complex environments legally, regulatorily, socially, technologically, and environmentally. There are issues that have not yet been addressed that likely will become major topics as the adoption of AI becomes more widespread. This includes AI and sustainability, specifically the large carbon footprint AI creates while being produced, and AI and workers' rights. This includes both the rights of workers not to be replaced by AI (largely a domestic issue), and AI workers who come from developing nations and suffer from poor working conditions. Those issues may dictate how AI is used by organizations in the future, and the choice about which platform to use may reflect the values and social responsibility of organizations.

Artificial intelligence also presents new issues for discrimination. Workplace systems that employ AI tools to screen resumes and create models to determine promotions can be the subject of inherent algorithmic biases that mirror those of humans. Some states and cities, notably New York City, have even addressed this by creating mandatory disclosure of AI systems used to screen applications.[16] Discriminatory practices with AI are compounded by a new legal reality in the United States where diversity, equity, and inclusion (DEI) initiatives are being questioned and legally challenged, especially in light of the 2023 U.S. Supreme Court ruling that struck down affirmative action in college admissions.[17] AI and DEI will likely become a significant social topic, especially within communication professions that focus on corporate, higher education, and political communication.

It is important to note that AI in the United States may have its regulation tempered by the desire to encourage innovation. This is particularly true because of the American desire to be a global leader in the space of AI innovation. The October 2023 Executive Order on AI acknowledges this, stating that part of the AI initiatives in the Biden administration is to promote interaction with key global U.S. allies, specifically data sharing.[18] The current AI race between the United States and China has not created a winner but has proliferated the growth and innovation of the technology. It remains to be seen what effects, good or bad, this may have.[19]

This reality of AI growth places PR practitioners in a unique situation. The regulation of AI is not going to change its proliferation into content creation. PR practitioners will have to learn the platform and utilize it and become more aware of its potential problems and benefits. The law will also continue to evolve in this area, likely not keeping up with technological innovation. To effectively manage this new reality, PR practitioners should lean into their own ethical and professional standards, analyzing what is best for clients and the profession. By doing this, public relations stands to not only weather the AI revolution but be an active part of shaping its future.

DISCUSSION QUESTIONS

1. What is the most important issue facing PR practice in the era of AI?

2. What are the legal considerations a PR practitioner should consider when using AI to create content?

3. Imagine the year 2030. What do you think PR practice will look like?

4. Suppose you are a PR practitioner using generative AI to create a logo for a client. The client likes the logo, and you use it on their website. Later you notice the logo is used on a competitor's site. What legal recourse do you have?

5. Which area of law do you think is the most important to establish, given the rate of AI development?

CASE SCENARIO

You use artificial intelligence to create a new logo for a client who sells landscaping equipment. The logo depicts a lawn mower with a vibrant green background and the company name at the bottom of the logo. The design takes several minutes to create as you refine the requirements of the logo through several detailed prompts. After the logo is created, you edit it for color and design before presenting it to the client. Does this logo have IP protection? If so, what type? Additionally, what potential IP infringement issues are there given that the logo was created through AI? Should you disclose your use of AI to the client? Why or why not?

Glossary

actual malice: The fault standard that public figures, limited-purpose public figures, and public officials must prove in a defamation case. This requires either reckless disregard for the truth or knowing falsity.

administrative law: Laws and regulations that regulate federal and state agencies. These laws are created and enforced by the agencies.

appeal: The process by which parties ask higher courts to review a lower court decision. Both states and federal courts have separate systems for appeals. The U.S. Supreme Court is the highest appellate court in the United States.

case law: Law created by judges in appellate decisions. Case laws are valid in specific jurisdictions in the United States. The U.S. Supreme Court's case law is the law in the United States.

Chevron deference: A standard of judicial review in administrative law established by the 1984 U.S. Supreme Court case *Chevron USA, Inc. v. Natural Resources Defense Counsel*. It requires courts to defer to interpretations of statutes made by those government agencies charged with enforcing them unless such interpretations are unreasonable. This standard is currently under review as of 2024 at the U.S. Supreme Court.

Constitution: The U.S. Constitution is the supreme law of the United States. It is comprised of seven articles: Article 1 (Legislative Branch), Article 2 (Executive Branch), Article 3 (Judicial

Branch), Article 4 (State Powers and Limitations), Article 5 (Constitutional Amendment Process), Article 6 (Supremacy Clause), and Article 7 (Constitutional Ratification), as well as 27 amendments. The first 10 amendments are called the Bill of Rights.

contract: A legally binding agreement between two or more parties. The parties can be either individuals or businesses. These agreements can be enforced in courts.

copyright: Federal and state laws that protect original works of authorship fixed in a tangible medium.

damages: Monetary compensation awarded for loss or injury from a lawsuit. Damages can take various forms such as:

compensatory damages: Money paid for actual damages. This can include general damages, such as pain and suffering or emotional distress and special damages, which compensate actual losses that can be calculated.

punitive damages: Money paid as a punishment to the defendant for egregious behavior. *statutory damages*: Money paid according to a statutory schedule.

defamation: A false statement, spoken or published, which results in reputational harm. Written defamation is called libel, and spoken defamation is slander. Both libel and slander are encapsulated in the larger term of defamation.

defendant: An individual, company, or institution sued by a plaintiff in a court of law.

fair use doctrine: This doctrine is an affirmative defense for limited use of copyrighted material without requiring permission from the rights holder. The fair use defense is based on four factors: purpose and character of the use, nature of copyrighted work, amount of copyrighted work used, and impact on the market.

First Amendment: The amendment to the U.S. Constitution that guarantees freedom of speech, freedom of religion (exercise and establishment), the right to assembly, freedom of the press, and the right to petition the government.

intellectual property: Property rights given to human creations. This includes copyright, trademark, patents, and trade secrets.

jurisdiction: The authority of a court to hear specific cases. This includes federal and state jurisdiction.

litigation: The process of bringing a lawsuit in court. Litigation follows procedural rules set either by federal or state procedure. In federal court, the procedure is established by the Federal Rules of Civil Procedure and Federal Rules of Criminal Procedure.

negligence: Failure of a party to take ordinary care, which results in damage or injury to another. In defamation, negligence is the standard of proof required for regular, nonpublic plaintiffs.

obscenity: Material that is unprotected by the First Amendment of the U.S. Constitution. The U.S. Supreme Court established a three-part test to determine obscenity in the 1973 case *Miller v. California*.

patent: A type of intellectual property that gives the owner the exclusive rights to manufacture and control an invention. The duration of a patent in the United States is 20 years.

plaintiff: An individual, group of individuals, or entity that brings a case against a defendant(s) in a court of law.

precedent: Prior law from a previous case in which a court made a decision. Depending on the jurisdiction, the prior case can be binding precedent or, where the case is outside the jurisdiction, the precedent is persuasive.

privacy laws: Laws that deal with the regulation of personal information. Privacy torts include intrusion upon seclusion, public disclosure of private facts, misappropriation, and false light.

statute: A written law passed by a legislative body and signed into law by an executive, either the president of the United States (federal) or governor (state). Federal statutes are codified in the United States Code, which has 54 titles. State statutes are codified in similar codes which have a varying number of titles.

statutory interpretation: The philosophical approach that judges and attorneys use to interpret statutes. Common approaches to statutory interpretation include textualism, purposivism, and legal realism, among others.

subpoena: A legal order compelling someone to attend court.

testimony: Written or spoken statement, given in a court of law under oath.

tort: An area of law that includes an act or an omission that constitutes a civil wrong that causes injury or loss to another person.

trademark: A type of intellectual property that is a symbol or word(s) that identifies a specific product or service. Trademarks may be registered by the U.S. Patent and Trademark Office. The duration of a trademark is potentially forever. However, trademarks can be lost through abandonment (i.e., not defending the mark when infringement occurs) or by genericity (i.e., the process where a mark loses its uniqueness).

verdict: The decision in a civil or criminal case, usually determined by a jury.

NOTES

CHAPTER 1

1. "Law," *Merriam-Webster Dictionary*, accessed July 25, 2023, https://www.merriam -webster.com/dictionary/law#legalDictionary.

2. "Ethics," *Merriam-Webster.com Dictionary*, accessed July 25, 2023, https://www.merriam -webster.com/dictionary/ethics.

3. Will Durant, The Story of Philosophy: The Lives and Opinions of the Greater Philos-ophers, 2nd ed. (New York: Simon and Schuster, 1933).

4. Public Relations Society of America, "PRSA Code of Ethics," accessed July 25, 2023, https://www.prsa.org/about/ethics/prsa-code-of-ethics.

5. Page Society, "Page Principles," accessed November 3, 2023, https://page.org/who-we -are/page-principles/.

6. "PRSA Code of Ethics."

7. International Association of Business Communicators (IABC), "Code of Ethics," accessed July 25, 2023, https://www.iabc.com/About/Purpose/Code-of-Ethics.

8. Marbury v. Madison, 5 U.S. (1 Cranch) 137 (1803); Brown v. Board of Education, 347 U.S. 483 (1954); Miranda v. Arizona, 384 U.S. 436 (1966).

9. Roe v. Wade, 410 U.S. 113 (1973); Dobbs v. Jackson Women's Health Organization, 597 U.S. 215 (2022).

10. The Federal Circuit Court is a specialized federal court that only hears cases in administrative law, intellectual property cases, and cases involving monetary claims against the U.S. government.

11. Only nine states have no intermediary court of appeal: Delaware, Maine, Montana, New Hampshire, Rhode Island, South Dakota, Vermont, West Virginia, and Wyoming.

12. En banc cases in federal circuits with more than 15 judges, such as the U.S. Court of Appeals for the Ninth Circuit which has 29 judges, have a special rule for the number of en banc judges. Though not required, the Ninth Circuit limits en banc hearings to 11 judges.

13. Andy Warhol Foundation for the Visual Arts v. Goldsmith, 598 U.S. 508 (2023).

14. Rosemary Feitelberg, "Supreme Court Victor Lynn Goldsmith Talks Warhol, Prince and Celebrity Facades," WWD, May 19, 2023, https://wwd.com/eye/people

/lynn-goldsmith-prince-photograph-andy-warhol-supreme-court-interview
-1235658276/.

15. "What Percentage of Lawsuits Settle Before Trial? What Are Some Statistics on Personal Injury Settlements?" *The Law Dictionary*, accessed July 28, 2023, https:// thelawdictionary.org/article/what-percentage-of-lawsuits-settle-before-trial-what -are-some-statistics-on-personal-injury-settlements/.

16. United States Courts, "About Federal Courts," accessed July 28, 2023, https:// www.uscourts.gov/about-federal-courts/educational-resources/about-educational -outreach/activity-resources/about.

17. Angie Gou, "As Unanimity Declines, Conservative Majority's Power Runs Deeper Than the Blockbuster Cases," *SCOTUSblog*, July 3, 2022, https://www.scotusblog .com/2022/07/as-unanimity-declines-conservative-majoritys-power-runs-deeper -than-the-blockbuster-cases/.

18. United States Courts, "Federal Judicial Caseload Statistics 2023," accessed March 29, 2024, https://www.uscourts.gov/statistics-reports/federal-judicial-caseload -statistics-2023.

19. U.S. Constitution, art. I–VII.

20. U.S. Constitution, amend. I–X.

21. There is another related philosophy of plain meaning, which is also not textualism. In plain meaning, courts look to dictionary definitions to determine the meaning behind words.

22. District of Columbia v. Heller, 554 U.S. 570 (2008).

23. Charles L. Barzun, "Three Forms of Legal Pragmatism," *Washington University Law Review* 95, no. 5 (2018): 1003–1034, https://openscholarship.wustl.edu/cgi/ viewcontent.cgi?article=6495&context=law_lawreview.

24. Thomas C. Grey, "Holmes and Legal Pragmatism," *Stanford Law Review* 41, no. 4 (April 1989): 787–870.

25. U.S. Constitution, amend. XIV, § 1.

26. Nicos Stavropoulos, "Interpretivist Theories of Law," *Stanford Encyclopedia of Philosophy*, last modified July 20, 2017, https://plato.stanford.edu/entries/law -interpretivist/. This theory was largely developed by legal scholar Ronald Dworkin, who was a professor at New York University Law School and the University of Oxford. Dworkin was a major critic of legal positivism and critiqued that area of legal interpretation in his book *Law's Empire*, which presents an idealized version of a judge, Judge Hercules, who combats the legal positivism of Judge Hermes. Ronald Dworkin, *Law's Empire* (Cambridge, MA: Harvard University Press, 1986).

27. David W. Kennedy, "Critical Theory, Structuralism and Contemporary Legal Schol- arship," *New England Law Review* 21 (1986): 209–289.

28. The White House, "Executive Order on the Safe, Secure, and Trustworthy Devel- opment and Use of Artificial Intelligence," last modified October 30, 2023, https: //www.whitehouse.gov/briefing-room/presidential-actions/2023/10/30/executive -order-on-the-safe-secure-and-trustworthy-development-and-use-of-artificial -intelligence/.

29. Antonin Scalia and Bryan A. Garner, Reading Law: The Interpretation of Legal Texts (St. Paul, MN: Thomson/West, 2012), 69–77.

30. Ibid., 78–92.

31. Ibid., 195–198.

32. Ibid., 16–28. In Scalia and Garner's book, purposivism is criticized as wrongly framing textualism as a conservative approach that only produces one type of interpretive outcome. Purposivism is a convention largely associated with liberal interpretations of the law. It is very common in the European Union and among progressive jurists.

33. Ibid., 428.

34. Ibid., 427–428.

35. Ibid.

36. Administrative Procedure Act, 5 U.S.C. §§ 500–596 (2023).

37. Chevron U.S.A., Inc. v. Natural Resources Defense Council, Inc., 467 U.S. 837 (1984).

38. Loper Bright Enterprises, et al. v. Raimondo, Secretary of Commerce, et al., No. 22–451, docketed Nov. 15, 2022 (U.S.), on appeal from 21–5166 (D.C. Cir. Aug. 12, 2022); Relentless, Inc. v. Dep't. of Commerce, No. 22–1219 (U.S. argued Jan. 17, 2024), on appeal from the 1st Circuit. These two companion cases potentially could overturn Chevron deference, but at the time of this writing the cases have had oral argument only. There has been a conservative movement to overturn Chevron deference, and with a 6–3 conservative majority on the Supreme Court there is speculation that the deference will be overturned or modified in a significant way. The Chevron doctrine has been in place since 1984, and Justice Elena Kagan estimates that Chevron deference is the basis of at least 70 U.S. Supreme Court decisions and approximately 17,000 lower court decision. Discarding or changing the doctrine would have a significant impact on agency power and would increase the role of courts in the United States. One argument against deference is that it usurps judicial power in a major way. In fact, during oral argument, attorney Roman Martinez said that Chevron deference would not permit the Supreme Court to overturn an agency interpretation of a rule so long as the interpretation was reasonable, even if all nine justices agreed that there was a better interpretation of the agency rule.

39. U.S. Constitution, art. VI, sec. 2.

40. Berne Convention for the Protection of Literary and Artistic Works, Sept. 9, 1886, as last revised in Paris on July 24, 1971, 828 U.N.T.S. 221.

41. Anu Bradford, *The Brussels Effect: How the European Union Rules the World* (Oxford University Press, 2020).

42. European Parliament and Council of the European Union, "Regulation (EU) 2016/679 of the European Parliament and of the Council of 27 April 2016 on the Protection of Natural Persons with Regard to the Processing of Personal Data and on the Free Movement of Such Data, and Repealing Directive 95/46/EC (General Data Protection Regulation)," *Official Journal of the European Union* L 119 (May 4, 2016): 1–88.

43. The statute of frauds is a legal concept that dates back to English law, when in 1677 Parliament enacted An Act for the Prevention of Frauds and Perjuries. The purpose behind this original statute of frauds was to prevent claims of contracts

where there was, in fact, none made. Over time this concept entered U.S. law, and the Universal Commercial Code (UCC) mandates contracts over a certain amount, usually goods and services totaling $500 or more, are to be made in writing.

44. The Latin term for this is *contra proferentem*.
45. The ancient Greek text of the Hippocratic oath from 245 CE, the earliest surviving document of the oath, does not contain the exact phrase "first do no harm."
46. The AMA created ethical guidelines for its members in 1847. The ABA established its rules of conduct in 1908 with Canons of Professional Ethics, last amended in 1963. The ABA published Model Rules of Professional Responsibility in 1969 and a major revision in 1989 for the Model Rules of Professional Conduct.
47. Karen Russell and Carl Bishop, "Understanding Ivy Lee's Declaration of Principles: U.S. Newspaper and Magazine Coverage of Publicity and Press Agentry, 1865–1904," Public Relations Review 35, no. 2 (June 2009): 91–101.
48. Tillman Act, ch. 420, 34 Stat. 864 (1907).
49. Cayce Myers, *Public Relations History: Theory, Practice and Profession* (New York: Routledge, 2021), 127–128.
50. Scott Cutlip and Allen Center, Effective Public Relations, 2nd ed. (Englewood Cliffs, NJ: Prentice Hall, Inc., 1958), 426.
51. Nicholas Browning, "Ethics and the Profession: The Crystallizing of Public Relations Practice from Association to Accreditation, 1936–1964," American Journalism 35, no. 2 (2018): 140–170, doi:10.1080/08821127.2018.1455400.
52. Rex Harlow, "A Timeline of Public Relations Development," *Public Relations Review* 6, no. 3 (Fall 1980): 3–13, https://doi.org/10.1016/s0363-8111(80)80007-5.
53. The early PRSA Grievance Board dealt with code issues facing practitioners in the 1960s. In 1963 the board was dealing with the ethical considerations around front groups, conflicts of interest, undisclosed special interests in organizations, and transparency issues within financial public relations practitioners who had to file disclosures with the Securities and Exchange Commission (SEC). In 1966 the Grievance Board began issuing formal guidance on code provisions and became more active in hearing minor grievances in 1970. By the 1990s, the enforcement of the code became voluntary and educational in spirit. The author of this book was a member of the PRSA Board of Ethics and Professional Standards for four years and was the PRSA National Board of Directors liaison to BEPS at the time of this writing.
54. Browning, "Ethics and the Profession," 148.
55. Myers, *Public Relations History*, 131.
56. International Public Relations Association (IPRA), Code of Athens, accessed July 26, 2023, https://www.ipra.org/static/media/uploads/pdfs/ipra_code_of_athens .pdf. The current version of the Code of Athens has a tone that is closely tied to the Universal Declaration of Human Rights, published by the United Nations in December 1948. There is a particular focus on human rights, dignity of humankind, and an express prohibition against disinformation.
57. Myers, *Public Relations History*, 131.

58. "Barcelona Principles 2.0," *PR News Online*, accessed July 26, 2023, https://www
.prnewsonline.com/barcelona-principles-2-0/.

59. "Common Good," *Stanford Encyclopedia of Philosophy*, accessed July 25, 2023, https://
plato.stanford.edu/entries/common-good/.

60. Durant, *The Story of Philosophy*, 55–86.

61. McKinsey & Company, "Patagonia Shows How Turning a Profit Doesn't Have to
Cost the Earth," accessed July 25, 2023, https://www.mckinsey.com/industries
/agriculture/our-insights/patagonia-shows-how-turning-a-profit-doesnt-have-to
-cost-the-earth.

62. John Stuart Mill, On Liberty, *Utilitarianism, and Other Essays* (London: Oxford University Press, 2015); Brown University, "Framework for Making Ethical Decisions,"
accessed July 25, 2023, https://www.brown.edu/academics/science-and-technology
-studies/framework-making-ethical-decisions.

63. Judith Rehak, "Tylenol Made a Hero of Johnson & Johnson: The Recall That
Started Them All," New York Times, March 23, 2002, https://www.nytimes.com
/2002/03/23/your-money/IHT-tylenol-made-a-hero-of-johnson-johnson-the
-recall-that-started.html.https://www.nytimes.com/2002/03/23/your-money/IHT
-tylenol-made-a-hero-of-johnson-johnson-the-recall-that-started.html. Adjusted
for inflation, $100 million in 1982 would be approximately three times that much
today.

64. Ayn Rand, The Fountainhead (New York: Bobbs-Merrill, 1943); Ayn Rand, Atlas
Shrugged (New York: Random House, 1957); Ayn Rand, The Virtue of Selfishness: A New Concept of Egoism (New York: Signet, 1964). It is important to note
that Rand's philosophy of libertarian egoist principles was rooted in the concept
of restricted government. She believed that egoist philosophy preserved individual
rights, and that embracing reason-based self-interestedness led to robust debate
and a protection of free speech.

65. Rand, *The Virtue of Selfishness*.

66. Milton Friedman, "The Social Responsibility of Business is to Increase its Profits,"
New York Magazine, September 13, 1970, http://websites.umich.edu/~thecore/doc/
Friedman.pdf. This article discusses Friedman's book *Capitalism and Freedom*. Associated with the 1970s and 1980s conservative government of Margaret Thatcher
and Ronald Reagan, Friedman was a proponent of free market capitalism. His
position was in opposition to Keynesian economic theory, which posited that the
markets work best when there is strong regulatory control.

67. Durant, *The Story of Philosophy*, 205–233.

68. "Categorical Imperatives and the Case for Deception: Part I," Teachers College,
Columbia University, *Institutional Review Board (IRB) Blog*, July 13, 2020, https:
//www.tc.columbia.edu/institutional-review-board/irb-blog/2020/categorical
-imperatives-and-the-case-for-deception-part-i/.

69. Kantian influence cannot be overstated in many other types of ethical philosophies.
John Locke's ethical approach to individual rights, sometimes called the rights
approach, is rooted in Kantian duty-based ethics. So is the fairness approach
advocated by philosophers such as the American John Rawls. Similarly, divinity

plays a role within Kantian ethics. The divine rights given to mankind by God are a justification for ethical decision making. The divine will of God's impact on ethical decision making and non-consequentialism is seen in the work of Søren Kierkegaard in his analysis of Abraham in the Old Testament who was willing to sacrifice his son Isaac as God commanded.

70. Durant, *The Story of Philosophy*, 211–224.
71. "Ren," *Encyclopedia Britannica*, accessed July 25, 2023, https://www.britannica.com/topic/ren.
72. Peter Drucker, "The Effective Decision," *Harvard Business Review*, January 1967, https://hbr.org/1967/01/the-effective-decision.
73. Emre Soyer and Robin Hogarth, "Fooled by Experience," *Harvard Business Review*, May 2015, https://hbr.org/2015/05/fooled-by-experience.
74. Brown University, "Framework for Making Ethical Decisions."
75. Ibid.
76. Ibid.
77. Melody Wilding, "How to Stop Overthinking and Start Trusting Your Gut," *Harvard Business Review*, March 2022, https://hbr.org/2022/03/how-to-stop-overthinking-and-start-trusting-your-gut.
78. Benjamin Finzi, "CEO Decision Making: Emotional Fortitude," Deloitte Insights, Spring 2021, https://www2.deloitte.com/us/en/insights/topics/leadership/ceo-decision-making-emotional-fortitude.html.
79. "The Psychology Behind Unethical Behavior," *Harvard Business Review*, April 2019, https://hbr.org/2019/04/the-psychology-behind-unethical-behavior.
80. Elisabeth Noelle-Neumann, "The Spiral of Silence: A Theory of Public Opinion," Journal of Communication 24 (1974): 43–51.
81. Dietram A. Scheufele and Patricia Moy, "Twenty-Five Years of the Spiral of Silence: A Conceptual Review and Empirical Outlook," International Journal of Public Opinion Research 12, no. 1 (2000): 3–28, https://search-ebscohost-com.ezproxy.lib.vt.edu/login.aspx?direct=true&db=ufh&AN=3236575&scope=site.
82. American Psychiatric Nurses Association, "A Systematic Approach to Ethical Decision Making for Nurses," accessed July 25, 2023, https://www.apna.org/news/a-systematic-approach-to-ethical-decision-making-for-nurses/; Licensed Professional Counselors Association of Georgia, "Models of Decision Making," accessed July 25, 2023, https://www.lpcaga.org/assets/Models%20of%20Decision%20Making%202.pdf; American Counseling Association, "The Ethics Model," accessed July 25, 2023, https://www.counseling.org/docs/default-source/vistas/the-ethics-model.pdf; National Criminal Justice Reference Service, "Making Ethical Decisions: A Practical Model," accessed July 25, 2023, https://www.ojp.gov/ncjrs/virtual-library/abstracts/making-ethical-decisions-practical-model.
83. Public Relations Society of America, "Ethics Case Study: Ethical Decision-Making Guide," accessed July 25, 2023, https://www.prsa.org/docs/default-source/about/ethics/ethics-case-studies/ethics-case-study-ethical-desision-making-guide.pdf?sfvrsn=8a55268f_4.
84. Ibid.

85. Josephson Institute, "The Seven-Step Path to Better Decisions," accessed July 25, 2023, https://josephsoninstitute.org/med-4sevensteppath/.

86. Laura Nash, "Ethics without the Sermon," *Harvard Business Review*, November 1981, https://hbr.org/1981/11/ethics-without-the-sermon.

87. Ibid.

88. Ibid.

89. Ethics & Compliance Initiative, "Global Business Ethics Survey," accessed July 24, 2023, https://www.ethics.org/global-business-ethics-survey/.

90. The White House, "Blueprint for an AI Bill of Rights: Making Automated Systems Work for the American People," accessed October 31, 2023, https://www.whitehouse.gov/ostp/ai-bill-of-rights/.

91. European Parliament, "EU AI Act: First Regulation on Artificial Intelligence," June 8, 2023, https://www.europarl.europa.eu/news/en/headlines/society/20230601STO93804/eu-ai-act-first-regulation-on-artificial-intelligence.

92. Title VII of the Civil Rights Act of 1964, 42 U.S.C. § 2000e (1964).

93. Students for Fair Admissions v. Harvard, 600 U.S. 181 (2023).

94. Roosevelt Institute, "The End of Affirmative Action?" June 29, 2023, https://rooseveltinstitute.org/2023/06/29/the-end-of-affirmative-action/?gclid=Cj0KCQjw5f2lBhCkARIsAHeTvljgNEwbux2LseZDit7VYK2ZrMYa9x2YR0LQydC3Afj5m-WSxzJA-uIaAmarEALw_wcB; National Equity Project, "SCOTUS Affirmative Action Decision," June 30, 2023, https://www.nationalequityproject.org/blog/scotus-affirmative-action-decision?gclid=Cj0KCQjw5f2lBhCkARIsAHeTvlhxh5W_Bbv0K55462rW-DS1_n8iR12Zn9K5aWMD87E5KD7QIuqbiy8aAto0EALw_wcB.

95. Michael Peregrine, "State Attorney Generals' Warning To CEOs May Chill DEI Initiatives," Fortune, July 18, 2023, https://www.forbes.com/sites/michaelperegrine/2023/07/18/state-attorney-generals-warning-to-ceos-may-chill-dei-initiatives/?sh=58f2cc8b1583. This letter was signed by 13 state attorney generals who warned companies that the Supreme Court decision had direct implications for DEI within employment law. Specifically, the letter emphasizes the requirement of race neutrality within employment practices.

96. Kenji Yoshino and David Glasgow, "What SCOTUS's Affirmative Action Decision Means for Corporate DEI," *Harvard Business Review*, July 12 2023, https://hbr.org/2023/07/what-scotuss-affirmative-action-decision-means-for-corporate-dei.

CHAPTER 2

1. Scott M. Cutlip and Allen H. Center, *Effective Public Relations*, 2nd ed. (Englewood Cliffs, NJ: Prentice-Hall, Inc., 1958), 3.

2. Ibid., 6.

3. Tom Kelleher, *Public Relations*, 2nd ed. (Oxford: Oxford University Press, 2021), 185. The PESO model was created by Gini Dietrich in her 2014 book, *Spin Sucks: Communication and Reputation Management in the Digital Age* (Indianapolis: Que Publishing, 2014).

4. Ganga S. Dhanesh, "Putting Engagement in its PRoper Place: State of the Field, Definition and Model of Engagement in Public Relations," Public Relations Review 43, no. 5 (December 2017): 925–933, https://doi.org/10.1016/j.pubrev.2017.04.001.
5. Cutlip and Center, *Effective Public Relations*; Kelleher, *Public Relations*.
6. U.S. Constitution, Amend. I.
7. Gitlow v. New York, 268 U.S. 652 (1925). Gitlow is a case that applies the First Amendment to the states through a process called incorporation. Incorporation is a process by which the Bill of Rights is applied to the states through the Fourteenth Amendment, enacted in 1868. The incorporation doctrine applies to some, but not all, of the Bill of Rights. More about this is found in Chapter 1.
8. Walter Berns, "Freedom of the Press and the Alien and Sedition Laws: A Reappraisal," *Supreme Court Review* 1970, no. 1 (1970): 109–159. Prior to that point, the only federal speech law in the United States was the heavily criticized Sedition Acts passed in 1798 during the administration of John Adams. That law made it a criminal offense to criticize or make false statements about the federal government. It was seen by many as a political maneuver by the Federalists to suppress the content in Democratic-Republican, pro–Thomas Jefferson newspapers. Its blatant partisanship became one of the lasting legacies of Adams's administration and represents a low point in free speech in the United States. It was not challenged in the courts, and ultimately expired in 1800 coinciding with Thomas Jefferson's election as president of the United States.
9. Schenk v. United States, 249 U.S. 47 (1919).
10. Ibid., 52.
11. Abrams v. United States, 250 U.S. 616 (1919).
12. Ibid., 630.
13. Connally v. General Construction Company, 269 U.S. 385, 391 (1926). The issue of vagueness in law is an ancient legal theory that dates back to Roman times when the idea that a law that could not be deciphered as to follow it was automatically invalid. The principle of *nulla crimen sine lege,* roughly translated as "no crime without law," was later enshrined in Blackstone's *Commentarieson the Laws of England,* informally known as *Blackstone's Commentaries,* by highly influential English jurist William Blackstone. In the American colonies, Blackstone's work was highly influential in the creation of American law and was widely read by American lawyers in the eighteenth century, including many founders. Later applications of the vagueness doctrine to speech laws are rooted in the Fifth and Fourteenth Amendment Due Process Clause; see Grayned v. City of Rockford, 408 U.S. 104 (1972).
14. Cantwell v. Connecticut, 310 U.S. 296 (1940); Thornhill v. Alabama, 310 U.S. 88 (1940).
15. United States v. Alvarez, 567 U.S. 709 (2012); United States v. Stevens, 559 U.S. 460 (2010).
16. Near v. Minnesota, 283 U.S. 697 (1931). In *Near,* the Supreme Court was not necessarily inventing a new legal theory against prior restraint. The excesses and injustices of British courts in the Tudor and Stuart reigns had proved to be examples of how courts could suppress political thought. Specifically, in *Near* the Court

discussed the Star Chamber, which was used from medieval times through the seventeenth century as a court to bring prominent figures to justice. However, the Star Chamber came to represent arbitrary and unfair injustices that are the byproduct of a flawed legal system.

17. New York Times Co. v. United States, 403 U.S. 713 (1971). This case involved the Nixon administration's attempt to prevent the *New York Times* and *Washington Post* from publishing classified information about the Vietnam War. Known as the Pentagon Papers, officially *Report of the Office of the Secretary of Defense Vietnam Task Force*, the information had been illegally obtained by Daniel Ellsberg. Later, Ellsberg was indicted by a grand jury, but his case was later declared a mistrial because agents working on behalf of the Nixon administration broke into Ellsberg's psychiatrist's office and offered the trial judge a directorship of the FBI, along with wiretapping incidents.

18. Sable Communications of California v. FCC, 492 U.S. 115 (1989)

19. Holder v. Humanitarian Law Project, 561 U.S. 1 (2010).

20. Williams-Yulee v. Florida Bar, 575 U.S. 433 (2015).

21. City of Los Angeles v. Alameda Books, 535 U.S. 425, 455 (2002) (Souter, J., dissenting).

22. Victoria L. Killion, "Free Speech: When and Why Content-Based Laws Are Presumptively Unconstitutional," *Congressional Research Service*, January 10, 2023, https://crsreports.congress.gov/product/pdf/IF/IF12308. See Reed v. Town of Gilbert, 576 U.S. 155, 163 (2015); National Institute of Family & Life Advocates v. Becerra, 138 S. Ct. 2361 (2018) where a law mandated that pregnancy centers provide information to patients about publicly funded family planning services.

23. Schenck v. United States, 249 U.S. 47, 52 (1919).

24. Chaplinsky v. New Hampshire, 315 U.S. 568, 571–72 (1942).

25. Terminiello v. City of Chicago, 337 U.S. 1, 4 (1949).

26. Gooding v. Wilson, 405 U.S. 518 (1972); R.A.V. v. City of St. Paul, 505 U.S. 377 (1992).

27. Dennis Baron, "Trump's Words on January 6 Were a Clear and Present Danger," *Web of Language* (blog), February 16, 2021, https://blogs.illinois.edu/view/25/502281961.

28. Jacobellis v. Ohio, 378 U.S. 187 (1964).

29. Act of Mar. 3, 1873, ch. 258, 17 Stat. 598. The old English law has some impact on U.S. definitions of obscenity. Borrowing from the standard of obscenity from the English case Regina v. Hicklin, [1868] LR 3 QB 360, the definition of obscenity was "whether the tendency of the matter . . . is to deprave and corrupt those whose minds are open to such immoral influences, and into whose hands a publication of this sort may fall." See David Hudson, "Obscenity and Pornography," Middle Tennessee State University, 2009, https://www.mtsu.edu:8443/first-amendment/article/1004/obscenity-and-pornography.

30. Roth v. United States, 354 U.S. 476, 489 (1957)

31. Memoirs v. Massachusetts, 383 U.S. 413, 418 (1966).

32. Miller v. California, 413 U.S. 15, 24 (1973).

33. Paris Adult Theater I v. Slaton, 413 U.S. 49 (1973).

34. Brown v. Entertainment Merchants Association, 564 U.S. 768 (2011).

35. Hudson, "Obscenity and Pornography."

36. Reno v. American Civil Liberties Union, 521 U.S. 844 (1997).

37. Ashcroft v. American Civil Liberties Union, 535 U.S. 564 (2002).

38. Federal Communications Commission, "Obscene, Indecent and Profane Broadcasts," January 13, 2021, https://www.fcc.gov/consumers/guides/obscene-indecent-and -profane-broadcasts.

39. During this time, a plaintiff in a defamation case, regardless of status, only needed to prove that a defendant speaker made their defamatory statements negligently. Negligence can be defined as lacking ordinary care that a reasonable person would use, which as a legal standard is nebulous. The standard tends to favor plaintiffs in defamation suits, and because of this defamation claims typically favored plaintiffs until 1964, when the actual malice standard was created by the U.S. Supreme Court in New York Times v. Sullivan.

40. New York Times Co. v. Sullivan, 376 U.S. 254 (1964).

41. Ibid., 280.

42. Curtis Publishing Co. v. Butts, 388 U.S. 130 (1967). This case involved a *Saturday Evening Post* article about University of Georgia former football coach and current athletic director, Wally Butts, claiming that Butts had conspired to fix a football game with Coach Paul "Bear" Bryant of Alabama. The *Saturday Evening Post* was sued and Butts eventually recovered $3.06 million, reduced to $460,000. Bryant settled for $300,000. The *Saturday Evening Post* later went out of business in 1969 in part because of the settlements and judgments in this case. See David Summer, Fumbled Call: The Bear Bryant–Wally Butts Football Scandal That Split the Supreme Court and Changed American Libel Law (Jefferson, NC: McFarland & Company, Inc., 2018).

43. Summer, Fumbled Call, 162.

44. Gertz v. Welch, 418 U.S. 323, 344 (1974).

45. Hustler Magazine v. Falwell, 485 U.S. 46 (1988).

46. Ibid. In this case, Falwell sued *Hustler Magazine* over a double-entendre Campari ad. Falwell sued the magazine for defamation, invasion of privacy, and intentional infliction of emotional distress. It is important to note that intentional infliction of emotional distress is not an element of defamation. In defamation, the harm is reputational damage. Emotional distress is typically the harm shown in a false light case, which is different than defamation.

47. Communications Decency Act of 1996, Pub. L. No. 104–104, 110 Stat. 133, 47 U.S.C. § 230 (1996).

48. Exec. Order No. 13,925, 85 *Fed. Reg.* 34,079 (May 28, 2020).

49. Gonzalez v. Google LLC, 598 U.S. 617 (2023); Twitter, Inc. v. Taamneh, 598 U.S. 471 (2023).

50. Telecommunications Act of 1996, Pub. L. No. 104–104, 110 Stat. 56 (1996).

51. Milkovich v. Lorain Journal Co., 497 U.S. 1 (1990).

52. Central Hudson Gas & Electric Corp. v. Public Service Commission, 447 U.S. 557 (1980).
53. Ibid., 563.
54. Ibid.
55. Valentine v. Chrestensen, 316 U.S. 52 (1942).
56. Bates v. State Bar of Arizona, 433 U.S. 350 (1977).
57. Bigelow v. Virginia, 421 U.S. 809 (1975); Virginia State Pharmacy Board v. Virginia Citizens Consumer Council, 425 U.S. 748 (1976).
58. Bolger v. Youngs Drug Products Corp., 463 U.S. 60 (1983).
59. Ibid., 67.
60. Lorillard Tobacco Co. v. Reilly, 533 U.S. 525 (2001).
61. 44 Liquormart, Inc. v. Rhode Island, 517 U.S. 484 (1996).
62. Sometimes the Supreme Court's decision in Eastern Railroad Conference v. Noerr Motors, 365 U.S. 127 (1961) is described as the case that gives PR First Amendment Protection. However, the case is more about First Amendment protection for lobbying. The case is discussed in the lobbying section of this chapter.
63. Kasky v. Nike, Inc., 93 Cal. Rptr. 2d 854 (Ct. App. 2000).
64. Ibid.
65. Ibid.
66. In re RMJ, 455 U.S. 191 (1982); Ibanez v. Florida Department of Business and Professional Regulation, Board of Accountancy, 512 U.S. 136 (1994).
67. Nike v. Kasky, 537 U.S. 1099 (2003) (cert. granted); Nike v. Kasky, 539 U.S. 654 (2003) (cert. denied). The denial of certiorari was based on the fact that the Superior Court of California had no final disposition of the case. The reversal of certiorari was a split decision, and the dissenters thought the case should go forward because the issue was one of major importance to the First Amendment. The case garnered some attention, with 34 amicus briefs being filed on various sides.
68. Cayce Myers, "What's the Legal Definition of PR?: An Analysis of Commercial Speech and Public Relations," *Public Relations Review* 42 (2016): 821–831.
69. Citizens United v. Federal Election Commission, 558 U.S. 310 (2010).
70. Dartmouth College v. Woodward, 17 U.S. (4 Wheat.) 518 (1819).
71. Santa Clara County v. Southern Pacific Railroad Co., 118 U.S. 394 (1886).
72. Brian Schwartz, "Total 2020 Election Spending to Hit Nearly $14 Billion, More Than Double 2016's Sum," *CNBC*, October 28, 2020, https://www.cnbc.com/2020/10/28/2020-election-spending-to-hit-nearly-14-billion-a-record.html.
73. Newberry v. United States, 256 U.S. 232 (1921).
74. Burroughs v. United States, 290 U.S. 534 (1934).
75. Public Utility Holding Company Act of 1935, 15 U.S.C. §§ 79 to 79z-6 (1935); Hatch Act of 1939, 5 U.S.C. §§ 1501–1508 (1939); Labor Management Relations Act of 1947, 29 U.S.C. §§ 141–197 (1947).
76. Federal Election Campaign Act of 1971, Pub. L. No. 92–225, 86 Stat. 3.
77. Buckley v. Valeo, 424 U.S. 1 (1976).
78. First National Bank of Boston v. Bellotti, 435 U.S. 765 (1978).
79. Bipartisan Campaign Reform Act of 2002, Pub. L. No. 107–155, 116 Stat. 81.

80. McConnell v. FEC, 540 U.S. 93 (2003).

81. FEC v. Wisconsin Right to Life, Inc., 551 U.S. 449 (2007).

82. Citizens United v. Federal Election Commission.

83. SpeechNow.org v. FEC, 599 F.3d 686 (D.C. Cir. 2010).

84. McCutcheon v. Federal Election Commission, 572 U.S. 185 (2014).

85. Lobbying Disclosure Act of 1995, Pub. L. No. 104–65, 109 Stat. 691, 2 U.S.C. §§ 1601–1612; Ethics Reform Act of 1989, Pub. L. No. 101–194, 103 Stat. 1760, 2 U.S.C. and 5 U.S.C.; Honest Leadership and Open Government Act of 2007, Pub. L. No. 110–81, 121 Stat. 735, 2 U.S.C. and 5 U.S.C.

86. United States v. Harriss, 347 U.S. 612, 620 (1954).

87. United States v. Rumely, 345 U.S. 41 (1953). This case was about a lobbyist, Edward Rumely, who refused to provide information to the U.S. House of Representatives Select Committee on Lobbying Activities about from whom he purchased books and pamphlets. His conviction was overturned on First Amendment grounds.

88. Eastern Railroad Presidents Conference v. Noerr Motor Freight, Inc., 365 U.S. 127 (1961).

89. Ibid., 129.

90. United Mine Workers of America v. Pennington, 381 U.S. 657 (1965).

91. California Motor Transport Co. v. Trucking Unlimited, 404 U.S. 508 (1972).

92. Federal Trade Commission Staff, "FTC Staff Report Concerning Enforcement Perspectives on the Noerr–Pennington Doctrine," October 2006, https://www.ftc.gov/sites/default/files/documents/reports/ftc-staff-report-concerning-enforcement-perspectives-noerr-pennington-doctrine/p013518enfperspectnoerr-penningtondoctrine.pdf.

93. Karla K. Gower and Margot Opdycke Lamme, "Public Relations on Trial: 'The Railroad–Trucker's Brawl,' Journalism History 29, no. 1 (Spring 2003): 12–20, https://doi.org/10.1080/00947679.2003.12062616.

94. First National Bank of Boston v. Bellotti, 435 U.S. 765 (1978).

95. New York Lobbying Act, 32 NY Leg. §§1-a-1-v (2016); Cayce Myers, "Public Relations or 'Grassroots Lobbying'? How Lobbying Laws Are Re-Defining PR Practice," Public Relations Review 44, no. 1 (2018): 11–21, https://doi.org/10.1016/j.pubrev.2017.11.006.

96. Nike v. Kasky, 537 U.S. 1099 (2003) (cert. granted); Nike v. Kasky, 539 U.S. 654 (2003) (cert. denied).

CHAPTER 3

1. An-Sofie Claeys and Michaël Opgenhaffen, "Why Practitioners Do (Not) Apply Crisis Communication Theory in Practice," Journal of Public Relations Research 28, no. 5–6 (2016): 232–247, doi: 10.1080/1062726X.2016.1261703; Timothy Coombs, "Choosing the Right Words," Management Communication Quarterly 8, no. 4 (1995): 447–476, doi: 10.1080/1062726X.2016.1261703; Timothy Coombs and Sherry Holladay, "Communication and Attributions in a Crisis: An Experimental Study in Crisis Communication," Journal of Public Relations Research 8, no. 4 (1996): 279–295, doi: 10.1207/s1532754xjprr0804_04; Colleen Shelton and

Lynne M. Sallot, "Image Repair in Politics: Testing Effects of Communication Strategy and Performance History in a Faux Pas," Journal of Public Relations Research 21, no. 1 (2009): 25–50, doi: 10.1080/10627260802520496; Iuliana Vlad, Lynne M. Sallot, and Bryan Reber, "Rectification Without Assuming Responsibility: Testing the Transgression Flowchart With the Vioxx Recall," Journal of Public Relations Research 18, no. 4 (2006): 357–379, doi: 10.1207/s1532754xjprr1804_4.

2. Suzanne Terilli, Slavko Splichal, and Paul Discol, "Lowering the Bar: Privileged Court Filings as Substitutes for Press Releases in the Court of Public Opinion," Communication Law & Policy 12, no. 2 (2007): 143–175, doi: 10.1080/10811680701266500; Susan Twardy, "Attorneys and Public Relations Professionals Must Work Hand-in-Hand when Responding to an Environmental Investigation," Public Relations Quarterly 39, no. 2 (1994): 15–16; David Yalof and Kenneth Dautrich, The First Amendment and the Media in the Court of Public Opinion (Cambridge: Cambridge University Press, 2002).

3. Cayce Myers, "Protecting Online Image in a Digital Age: How Trademark and Parody Issues Affect PR Practice," Research Journal for the Institute for Public Relations 3, no. 1 (2016): 1–18.

4. Cayce Myers, "An Analysis of Social Media Ownership Litigation Between Organizations and PR Practitioners," Public Relations Review 41, no. 4 (2015): 515–522, doi: 10.1016/j.pubrev.2015.05.003.

5. Kathy Fitzpatrick and Mark Rubin, "Public Relations vs. Legal Strategies in Organizational Crisis Decisions," Public Relations Review 21, no. 1 (1995): 21–33, doi: 10.1016/0363-8111(95)90037-3; Kathy Fitzpatrick, "Public Relations and the Law: A Survey of Practitioners," Public Relations Review 22, no. 1 (1996): 1–8, doi: 10.1016/S0363-8111(96)90067-3; Jongmin Lee, Susan Jares, and Robert Heath, "Decision-Making Encroachment and Cooperative Relationships Between Public Relations and Legal Counselors in the Management of Organizational Crisis," Journal of Public Relations Research 11, no. 3 (1999): 243–270, doi: 10.1207/s1532754xjprr1103_03.

6. Cayce Myers, "The Law in Modern Society," in Communication and the Law, 2020 ed., ed. W. Hopkins (Northport, AL: Vision Press, 2023), 1–21.

7. Ibid.

8. Ibid.

9. American Society of Trial Consultants, accessed September 17, 2023, https://www.astcweb.org/.

10. Ibid.

11. Myers, "The Law in Modern Society," 10.

12. Federal Rules of Criminal Procedure, Rule 24(b)(1); Federal Rules of Criminal Procedure, Rule 24(b)(2); Federal Rules of Civil Procedure, Rule 47(b).

13. Batson v. Kentucky, 476 U.S. 79 (1986); J.E.B. v. Alabama ex rel. T.B., 511 U.S. 127 (1994).

14. In re Winship, 397 U.S. 358 (1970); Jackson v. Virginia, 443 U.S. 307 (1979); Cage v. Louisiana, 498 U.S. 39 (1990); Sullivan v. Louisiana, 508 U.S. 275 (1993); Victor v. Nebraska, 511 U.S. 1 (1994).

15. Yuval Sinai, "The Doctrine of Affirmative Defense in Civil Cases—Between Common Law and Jewish Law," North Carolina Journal of International Law 34, no. 1 (Fall 2008): 111–178,https://scholarship.law.unc.edu/cgi/viewcontent.cgi?referer=&httpsredir=1&article=1863&context=ncilj.

16. Guinness World Records, "Longest Jury Deliberation," accessed September 21, 2023, https://www.guinnessworldrecords.com/world-records/93247-longest-jury-deliberation. This trial was over a Fair Housing Act in which the plaintiffs accused the City of Long Beach from preventing them from developing a chain of residential houses.

17. "O. J. Simpson Trial," Encyclopedia Britannica, accessed September 21, 2023, https://www.britannica.com/event; "Jury Acquits Simpson: Throngs Cheer Verdict," Los Angeles Times, October 4, 1995, https://www.latimes.com/archives/la-xpm-1995.

18. Allen v. United States, 164 U.S. 492 (1896).

19. Andy Warhol Foundation for the Visual Arts v. Goldsmith, 598 U.S. 508 (2023).

20. "Lynn Goldsmith on Her Prince Photograph, Andy Warhol and the Supreme Court," WWD, May 19, 2023, https://wwd.com/eye/people/lynn-goldsmith-prince-.

21. Judiciary Act of 1869, ch. 22, 16 Stat. 44 (1869). The number of Supreme Court judges is not set in the Constitution but is decided by Congress. There has been political talk of "court packing" by politicians when the Supreme Court ideologically changes to one side or another. Famously, President Franklin D. Roosevelt attempted to pack the court in 1937 when his New Deal programs were being struck down as unconstitutional by a conservative court. The attempt backfired and was partly the reason why Democrats suffered politically in the 1938 midterm elections where Republicans gained 8 seats in the Senate and 81 seats in the House of Representatives.

22. Fed. R. App. P. 35. It is important to note that en banc hearings are the exception, not the rule for federal appellate courts. En banc decisions typically occur when there is a truly novel question in appellate law before the court or where there is a case in which the court wishes to ensure a maximum level of uniformity. That case's significance warrants en banc status if an absolute majority of the appeals judges agree to the en banc status of the case. The U.S. Supreme Court has never issued a ruling on what constitutes en banc status, so the determination of when a case qualifies as important or qualifies for circuit consistency is up to the judges of the federal appellate court. Parties to an appeal may request an en banc hearing or rehearing. The Federal Rules of Appellate Procedure Rule 35 states that "(1) The petition must begin with a statement that either: (A) the panel decision conflicts with a decision of the United States Supreme Court or of the court to which the petition is addressed (with citation to the conflicting case or cases) and consideration by the full court is therefore necessary to secure and maintain uniformity of the court's decisions; or (B) the proceeding involves one or more questions of exceptional importance, each of which must be concisely stated; for example, a petition may assert that a proceeding presents a question of exceptional importance if it involves an issue on which the panel decision conflicts with the authoritative decisions of other United States Courts of Appeals that have addressed the issue."

23. "Certiorari," Legal Information Institute, Cornell Law School, accessed September 21, 2023, https://www.law.cornell.edu/wex/certiorari.

24. "Supreme Court Research Guide," Georgetown Law Library, accessed September 21, 2023, https://guides.ll.georgetown.edu/c.php?g=316498&p=2114300.

25. Fed. R. Evid. 801(d)(2).

26. Fed. R. Evid. 801(d)(2)(a-e).

27. Cayce Myers, "Apology, Sympathy, and Empathy: The Legal Ramifications of Admitting Fault in U.S. Public Relations Practice," Public Relations Review 42, no. 1 (March 2016): 176–183.

28. "In re Judith Miller," Historical Society of the District of Columbia Circuit, accessed October 31, 2023, https://dcchs.org/in-re-judith-miller/. Miller was a *New York Times* reporter who was put in jail for contempt of court for refusing to comply with a grand jury subpoena demanding her to state who had revealed that Valerie Plame was a CIA operative.

29. Branzburg v. Hayes, 408 U.S. 665 (1972).

30. See, e.g., Cal. Evid. Code § 1070 (California); N.Y. Civ. Rights Law § 79-h (New York); 42 Pa. Cons. Stat. Ann. § 5942(a) (Pennsylvania); U.S. Department of Justice, "Use of Compulsory Process to Obtain Information from, or Records of, Members of the News Media," July 2021, https://www.justice.gov/d9/2022-12/media_memo_07-19-2021.pdf.

31. United States v. Kovel, 296 F.2d 918, 922 (2d. Cir. 1962).

32. In re Copper Mkt. Antitrust Litig., 200 F.R.D. 213 (S.D.N.Y. 2001).

33. In re Signet Jewelers Ltd. Sec. Litig., 332 F.R.D. 131 (S.D.N.Y. 2019).

34. Church & Dwight Co. Inc. v. SPD Swiss Precision Diagnostics, 2014 WL 7238354 (S.D.N.Y. 2014).

35. U.S. ex rel. Strom v. Scios, Inc., 2011 WL 4831193, *4 (N.D. Cal. 2011).

36. Digital Mentor v. Ovivo, 2020 WL 550746 (W.D. Wash. 2020).

37. BouSamra v. Excela Health, 210 A.3d 967 (Pa. 2019).

38. Ibid. The Pennsylvania Supreme Court noted that attorney–client privilege is complex, especially for corporations, because corporations cannot communicate directly to attorneys as they are inanimate objects. See, for example, Commodity Futures Trading Commission v. Weintraub, 471 U.S. 343 (1985) (analyzing who holds attorney–client privilege when a corporation goes into bankruptcy).

39. Myers, "Apology, Sympathy, and Empathy."

40. Public Relations Society of America, "PRSA Code of Ethics," accessed September 25, 2023, https://www.prsa.org/about/ethics/prsa-code-of-ethics.

41. Cayce Myers, "Public Relations Confidentiality: An Analysis of PR Practitioner–Client Privilege in High Profile Litigation," Public Relations Review 41, no. 1 (March 2015): 14–21.

CHAPTER 4

1. Pasi Ikonen, Vilma Luoma-aho, and Shannon A. Bowen, "Transparency for Sponsored Content: Analysing Codes of Ethics in Public Relations, Marketing, Advertising

and Journalism," *International Journal of Strategic Communication* 11, no. 2 (April–June 2017): 165–178, https://doi.org/10.1080/1553118X.2016.1252917.

2. Chang Woo, Michael Gulotaa, and April Gulotta, "Penn State's After-Sanction Response Strategy," in *The Moral Compass of Public Relations*, ed. Brigitta Brunner (New York: Routledge, 2017), 28–42, 32.

3. Cayce Myers, "Regulating Public Relations: How U.S. Legal Policies and Regulations Shaped Early Corporate Public Relations," *American Journalism* 37, no. 2 (Spring 2020): 139–164, https://doi.org/10.1080/08821127.2020.1750883.

4. International Public Relations Association, "Code of Conduct," accessed September 26, 2023, https://www.ipra.org/member-services/code.

5. Public Relations Society of America, "PRSA Code of Ethics," accessed September 26, 2023, https://www.prsa.org/about/ethics/prsa-code-of-ethics.

6. Karla Gower, *Legal and Ethical Considerations for Public Relations*, 3rd ed. (Long Grove, IL: Waveland Press, 2018), 8.

7. "National Advertising Division," Better Business Bureau Programs, accessed September 26, 2023, https://bbbprograms.org/programs/all-programs/national-advertising -division.

8. Ibid.

9. Terri Seligman and Hannah Taylor, "Navigating the National Advertising Division," *Landslide*, March–April 2018–2019, https://www.americanbar.org/groups/ intellectual_property_law/publications/landslide/2018-19/march-april/navigating -national-advertising-division/.

10. One such state is California, which has a robust false advertising law found in Cal. Bus. & Prof. Code § 17500 (2022).

11. Nike, Inc. v. Kasky, 539 U.S. 654 (2003).

12. Lanham Act, 15 U.S.C. §§ 1051–1127.

13. 15 U.S.C. § 1125(a)(1)(A-B).

14. Federal Trade Commission Act of 1914, 15 U.S.C. §§ 41–58.

15. Federal Trade Commission, "Federal Trade Commission Act," accessed September 26, 2023, https://www.ftc.gov/legal-library/browse/statutes/federal-trade-commission -act.

16. Federal Trade Commission, "Coronavirus: Enforcement Warning Letters," accessed September 26, 2023, https://www.ftc.gov/news-events/features/coronavirus/ enforcement/warning-letters.

17. Federal Trade Commission, "Glossary of Scams and Legal Terms," accessed September 26, 2023, https://www.ftc.gov/news-events/topics/glossary-scams-legal-terms.

18. Federal Trade Commission, "Native Advertising: A Guide for Businesses," 2015, https: //www.ftc.gov/business-guidance/resources/native-advertising-guide-businesses.

19. A. Aribarg and E. M. Schwartz, "Native Advertising in Online News: Trade-Offs Among Clicks, Brand Recognition, and Website Trustworthiness," *Journal of Marketing Research* 57, no. 1 (2020): 20–34, https://doi.org/10.1177/0022243719879711.

20. "Native Advertising: A Guide for Businesses."

21. "Native Advertising: A Guide for Businesses"; Federal Trade Commission, "Enforcement Policy Statement on Deceptively Formatted Advertisements," December

22, 2015, https://www.ftc.gov/system/files/documents/public_statements/896923/151222deceptiveenforcement.pdf.

22. Federal Trade Commission, "Statement in Regard to Advertisements That Appear in Feature Article Format," Press release, November 28, 1967.

23. JS&A Grp., Inc., 111 F.T.C. 522 (1989) (consent).

24. Federal Trade Commission, "FTC Consumer Protection Staff Updates Agency's Guidance to Search Engine Industry on the Need to Distinguish Between Advertisements and Search Results," press release, June 25, 2013, www.ftc.gov/news-events/press-releases/2013/06/ftc-consumer-protection-staff-updates-agencys-guidance-search.

25. Controlling the Assault of Non-Solicited Pornography and Marketing (CAN-SPAM) Act of 2003, 15 U.S.C. §§ 7701–7713 (2003).

26. "Native Advertising: A Guide for Businesses."

27. Federal Trade Commission. ".com Disclosures: How to Make Effective Disclosures in Digital Advertising," March 2013, https://www.ftc.gov/business-guidance/resources/com-disclosures-how-make-effective-disclosures-digital-advertising."

28. "Native Advertising: A Guide for Businesses."

29. Federal Trade Commission v. Garvey, 383 F.3d 891, 901 (9th Cir. 2004).

30. Deception Policy Statement, 103 F.T.C. 174 (1984).

31. Federal Trade Commission v. Direct Marketing Concepts, Inc., 569 F.Supp.2d 285 (D. Mass. 2008).

32. Federal Trade Commission, "FTC Policy Statement Regarding Advertising Substantiation," November 23, 1984, https://www.ftc.gov/legal-library/browse/ftc-policy-statement-regarding-advertising-substantiation; Federal Trade Commission, "FTC Policy Statement on Deception," October 14, 1983, https://www.ftc.gov/system/files/documents/public_statements/410531/831014deceptionstmt.pdf.

33. "FTC Policy Statement Regarding Advertising Substantiation."

34. Telebrand Corps., TV Sav., LLC, & Ajit Khubani, 140 F.T.C. 278, 291 (2005).

35. Federal Trade Commission, "Substantiation: Federal Trade Commission Advertising Guide," accessed September 26, 2023, https://www.ftc.gov/sites/default/files/attachments/training-materials/substantiation.pdf.

36. Ibid.

37. Carlill v. Carbolic Smoke Ball Co., 1 Q.B. 256 (U.K. Ct. of Appeal 1893).

38. Vulcan Metals Co. v. Simmons Mfg. Co., 248 F. 853, 857 (2d Cir. 1918).

39. Roger Colaizzi, Chris Crook, Claire Wheeler, and Taylor Sachs, "Best Explanation and Update on Puffery You Will Ever Read," Antitrust 31, no. 3 (Summer 2017): 88–90, https://www.venable.com/files/Publication/073d0951-9fa6-4977-9e68-4deb21a819d8/Presentation/PublicationAttachment/c245d881-6fd8-434e-b068-52959159e864/Best-Explanation-and-Update-on-Puffery-You-Will-Ever-Read-Antitrust-Summer-2017.pdf.

40. Pizza Hut, Inc. v. Papa Johns, Inc., 227 F.3d 489 (5th Cir. 2000), citing J. Thomas McCarthy, McCarthy on Trademark and Unfair Competition, 4th ed. (1996), § 27.38. McCarthy's commentary on puffery also states that a claim where a product is merely better than someone else's cannot be puffery.

41. Pizza Hut, Inc. v. Papa Johns, Inc., 227 F.3d 489 (5th Cir. 2000), citing W. Page Keeton et al., Prosser and Keeton on the Law of Torts, 5th ed. (1984), § 109, at 757.
42. Colaizzi et al., "Best Explanation on Puffery," 88–90.
43. Fine F. Leung, Jonathan Z. Zhang, Flora F. Gu, Yiwei Li, and Robert W. Palmatier, "Does Influencer Marketing Really Pay Off?" Harvard Business Review, November 2022, https://hbr.org/2022/11/does-influencer-marketing-really-pay-off.
44. Alexandra Sternlicht, "Top Creators 2022," Forbes, September 6, 2022, https://www.forbes.com/sites/alexandrasternlicht/2022/09/06/top-creators-2022/?sh=1884fe1c67a1.
45. Guides Concerning the Use of Endorsements and Testimonials in Advertising, Code of Federal Regulations, 16 CFR § 255, 2023.
46. 16 CFR § 255(b).
47. 16 CFR § 255.1(b).
48. 16 CFR § 255.5 (a).
49. Ibid.
50. 16 CFR § 255.5 (b)(7).
51. 16 CFR § 255.1(d)(1–3).
52. Federal Trade Commission, "The FTC's Endorsement Guides: What People Are Asking," last modified June 2023, https://www.ftc.gov/business-guidance/resources/ftcs-endorsement-guides-what-people-are-asking#SocialNetworkingSites.
53. "Disclosures 101 for Social Media Influencers," Federal Trade Commission, November 2019, https://www.ftc.gov/business-guidance/resources/disclosures-101-social-media-influencers.
54. "The FTC's Endorsement Guides."
55. Ibid.
56. Ibid.
57. Federal Trade Commission, "Fashion Nova Will Pay $4.2 Million as Part of Settlement with FTC over Allegations It Blocked Negative Reviews," January 2022, https://www.ftc.gov/news-events/news/press-releases/2022/01/fashion-nova-will-pay-42-million-part-settlement-ftc-allegations-it-blocked-negative-reviews. This was the second settlement with Fashion Nova. In 2020, the FTC entered an agreement with Fashion Nova in which the company agreed to pay $9.3 million in a settlement because of failure to provide notice to customers that they could cancel orders not received in a timely manner.
58. Federal Trade Commission, "Letter Regarding Fashion Nova Settlement," January 2022, https://www.ftc.gov/system/files/attachments/press-releases/fashion-nova-will-pay-42-million-part-settlement-ftc-allegations-it-blocked-negative-reviews/generic_letter.pdf.
59. Consumer Review Fairness Act of 2016, Pub. L. No. 114–258, 130 Stat. 1355.
60. Federal Trade Commission, "Consumer Review Fairness Act: What Businesses Need to Know," accessed September 26, 2023, https://www.ftc.gov/business-guidance/resources/consumer-review-fairness-act-what-businesses-need-know.
61. "The FTC's Endorsement Guides: What People Are Asking."

62. Simon Constable, "How the Enron Scandal Changed American Business Forever," *Time*, December 2, 2021, https://time.com/6125253/enron-scandal-changed -american-business-forever/.

63. Ibid.

64. Cayce Myers, *Public Relations History: Theory, Practice and Profession* (New York: Routledge, 2021), 91–111.

65. Banking Act of 1933, 12 U.S.C. §§ 227 et seq.; Securities Act of 1933, 15 U.S.C. §§ 77a et seq.; Securities Exchange Act of 1934, 15 U.S.C. §§ 78a et seq. The Banking Act of 1933, commonly referred to as Glass-Steagall, was eliminated in 1999 by the Gramm-Leach-Bliley Act, Pub. L. No. 106–102, 113 Stat. 1338 (1999).

66. 15 U.S.C.A. § 77q (2011).

67. U.S. Securities and Exchange Commission, "About the SEC: What We Do," last modified October, 1, 2013, https://www.sec.gov/about/about-securities -laws#secact1933.

68. U.S. Securities and Exchange Commission, "Regulation S-K," 17 CFR 229 (2023).

69. U.S. Securities and Exchange Commission, "Regulation S-X," 17 CFR Part 210 (2023).

70. Securities Act of 1933, Rule 134, 17 C.F.R. § 230.134 (2023).

71. Gilmartin Group, "Quiet Period: What It Means for Public and Private Companies," accessed September 27, 2023, https://gilmartinir.com/what-is-a-quiet-period/.

72. Gary Rivlin, "Talkative Chief Complicates an Offering by Salesforce," New York Times, June 5, 2004, https://www.nytimes.com/2004/06/05/business/talkative -chief-complicates-an-offering-by-salesforce.html.

73. Tom McDonald, "Six Commonly Asked Questions and Answers about Quiet Periods," IR Magazine, September 11, 2020, https://www.irmagazine.com/reporting/ six-commonly-asked-questions-and-answers-about-quiet-periods.

74. Securities Exchange Act of 1934, Pub. L. No. 73–291, 48 Stat. 881.

75. U.S. Securities and Exchange Commission, "The Laws That Govern the Securities Industry," last modified October 1, 2013, https://www.sec.gov/about/about -securities-laws#secexact1934.

76. Sarbanes-Oxley Act of 2002, Pub. L. No. 107–204, 116 Stat. 745 (2002). SOX was passed in part because of Enron, but other major financial catastrophes were also catalysts for the law, e.g., Worldcom and Tyco.

77. 15 U.S.C. § 7241; 18 U.S.C. § 1519.

78. 15 U.S. Code § 78m.

79. Stephen Wagner and Lee Dittmar, "The Unexpected Benefits of Sarbanes-Oxley," Harvard Business Review, April 2006, https://hbr.org/2006/04/the-unexpected -benefits-of-sarbanes-oxley.

80. Donnalyn Pompper, "The Sarbanes-Oxley Act: Impact, Processes, and Roles for Strategic Communication," International Journal of Strategic Communication 8, no. 3 (2014): 130–145, https://doi.org/10.1080/1553118X.2014.905476.

81. U.S. Copyright Office, "Copyright and Artificial Intelligence," accessed November 1, 2023, https://www.copyright.gov/ai/.

CHAPTER 5

1. Communications Decency Act of 1996, 47 U.S.C. § 230 (1996).
2. Samantha Barbas, "The Press and Libel before New York Times v. Sullivan," Columbia Journal of Law & The Arts 44, no. 4 (2021): 511–544. https://doi.org/10.52214/jla.v44i4.8195.
3. Ibid.
4. Kathleen Olson, "First Amendment Theory and Practice," in Communication and the Law, ed. W. Wat Hopkins (Northport, AL: Vision Press, 2022), 26.
5. Kyu Ho Youm, "Defamation," in Communication and the Law, ed. W. Wat Hopkins (Northport, AL: Vision Press, 2022), 88.
6. Barbas, "The Press and Libel before New York Times v. Sullivan," 517. Barbas explains that during this era of legal history, defamation lawsuits were important because of the values of the time. Professionals of all types had to preserve their reputation because of the growing commercial marketplace. Even more important was the reputation of women, particularly in terms of chastity. This is why libel per se traditionally include allegations of unchaste behavior.
7. Ibid., 520.
8. New York Times Co. v. Sullivan, 376 U.S. 254 (1964); Gertz v. Robert Welch, Inc., 418 U.S. 323 (1974).
9. Barbas, "The Press and Libel before New York Times v. Sullivan," 526.
10. Ibid., 525.
11. Curtis Publishing Co. v. Butts, 388 U.S. 130 (1967). This case involved a defamation suit by a college football athletic director at the University of Georgia, Wally Butts. In that case, the *Saturday Evening Post* alleged that Butts and University of Alabama Coach Paul "Bear" Bryant had conspired to fix the Georgia–Alabama football game in 1962 during a phone call on a party line. The source for the information was a third party who overheard this conversation on the party line. Butts sued and won over a $3 million in a verdict. Even though the Supreme Court expanded actual malice to public officials in a 5–4 decision, Butts's judgment was upheld because the court found that he could prove actual malice in the case. This case ultimately led to the financial downfall of the *Saturday Evening Post*.
12. Lundell Manufacturing Co., Inc. v. ABC, Inc., 98 F.3d 351 (8th Cir. 1996); Steaks Unlimited, Inc. v. Deaner, 623 F.2d 264, 273–74 (3d Cir. 1980); Jadwin v. Minneapolis Star & Tribune Co., 367 N.W.2d 476 (Minn. 1985).
13. Reporters Committee for Freedom of the Press, "Anti-SLAPP Laws," accessed October 3, 2023, https://www.rcfp.org/resources/anti-slapp-laws/.
14. Bose Corp. v. Consumers Union of United States, Inc., 466 U.S. 485 (1984).
15. David Bauder, Randall Chase, and Geoff Mulvihill, "Fox, Dominion reach $787M settlement over election claims," Associated Press, April 18, 2023, https://apnews.com/article/fox-news-dominion-lawsuit-trial-trump-2020-0ac71f75acfacc52ea80b3e747fb0afe.
16. Youm, "Defamation," 91.
17. Goldwater v. Ginzburg, 414 F.2d 324 (2d Cir. 1969).
18. Ibid.

19. Goldwater v. Ginzburg, 261 F.Supp. 784 (S.D.N.Y. 1966).
20. Masson v. New Yorker Magazine, Inc., 501 U.S. 496 (1991). In this case, the Supreme Court held that although misquotes can show falsity, that is not always the case.
21. Ibid., 514. This case involved a *New Yorker* article about a Jeffrey Masson's disillusionment with the theories of Sigmund Freud after he became curator of the Freud archives. He was later interviewed for a two-part story in the *New Yorker* that was then turned into a book published by Knopf. The piece in the *New Yorker* criticized Masson, and he sued the magazine for defamation, alleging that many of the statements in the article and later book used quotation marks around statements that he did not say.
22. Ibid., 515.
23. Wat Hopkins, Actual Malice Twenty-Five Years After Times v. Sullivan (New York: Prager, 1989).
24. Society of Professional Journalists, "SPJ Code of Ethics," accessed October 3, 2023, https://www.spj.org/ethicscode.asp.
25. Garrison v. Louisiana, 379 U.S. 64, 74 (1964).
26. St. Amant v. Thompson, 390 U.S. 727, 731 (1968).
27. *Black's Law Dictionary* (St. Paul, MN: Thomson West, 2004), 1298.
28. Bentley v. Bunton, 94 S.W.3d 561 (Tex. 2002).
29. Gertz v. Robert Welch, Inc., 418 U.S. 323 (1974).
30. Philadelphia Newspapers, Inc. v. Hepps, 475 U.S. 767 (1986).
31. Ibid., 776–777.
32. Milkovich v. Lorain Journal Co., 497 U.S. 1 (1990).
33. Masson v. New Yorker Magazine, Inc..
34. Guccione v. Hustler Magazine, 800 F.2d 298 (2d Cir. 1986).
35. Dykstra v. St. Martin's Press LLC, 2020 WL 2789913 (N.Y. Sup. May 9, 2020).
36. Ibid.
37. Ali Breland, "Yelp becomes Weapon in Online Political War," The Hill, July 1, 2018, https://thehill.com/policy/technology/394922-yelp-becomes-weapon-in-online-political-war/.
38. Communications Decency Act of 1996, 47 U.S.C. § 230 (1996).
39. Electronic Communications Privacy Act of 1986, Pub. L. No. 99–508, 100 Stat. 1848 (1986).
40. Dendrite International, Inc. v. Doe No. 3, 342 N.J. Super. 134, 775 A.2d 756 (App. Div. 2001). The Dendrite standard was established by the Superior Court of New Jersey. For more analysis of anonymous online subpoenas, see Cayce Myers, "To Reveal or Conceal?: Introducing the Anonymous Public Concern Test for US Defamation Lawsuits," Journal of Information Policy 5 (2015): 71–108.
41. Communications Decency Act of 1996, 47 U.S.C. § 230 (1996).
42. Telecommunications Act of 1996, Pub. L. No. 104–104, 110 Stat. 56 (1996).
43. Communications Decency Act of 1996, 47 U.S.C. § 230 (1996).
44. Rashawn Ray and Joy Anyanwu, "Why Is Elon Musk's Twitter Takeover Increasing Hate Speech?" Brookings Institution, November 23, 2022, https://www.brookings.edu/articles/why-is-elon-musks-twitter-takeover-increasing-hate-speech/.

45. Reno v. ACLU, 521 U.S. 844 (1997); Batzel v. Smith, 333 F.3d 1018 (9th Cir. 2003); Green v. AOL, 318 F.3d 465 (3d Cir. 2003); Doe v. MySpace, 528 F.3d 413 (5th Cir. 2008); Chicago Lawyers' Comm. for Civil Rights Under Law, Inc. v. Craigslist, Inc., 519 F.3d 666 (7th Cir. 2008).
46. Zeran v. America Online, Inc., 129 F.3d 327 (4th Cir. 1997).
47. Fair Housing Council of San Fernando Valley v. Roommates.Com, LLC, 521 F.3d 1157 (9th Cir. 2008) (en banc).
48. Donald Trump, @realDonaldTrump, "Revoke 230," Twitter, May 29, 2020, https://twitter.com/realDonaldTrump/status/1266387743996870656.
49. Exec. Order No. 13,925, 85 Fed. Reg. 34,079 (May 28, 2020).
50. Gonzalez v. Google LLC, 598 U.S. 617 (2023); Twitter, Inc. v. Taamneh, 598 U.S. 471 (2023).
51. Antiterrorism and Effective Death Penalty Act of 1996, Pub. L. No. 104–132, 110 Stat. 1214 (1996).
52. Ibid.
53. Complaint, Walters v. OpenAI, L.L.C., Civil Action No. 23-A-04860-2 (Ga. Super. Gwinnett Cnty. June 2, 2023).
54. Isaiah Poritz, "First ChatGPT Defamation Lawsuit to Test AI's Legal Liability," Bloomberg Law, June 12, 2023, https://news.bloomberglaw.com/ip-law/first-chatgpt-defamation-lawsuit-to-test-ais-legal-liability.
55. 29 U.S. Code § 157.
56. National Labor Relations Board, "Employee Rights," accessed October 30, 2023, https://www.nlrb.gov/about-nlrb/rights-we-protect/your-rights/employee-rights.
57. Ibid.
58. Office of the General Counsel, Division of Operations-Management, "Report of the Acting General Counsel Concerning Social Media Cases," Memorandum OM 12–31, January 24, 2012.
59. Office of the General Counsel, Division of Operations-Management, "Report of the Acting General Counsel Concerning Social Media Cases," Memorandum OM 12–59, May 30, 2012, 10–11.
60. Ibid, 3–4.
61. Ibid.
62. Ibid., 8.
63. Ibid.
64. National Labor Relations Act, sec. 7, 29 U.S.C. § 157 (1935).
65. Office of the General Counsel, Division of Operations-Management, "Report of the Acting General Counsel Concerning Social Media Cases," Memorandum OM 12–59, 10.
66. Office of the General Counsel, Division of Operations-Management, "Report of the Acting General Counsel Concerning Social Media Cases," Memorandum OM 11–74, August 18, 2011.
67. Office of the General Counsel, Division of Operations-Management, "Report of the Acting General Counsel Concerning Social Media Cases," Memorandum OM 12–59, 10.

68. Ibid., 11.
69. Cayce Myers, "The New Water Cooler: Implications for Practitioners Concerning the NLRB's Stance on Social Media and Workers' Rights," Public Relations Review 40 (2014): 547–555.

CHAPTER 6

1. Christian Wiencierz and Ulrike Röttger, "The Use of Big Data in Corporate Communication," Corporate Communications: An International Journal 22, no. 3 (2017): 258–272, https://doi.org/10.1108/CCIJ-02-2016-0015.
2. Markets and Markets, "Big Data Market by Component, Deployment Mode, Organization Size, Business Function (Finance, Marketing & Sales, HR, and Operations) & Vertical (BFSI, Manufacturing, Healthcare & Life Sciences, and Retail & Consumer Goods)—Global Forecast to 2027," accessed October 6, 2023, https://www.marketsandmarkets.com/Market-Reports/big-data-market-1068.html.
3. Samuel D. Warren and Louis D. Brandeis, "The Right to Privacy," Harvard Law Review 4 (1890): 193–220, 196.
4. Cayce Myers, "Warren, Samuel & Louis Brandeis. The Right to Privacy, 4 Harv. L. Rev. 193 (1890)," Communication Law and Policy 25, no. 4 (2020): 519–522, https://doi.org/10.1080/10811680.2020.1805984.
5. Roberson v. Rochester Folding Box Co., 64 N.E. 442 (N.Y. 1902); Pavesich v. New England Life Ins. Co., 50 S.E. 68 (Ga. 1905).
6. William Prosser, "Privacy," California Law Review 48 (1960): 383–423.
7. Ibid., 415. Presumably this quote comes from the famed recluse Greta Garbo, who is not specifically mentioned but was alive when this article was published.
8. California Consumer Privacy Rights Act (CPRA), Proposition 24, approved November 2020, effective January 1, 2023.
9. California Consumer Privacy Act of 2018, Cal. Civ. Code §§ 1798.100 et seq.
10. Virginia Consumer Data Protection Act, Va. Code Ann. §§ 59.1-572 to -578 (2021); Colorado Privacy Act, Colo. Rev. Stat. §§ 6-1-1301 to -1305 (2021).
11. California Business and Professions Code §§ 22580–22582.
12. National Conference of State Legislatures, "Privacy of Employee and Student Social Media Accounts," last modified August 8, 2022, https://www.ncsl.org/technology-and-communication/privacy-of-employee-and-student-social-media-accounts. One state, Wisconsin, also has a similar law regarding landlords and tenants.
13. Fair Credit Reporting Act, 15 U.S.C. § 1681 et seq. (1970).
14. Privacy Act of 1974, Pub. L. No. 93–579, 88 Stat. 1896 (1974).
15. Freedom of Information Act, 5 U.S.C. § 552 (1966); Privacy Act of 1974, 5 U.S.C. § 552a (1974).
16. Family Educational Rights and Privacy Act, 20 U.S.C. § 1232g (1974).
17. Electronic Communications Privacy Act of 1986, Pub. L. No. 99–508, 100 Stat. 1848 (1986). This act has two sections: the Wiretap Act and the Stored Communications Act. Recording of phone conversations is governed by state laws with most states being a one-party state for consent for recording phone conversations. However, some states require the consent of both parties. At the time of this writing the

two-party states are California, Delaware, Florida, Illinois, Maryland, Massachusetts, Montana, Nevada, New Hampshire, Pennsylvania, and Washington. The general rule is that the one- or two-party consent of recording depends on the state in which the recording is taking place. The rules for one-party states are also nuanced, so a person should not assume that one party always means just one-party consent. For example, Nevada's one-party law is interpreted to be an all-party consent according to the law's interpretation. Note that under the ECPA there are also exemptions to the ban on wiretapping when there is a court order, part of regular maintenance of services, warrant by law enforcement, FCC enforcement services, and surveillance under the Foreign Services Enforcement Act.

18. Children's Online Privacy Protection Act of 1998, 15 U.S.C. §§ 6501–6506 (1998).
19. Health Insurance Portability and Accountability Act of 1996, Pub.L. 104–191, 110 Stat. 1936.
20. Banking Act of 1933, Pub. L. No. 73–66, 48 Stat. 162 (1933).
21. Gramm-Leach-Bliley Act, Pub. L. No. 106–102, 113 Stat. 1338 (1999).
22. WJLA-TV v. Levin, 564 S.E.2d 383, 395 n.5 (Va. 2000).
23. Prosser, "Privacy," 383.
24. Restatement (Second) of Torts § 652E (1977).
25. Time v. Hill, 385 U.S. 374 (1967). The Time v. Hill case is particularly interesting for professionals working in entertainment and book publishing. The underlying facts of the case involved a married couple, the Hills, and their five children who were held hostage in their Pennsylvania home by three escaped convicts. While being held hostage the Hills were treated well, and the hostage takers were eventually arrested. The case had a high level of publicity, and was the basis of a book, *The Desperate Hours*, in which the hostage event was changed to portray the family as having been threatened and sexually assaulted by the hostage takers. The book was a best-seller and was the basis of a Broadway play, which was then covered by *Life* magazine. The magazine's coverage of the play included a recounting of the actual events of the hostage situation, and the article indicated that the Hills had experienced the events that were portrayed in the fictionalized play. Richard Nixon, then in the private practice of law, was the Hills's attorney.
26. Cantrell v. Forest City Publishing Co., 419 U.S. 245 (1974).
27. Ibid., 248–249.
28. West v. Media General Convergence, Inc., 53 S.W.3d 640 (Tenn. 2001); Eastwood v. National Enquirer, Inc., 210 Cal. App. 3d 77 (1989).
29. Roberson v. Rochester Folding Box Co., 64 N.E. 442 (NY 1902); Pavesich v. New · England Life Insurance Co., 50 S.E. 68 (GA 1905); Haelan Laboratories, Inc. v. Topps Chewing Gum, Inc., 202 F.2d 866 (2d Cir. 1953).
30. Restatement (Second) of Torts § 652C (Am. Law Inst. 1977).
31. Namath v. Sports Illustrated, 48 A.D.2d 487 (N.Y. App. Div. 1975); Hoffman v. Capitol Cities, 255 F.3d 1180 (9th Cir. 2001); Comedy III Productions, Inc. v. Gary Saderup, Inc., 25 Cal. 4th 387 (2001). Sometimes courts look at transformativeness, like copyright fair use, to determine if there is appropriation.

32. Zacchini v. Scripps Howard Broadcasting Co., 433 U.S. 562 (1977). This is a famous Supreme Court case in that it involved the televised act of being shot out of a cannon. The court likened the nonimmunization of media to appropriation to that of trademark and copyright infringement.
33. Celebrities Rights Act, Cal. Civ. Code § 3344.1 (West 2023).
34. Isaiah Poritz, "AI Deepfakes Bill Pushes Publicity Rights, Spurs Speech Concerns," Bloomberg Law, October 17, 2023, https://news.bloomberglaw.com/ip-law/ai -deepfakes-bill-pushes-publicity-rights-spurs-speech-concerns.
35. Restatement (Second) of Torts § 652D (Am. Law Inst. 1977).
36. Community Health Network v. McKenzie, 185 N.E.3d 368 (Ind. 2022), 382.
37. Gilbert v. Medical Economics Co., 665 F.2d 305 (10 Cir. 1981).
38. Sidis v. F-R Publ. Corp., 113 F.2d 806 (2d Cir. 1940), 807–808.
39. Virgil v. Time, Inc., 527 F.2d 1122 (9th Cir. 1975); Sipple v. Chronicle Pub. Co., 154 Cal. App. 3d 1040 (1984).
40. Sipple v. Chronicle Pub. Co., 154 Cal. App. 3d 1040. Sipple was a friend and supporter of Harvey Milk, the San Francisco Board of Supervisors member who was the first openly gay elected official in the United States. Many of Sipple's supporters claimed Sipple was not invited to the White House following his heroic act because of his sexual orientation. The publicity, however, was highly damaging to Sipple's health. He died at 47 years old in 1989.
41. Barber v. Time, Inc., 159 S.W.2d 291 (Mo. 1942).
42. Restatement (Second) of Torts § 652B (Am. Law Inst. 1977).
43. Ibid.
44. Shulman v. Group W Productions, Inc., 18 Cal. 4th 200 (1998).
45. Dietemann v. Time, Inc., 449 F.2d 245 (9th Cir. 1971).
46. Nader v. General Motors Corp., 255 N.E.2d 765 (N.Y. 1970).
47. Justia, "Recording Phone Calls and Conversations: 50-State Survey," last modified October 2022, https://www.justia.com/50-state-surveys/recording-phone-calls -and-conversations/. According to this survey, 15 states require more than one-party consent, while most U.S. states require only one-party consent. Federal law, 18 U.S.C. § 2511, also requires one-party consent.
48. European Union, "Regulation (EU) 2016/679 of the European Parliament and of the Council of 27 April 2016," *Official Journal of the European Union* L 119, May 4, 2016.
49. Ben Wolford, "What Are the GDPR Fines?" GDPR.eu, accessed October 24, 2023, https://gdpr.eu/fines/.
50. Anu Bradford, The Brussels Effect: How the European Union Rules the World (New York: Oxford University Press, 2020).
51. Ben Wolford, "Does the GDPR Apply to Companies Outside of the EU?" GDPR.eu, accessed October 24, 2023, https://gdpr.eu/companies-outside-of-europe/.
52. Ben Wolford, "What Is GDPR, the EU's New Data Protection Law?" GDPR.edu, accessed October 24, 2023, https://chat.openai.com/c/d3ea7f12-f306-4e6e-922b -309dec15ed05. The assignment of a DPO is subject to many misinterpretations. According to the EU, a DPO is required under certain circumstances such as when

an organization is a public authority that has surveillance capabilities and processes large amounts of personal data.

53. Wolford, "What Is GDPR, the EU's New Data Protection Law?" This list is derived from the GDPR, Chapter 3, Rights of the Data Subject.
54. General Data Protection Regulation (GDPR), art. 17.
55. Rehabilitation of Offenders Act 1974, c. 53.
56. Google v. Garcia, 786 F.3d 733 (9th Cir. 2015); Martin v. Hearst Corporation, 777 F.3d 546 (2d Cir. 2015).
57. General Data Protection Regulation (GDPR), art. 17.
58. Federal Trade Commission, "Big Data: A Tool for Inclusion or Exclusion? Understanding the Issues," January 2016, https://www.ftc.gov/system/files/documents/reports/big-data-tool-inclusion-or-exclusion-understanding-issues/160106big-data-rpt.pdf; Lina M. Khan, "Joint Statement on Enforcement Efforts Against Discrimination and Bias in Automated Systems," Federal Trade Commission, April 25, 2023, https://www.ftc.gov/system/files/ftc_gov/pdf/EEOC-CRT-FTC-CFPB-AI-Joint-Statement%28final%29.pdf.
59. The White House, "Blueprint for an AI Bill of Rights," 2023, https://www.whitehouse.gov/ostp/ai-bill-of-rights.
60. Federal Trade Commission, "FTC Chair Khan and Officials from DOJ, CFPB and EEOC Release Joint Statement on AI," April 25, 2023, https://www.ftc.gov/news-events/news/press-releases/2023/04/ftc-chair-khan-officials-doj-cfpb-eeoc-release-joint-statement-ai.
61. The White House, "Executive Order on the Safe, Secure, and Trustworthy Development and Use of Artificial Intelligence," October 30, 2023, https://www.whitehouse.gov/briefing-room/presidential-actions/2023/10/30/executive-order-on-the-safe-secure-and-trustworthy-development-and-use-of-artificial-intelligence/.
62. AI.gov, "AI.gov," accessed November 2, 2023, https://ai.gov/.

CHAPTER 7

1. U.S. Copyright Office, "An Act for the Encouragement of Learning," Statutes at Large 1 (1790): 124, accessed November 2, 2023, https://www.copyright.gov/history/1790act.pdf.
2. Zvi S. Rosen, "Federal Trademark Law: From Its Beginnings," Landslide 11, no. 4 (2019), https://www.americanbar.org/groups/intellectual_property_law/publications/landslide/2018-19/march-april/federal-trademark-law/.
3. In re Trademark Cases, 100 U.S. 82 (1879).
4. Act of Mar. 3, 1881, 21 Stat. 502.
5. Act of Feb. 20, 1905, ch. 592, § 1, 33 Stat. 724; Rosen, "Federal Trademark Law: From Its Beginnings." Rosen notes that the problem with domestic trademark infringement laws in the nineteenth century was their focus on international infringement; courts continually struck down trademark application for domestic infringement. He states that prior to 1905, registrations for trademarks totaled around 2,000 a year. For comparison, trademark registrations in the U.S. Patent and Trademark Office for the fourth quarter of 2023 exceeded 400,000 as of November 2, 2023.

"Trademarks Data Q4 2023 at a glance," U.S. Patent and Trademark Office, accessed November 2, 2023, https://www.uspto.gov/dashboard/trademarks/.

6. Act of Aug. 14, 1876, chs. 273–274, 19 Stat. 141.

7. 17 U.S.C. §101.

8. Feist Publications v. Rural Telephone Service, 499 U.S. 340, 359 (1991).

9. Ibid.

10. Thaler v. Perlmutter, ___ F.3d___, 2023 WL 533236 (D.D.C. 2023).

11. Ibid., *4.

12. Naruto v. Slater, 916 F.3d 1148 (9th Cir. 2018).

13. U.S. Copyright Office, "Copyright and Artificial Intelligence," accessed November 2, 2023, https://www.copyright.gov/ai/.

14. 17 U.S.C. §101.

15. MAI Systems Corp. v. Peak Computer, Inc., 991 F.2d 511 (9th Cir. 1993); Cartoon Network LP v. CSC Holdings, Inc., 536 F.3d 121 (2d Cir. 2008).

16. 17 U.S.C. §102(b).

17. Berkic v. Crichton, 761 F.2d 1289 (9th Cir. 1985); Hoehling v. Universal City Studios, Inc., 618 F.2d 972 (2d Cir. 1980).

18. 17 U.S.C. §102(a)(1–8).

19. 17 U.S.C. §106.

20. Cayce Myers, "Intellectual Property Issues and RFPs: Protecting Your Work," PRSay, PRSA, September 28, 2022, https://prsay.prsa.org/2022/09/28/intellectual-property-issues-and-rfps-protecting-your-work/.

21. Peter B. Hirtle, "Copyright Term and the Public Domain," Cornell University Library, last updated August 2, 2023, https://guides.library.cornell.edu/copyright/publicdomain. This chart, updated annually, is an excellent resource for seeing all of the nuances of duration of copyright both in a U.S. context and abroad.

22. Copyright Renewal Act of 1992, Pub. L. No. 102–307, 106 Stat. 264 (1992); Sonny Bono Copyright Term Extension Act, Pub. L. No. 105–298, 112 Stat. 2827 (1998). The 1992 renewal act gave automatic copyright renewal to all works made from January 1, 1964, to December 31, 1977. The Sonny Bono Term Extension Act, named for famed musician Sonny Bono of Sonny and Cher, provided for extensions to copyrights from life of the author plus 50 years to life of the author plus 75 years, and provided for an extension of valid copyrights from 1923 onward, making 2019 the effective date these older 1923 copyrights would enter the public domain. This extension is sometimes called the Mickey Mouse Act because it allowed for valuable Disney copyrights to be extended, especially Mickey Mouse, created in 1928 with the cartoon "Steamboat Willie." That copyright is set to expire in 2024, which has caused much speculation on the market impact of Disney losing this valuable copyright. The extensions under the Sonny Bono Term Extension Act were enacted to bring the U.S. copyright law in line with that of the European Union.

23. Copyright registration occurs within the U.S. Copyright Office. This can be done online and requires paying a fee.

24. Lydia Hutchinson, "George Harrison's 'My Sweet Lord,'" Performing Songwriter, February 10, 2015, https://performingsongwriter.com/george-harrison-my-sweet -lord/.

25. 17 U.S.C.A. § 107.

26. Campbell v. Acuff-Rose, 510 U.S. 569, 579 (1994) (citing Sony Corp. of America v. Universal City Studios, 464 U.S. 417 (1984).

27. Andy Warhol Foundation for the Visual Arts v. Goldsmith, 598 U.S. 508, 143 S.Ct. 1258, 1274–1275 (2023).

28. Ibid., 1292.

29. Peter J. Karol, "The transformative impact of Warhol v. Goldsmith," Artforum, June 5, 2023, https://www.artforum.com/columns/the-transformative-impact-of-_warhol -v-goldsmith_-252757/.

30. U.S. Copyright Office, "Fair Use Index," last updated February 2023, https://www .copyright.gov/fair-use/; "Measuring Fair Use: The Four Factors," Stanford University Libraries, accessed October 28, 2023, https://fairuse.stanford.edu/overview /fair-use/four-factors/.

31. Harper & Row Publishers v. Nation Enterprises, 471 U.S. 539 (1985).

32. Harper & Row Publishers v. Nation Enterprises; Gerald Ford, *A Time to Heal: The Autobiography of Gerald R. Ford* (New York: Harper & Row, 1979).

33. Ibid.

34. Margaret Mitchell, Gone with the Wind (New York: Macmillan, 1936); Alice Randall, The Wind Done Gone (Boston: Houghton Mifflin Harcourt, 2001).

35. Campbell v. Acuff Rose, 510 U.S. 569, 590 (1994).

36. Andy Warhol Foundation for the Visual Arts v. Goldsmith, 598 U.S. 508 (2023).

37. 15 U.S.C. § 1127.

38. Two Pesos, Inc. v. Taco Cabana, 505 U.S. 763 (1992).

39. Qualitex Co. v. Jacobson Products Co., 514 U.S. 159, 163–64 (1995).

40. Lanham Act, 15 U.S.C. §§ 1051–1129 (1946).

41. U.S. Patent and Trademark Office, "What Is a Trademark?" accessed October 28, 2023, https://www.uspto.gov/trademarks/basics/what-trademark.

42. U.S. Patent and Trademark Office, "Strong Trademarks," accessed November 6, 2023, https://www.uspto.gov/trademarks/basics/strong-trademarks.

43. Ibid.

44. Ibid.

45. Nola Spice Designs L.L.C. v. Haydel Enterprises, Inc., 783 F.3d 527,544 (5th Cir. 2015).

46. U.S. Patent and Trademark Office, "Strong Trademarks."

47. International Information Systems Security Certification Consortium, Inc. v. Security University, 823 F.3d 153, 161 (2d Cir. 2016).

48. Multi Time Machine Inc., v. Amazon.com, 804 F.3d 930 (9th Cir. 2015). The U.S. Court of Appeals for the Ninth Circuit held that consumer confusion does not exist when there are competitor's products offered as an alternative. The Ninth Circuit addressed this issue in a trademark infringement case where Amazon offered competitors' watches when customers searched for MTM Special Ops (a watch

Amazon does not sell) manufactured by Multi Time Machine, Inc. The court held that Amazon did not violate the Lanham Act when it displayed alternative watches that clearly were not MTM Special Ops.

49. This discussion of "No Coke. Pepsi" comes from the dissent in Multi Time Machine, Inc. v. Amazon.com, 792 F.3d 1070 (9th Cir. 2015). The phrase is adopted from the famed Olympia Diner sketch from *Saturday Night Live*, with John Belushi responding "No Coke. Pepsi" when asked for a Coke by a customer played by Jane Curtin.

50. 15 U.S.C. §1125(c)(2)(A)(i–iv).

51. Starbucks Corp. v. Wolfe's Borough Coffee, Inc., 588 F.3d 97 (2d Cir. 2009); Starbucks Corp. v. Wolfe's Borough Coffee, Inc., No. 01 Civ. 5981, 2011 WL 6747431 (S.D.N.Y. Dec. 23, 2011).

52. Toys "R" Us, Inc. v. Akkaoui, No. C 96–3381 CW, 1996 WL 772709 (N.D. Cal. 1996).

53. Vulcan Golf, LLC v. Google Inc., 726 F.Supp.2d 911 (N.D.Ill. 2010).

54. Anticybersquatting Consumer Protection Act, 15 U.S.C. § 1125(d) (1999).

55. N. Barbantonis, "Should Contributory Cybersquatting Be Actionable?" North Carolina Journal of Law & Technology 17 (2015–2016): 79–121.

56. Academy of Motion Pictures Arts and Sciences v. GoDaddy.com, Inc., No. CV 10–03738 AB, 2015 WL 5311085 (C.D. Cal. Sep. 10, 2015); Petroliam Nasional Berhad v. GoDaddy.com, Inc., 737 F.3d 546 (9th Cir. 2013).

57. Cayce Myers, "Protecting Online Image in a Digital Age: How Trademark Issues Affect PR Practice," Research Journal of the Institute for Public Relations 3, no. 1 (August 2016): 1–18.

58. Ibid., 12–16.

59. 15 U.S.C. § 1127.

60. Major League Baseball Properties v. Sed Non Olet Denarius, 817 F.Supp. 1103 (S.D.N.Y. 1994); Major League Baseball Properties v. Sed Non Olet Denarius, 859 F.Supp. 80 (2d Cir. 1994).

61. Volkswagenwerk Aktiengesellschaft v. Church, 411 F.2d 350 (9th Cir. 1969); Mattel, Inc. v. MCA Records, Inc., 296 F.3d 894 (9th Cir. 2002).

62. Linda A. Friedman, "Online Use of Third Party Trademarks: Can Your Trademark Be Used without Your Permission?" Business Law Today, American Bar Association, February 20, 2016, https://www.americanbar.org/groups/business_law/resources/business-law-today/2016-february/online-use-of-third-party-trademarks/.

63. KP Permanent Makeup Inc. v. Lasting Impression I, 543 U.S. 111 (2004).

64. Patents have a set duration of protection, usually 20 years from the date of application. A patent has the core requirements of being new, useful, and nonobvious. However, the actual requirement of patents is quite complex.

65. As of the latest information provided by the Uniform Law Commission, only New York and North Carolina have not enacted the USTA. New York has introduced the bill. North Carolina is the only state where there is no enactment nor legislative bill introducing the USTA for adoption.

66. Uniform Trade Secrets Act with 1985 Amendments §1(4).

67. Economic Espionage Act of 1996, Pub. L. No. 104–294, 110 Stat. 3488; Defend Trade Secrets Act of 2016, Pub. L. No. 114–153, 130 Stat. 376.

68. Eagle v. Morgan, 2011 WL 6739448 (E.D. Pa. 2011).

69. Phonedog v. Kravitz, 2012 WL 273323 (N.D. Cal. 2012).

70. Cayce Myers, "An Analysis of Social Media Ownership Litigation between Organizations and PR Practitioners," Public Relations Review 41 (2015): 515–522.

71. Lang Van, Inc. v. VNG Corp., 40 F.4th 1034 (9th Cir. 2022). This case was about copyright infringement but was rooted in the Federal Rules of Civil Procedure, Rule 4(k)(2), which is considered a catchall provision for personal jurisdiction. This rule occurs when a court has no general jurisdiction over a foreign defendant, but when the defendant has met certain threshold factors, they are subject to jurisdiction in the United States. Those factors are (1) the claim is based in federal law, (2) the foreign defendant is not subject to general jurisdiction elsewhere, and (3) the foreign defendant availed itself to the privileges of doing business in the United States.

CHAPTER 8

1. Cynthia Littleton, "Writers' Fear of Joining the 'Gig Economy' Fuels WGA Picket Lines," Variety, May 10, 2023, https://variety.com/2023/tv/news/gig-economy-writers-strike-1235608830/.

2. Hillel Italie, "'Game of Thrones' Creator and Other Authors Sue ChatGPT-maker OpenAI for Copyright Infringement," AP News, updated September 21, 2023, 2:03 PM EST, https://apnews.com/article/openai-lawsuit-authors-grisham-george-rr-martin-37f9073ab67ab25b7e6b2975b2a63bfe.

3. Jake Coyle, "In Hollywood Writers' Battle against AI, Humans Win (for Now)," AP News, updated September 27, 2023, 5:35 PM EST, https://apnews.com/article/hollywood-ai-strike-wga-artificial-intelligence-39ab72582c3a15f77510c9c30a45ffc8.

4. McKinsey & Company, "Jobs Lost, Jobs Gained: Workforce Transitions in a Time of Automation," December 2017, https://www.mckinsey.com/~/media/mckinsey/industries/public%20and%20social%20sector/our%20insights/what%20the%20future%20of%20work%20will%20mean%20for%20jobs%20skills%20and%20wages/mgi-jobs-lost-jobs-gained-executive-summary-december-6-2017.pdf.

5. Communications Decency Act of 1996, Pub. L. No. 104–104, 110 Stat. 133 (1996).

6. Sarah Andersen et al. v. Stability AI Ltd. et al., No. 3:23-cv-00201 (N.D. Cal. filed January 13, 2023).

7. Silverman v. OpenAI Inc., No. 2:23-cv-03416, (N.D. Cal. 2023); Tremblay v. OpenAI Inc., No. 2:23-cv-03223, (N.D. Cal. 2023).

8. The White House, "Executive Order on the Safe, Secure, and Trustworthy Development and Use of Artificial Intelligence," last modified October 30, 2023, https://www.whitehouse.gov/briefing-room/presidential-actions/2023/10/30/executive-order-on-the-safe-secure-and-trustworthy-development-and-use-of-artificial-intelligence/.

9. Frontier Technologies, "Frontier Tech: 6th Factsheet," World Intellectual Property Organization, accessed November 3, 2023, https://www.wipo.int/export/sites/www/about-ip/en/frontier_technologies/pdf/frontier-tech-6th-factsheet.pdf. The "internet of things" is a term used for interconnected devices that communicate between each other, such as household appliances. Blockchain, which is used in cryptocurrencies, is a data ledger that shares information among users and stores that data for a record.

10. Ibid.

11. Regulation (EU) 2016/679 of the European Parliament and of the Council of 27 April 2016 on the Protection of Natural Persons Regarding the Processing of Personal Data and on the Free Movement of Such Data (General Data Protection Regulation), *Official Journal of the European Union* L 119 (May 4, 2016).

12. European Parliament, "Artificial Intelligence: Threats and Opportunities," last updated June 20, 2023, https://www.europarl.europa.eu/news/en/headlines/priorities/artificial-intelligence-in-the-eu/20200918STO87404/artificial-intelligence-threats-and-opportunities.

13. European Parliament, "EU AI Act: First Regulation on Artificial Intelligence," last updated June 14, 2023, https://www.europarl.europa.eu/news/en/headlines/society/20230601STO93804/eu-ai-act-first-regulation-on-artificial-intelligence.

14. Ibid.

15. Ephrat Livni, Sarah Kessler, and Ravi Mattu, "Who Is Liable for AI Creations?" *New York Times*, June 3, 2023, https://www.nytimes.com/2023/06/03/business/who-is-liable-for-ai-creations.html.

16. "States and Cities Limit AI Use in Employment Decisions," *JD Supra*, January 23, 2023, https://www.jdsupra.com/legalnews/states-and-cities-limit-ai-use-in-8779184/. Cities and states that have this regulation as of October 2023 are New York City, Illinois, and Maryland.

17. Students for Fair Admissions v. Harvard, 600 U.S. 181 (2023).

18. The White House, "Executive Order on the Safe, Secure, and Trustworthy Development and Use of Artificial Intelligence."

19. Mariano-Florentino Cuéllar, "AI Is Winning the AI Race: Success Isn't Just Staying Ahead of China," *Foreign Policy*, June 19, 2023, https://foreignpolicy.com/2023/06/19/us-china-ai-race-regulation-artificial-intelligence/.

BIBLIOGRAPHY

42 Pa. Cons. Stat. Ann. § 5942(a).

44 Liquormart, Inc. v. Rhode Island, 517 U.S. 484 (1996).

Abrams v. United States, 250 U.S. 616 (1919).

Academy of Motion Picture Arts and Sciences v. GoDaddy.com, Inc., No. CV 10-03738 AB, 2015 WL 5311085 (C.D. Cal. Sep. 10, 2015).

Administrative Procedure Act, 5 U.S.C. §§ 500–596 (2023).

AI.gov. "AI.gov." Accessed November 2, 2023. https://ai.gov/.

Allen v. United States, 164 U.S. 492 (1896).

American Bar Association. "Canons of Professional Ethics." Amended 1963.

American Bar Association. "Model Rules of Professional Responsibility." 1969. Revised 1989.

American Counseling Association. "The Ethics Model." Accessed July 25, 2023. https://www.counseling.org/docs/default-source/vistas/the-ethics-model.pdf.

American Medical Association. "AMA's Code of Medical Ethics." 1847.

American Psychiatric Nurses Association. "A Systematic Approach to Ethical Decision Making for Nurses." Accessed July 25, 2023. https://www.apna.org/news/a-systematic-approach-to-ethical-decision-making-for-nurses/

American Society of Trial Consultants. Accessed September 17, 2023. https://www.astcweb.org/.

Andersen et al. v. Stability AI Ltd., et al., No. 3:23-cv-00201 (N.D. Cal. filed January 13, 2023).

Andy Warhol Foundation for the Visual Arts v. Goldsmith, 598 U.S. 508 (2023).

Anticybersquatting Consumer Protection Act, 15 U.S.C. § 1125(d).

Antiterrorism and Effective Death Penalty Act of 1996, Pub. L. No. 104-132, 110 Stat. 1214 (1996).

Aribarg, A., and E. M. Schwartz. "Native Advertising in Online News: Trade-Offs Among Clicks, Brand Recognition, and Website Trustworthiness." Journal of Marketing Research 57, no. 1 (2020): 20–34. https://doi.org/10.1177/0022243719879711.

Ashcroft v. American Civil Liberties Union, 535 U.S. 564 (2002).

Banking Act of 1933. 12 U.S.C. §§ 227 et seq.

Barbantonis, N. "Should Contributory Cybersquatting Be Actionable?" North Carolina Journal of Law & Technology 17 (2015–2016): 79–121.

Barbas, Samantha. "The Press and Libel Before New York Times v. Sullivan." *Columbia Journal of Law & The Arts 44*, no. 4 (2021): 511–544. https://doi.org/10.52214/jla .v44i4.8195.

Barber v. Time, Inc. 159 S.W.2d 291 (Mo. 1942).

"Barcelona Principles 2.0." *PR News Online*. Accessed July 26, 2023. https://www .prnewsonline.com/barcelona-principles-2-0/.

Baron, Dennis. "Trump's Words on January 6 Were a Clear and Present Danger." *Web of Language* (blog), February 16, 2021. https://blogs.illinois.edu/view/25/502281961.

Barzun, Charles L. "Three Forms of Legal Pragmatism." *Washington University Law Review* 95, no. 5 (2018): 1003–1034. https://openscholarship.wustl.edu/cgi/ viewcontent.cgi?article=6495&context=law_lawreview.

Bates v. State Bar of Arizona, 433 U.S. 350 (1977).

Batson v. Kentucky, 476 U.S. 79 (1986).

Batzel v. Smith, 333 F.3d 1018 (9th Cir. 2003).

Bauder, David, Randall Chase, and Geoff Mulvihill. "Fox, Dominion Reach $787m Settlement Over Election Claims." Associated Press, April 18, 2023. https://apnews .com/article/fox-news-dominion-lawsuit-trial-trump-2020-0ac71f75acfacc52ea8 0b3e747fb0afe.

Bentley v. Bunton, 94 S.W.3d 561 (Tex. 2002).

Berkic v. Crichton, 761 F.2d 1289 (9th Cir. 1985).

Berne Convention for the Protection of Literary and Artistic Works, Sept. 9, 1886, last revised July 24, 1971, 828 U.N.T.S. 221.

Berns, Walter. "Freedom of the Press and the Alien and Sedition Laws: A Reappraisal." *Supreme Court Review* 1970, no. 1 (1970): 109–159.

Bigelow v. Virginia, 421 U.S. 809 (1975).

Bipartisan Campaign Reform Act of 2002, Pub. L. No. 107-155, 116 Stat. 81.

Black's Law Dictionary. St. Paul, MN: Thomson West, 2004.

Bolger v. Youngs Drug Products Corp., 463 U.S. 60 (1983).

Bose Corp. v. Consumers Union of United States, Inc., 466 U.S. 485 (1984).

BouSamra v. Excela Health, 210 A.3d 967 (Pa. 2019).

Bradford, Anu. *The Brussels Effect: How the European Union Rules the World*. Oxford: Oxford University Press, 2020.

Branzburg v. Hayes, 408 U.S. 665 (1972).

Ali Breland, "Yelp becomes Weapon in Online Political War." The Hill, July 1, 2018. https://thehill.com/policy/technology/394922-yelp-becomes-weapon-in -online-political-war/.

Brown v. Board of Education, 347 U.S. 483 (1954).

Brown v. Entertainment Merchants Association, 564 U.S. 768 (2011).

Brown University. "Framework for Making Ethical Decisions." Accessed July 25, 2023. https://www.brown.edu/academics/science-and-technology-studies/ framework-making-ethical-decisions.

Browning, Nicholas. "Ethics and the Profession: The Crystallizing of Public Relations Practice from Association to Accreditation, 1936–1964." *American Journalism* 35, no. 2 (2018): 140–170. doi:10.1080/08821127.2018.1455400.

Buckley v. Valeo, 424 U.S. 1 (1976).
Burroughs v. United States, 290 U.S. 534 (1934).
Cage v. Louisiana, 498 U.S. 39 (1990).
California Business and Professions Code § 17500 (2022).
California Business and Professions Code §§ 22580–22582.
California Consumer Privacy Act of 2018. Cal. Civ. Code §§ 1798.100 et seq.
California Consumer Privacy Rights Act. Proposition 24. Approved November 2020.
California Evidence Code § 1070.
California Motor Transport Co. v. Trucking Unlimited, 404 U.S. 508 (1972).
Campbell v. Acuff-Rose, 510 U.S. 569, 579 (1994).
Cantrell v. Forest City Publishing Co., 419 U.S. 245 (1974).
Cantwell v. Connecticut, 310 U.S. 296 (1940).
Carlill v. Carbolic Smoke Ball Co., 1 Q.B. 256 (UK Ct. of Appeal 1893).
Cartoon Network LP v. CSC Holdings, Inc., 536 F.3d 121 (2d Cir. 2008).
"Categorical Imperatives and the Case for Deception: Part I," Teachers College, Columbia University. *Institutional Review Board (IRB) Blog*, July 13, 2020. https://www.tc .columbia.edu/institutional-review-board/irb-blog/2020/categorical-imperatives -and-the-case-for-deception-part-i/.
Celebrities Rights Act, Cal. Civ. Code § 3344.1 (West 2023).
Central Hudson Gas & Electric Corp. v. Public Service Commission, 447 U.S. 557 (1980).
"Certiorari." Legal Information Institute, Cornell Law School. Accessed September 21, 2023. https://www.law.cornell.edu/wex/certiorari.
Chaplinsky v. New Hampshire, 315 U.S. 568 (1942).
Chevron U.S.A., Inc. v. Natural Resources Defense Council, Inc., 467 U.S. 837 (1984).
Chicago Lawyers' Comm. for Civil Rights Under Law, Inc. v. Craigslist, Inc., 519 F.3d 666 (7th Cir. 2008).
Children's Online Privacy Protection Act of 1998. 15 U.S.C. §§ 6501–6506 (1998).
Church & Dwight Co., Inc. v. SPD Swiss Precision Diagnostics, 2014 WL 7238354 (S.D.N.Y. 2014).
Citizens United v. Federal Election Commission, 558 U.S. 310 (2010).
City of Los Angeles v. Alameda Books, 535 U.S. 425, 455 (2002) (Souter, J., dissenting).
Claeys, An-Sofie, and Michaël Opgenhaffen. "Why Practitioners Do (Not) Apply Crisis Communication Theory in Practice." *Journal of Public Relations Research* 28, no. 5–6 (2016): 232–247. doi: 10.1080/1062726X.2016.1261703.
Colaizzi, Roger, Chris Crook, Claire Wheeler, and Taylor Sachs. "Best Explanation and Update on Puffery You Will Ever Read." Antitrust 31, no. 3 (Summer 2017): 88–90. https://www.venable.com/files/Publication/073d0951-9fa6-4977 -9e68-4deb21a819d8/Presentation/PublicationAttachment/c245d881-6fd8-434e -b068-52959159e864/Best-Explanation-and-Update-on-Puffery-You-Will-Ever -Read-Antitrust-Summer-2017.pdf.
Colorado Privacy Act, Colo. Rev. Stat. §§ 6-1-1301 to -1305 (2021).
Comedy III Productions, Inc. v. Gary Saderup, Inc., 25 Cal. 4th 387 (2001).
Commodity Futures Trading Commission v. Weintraub, 471 U.S. 343 (1985).

"Common Good." *Stanford Encyclopedia of Philosophy.* Accessed July 25, 2023. https://plato.stanford.edu/entries/common-good/.

Communications Decency Act of 1996. Pub. L. No. 104-104, 110 Stat. 133, 47 U.S.C. § 230 (1996).

Community Health Network v. McKenzie. 185 N.E.3d 368 (Ind. 2022), 382.

Connally v. General Construction Company, 269 U.S. 385 (1926).

Constable, Simon. "How the Enron Scandal Changed American Business Forever." *Time,* December 2, 2021. https://time.com/6125253/enron-scandal-changed-american-business-forever/.

Constitution of the United States. Amendment 1.

Consumer Review Fairness Act of 2016. Pub. L. No. 114-258, 130 Stat. 1355.

Controlling the Assault of Non-Solicited Pornography and Marketing (CAN-SPAM) Act, 15 U.S.C. §§ 7701–7713 (2003).

Coombs, Timothy. "Choosing the Right Words: The Development of Guidelines for the Selection of the 'Appropriate' Crisis-Response Strategies." *Management Communication Quarterly* 8, no. 4 (1995): 447–476. doi: 10.1177/0893318995008004003.

Coombs, Timothy, and Sherry Holladay. "Communication and Attributions in a Crisis: An Experimental Study in Crisis Communication." *Journal of Public Relations Research* 8, no. 4 (1996): 279–295. doi: 10.1207/s1532754xjprr0804_04.

Copyright Renewal Act, Pub. L. No. 102-307, 106 Stat. 264 (1992).

Coyle, Jake. "In Hollywood Writers' Battle Against AI, Humans Win (For Now)." AP News. Updated September 27, 2023, 5:35 PM EST. https://apnews.com/article/hollywood-ai-strike-wga-artificial-intelligence-39ab72582c3a15f77510c9c30a45ffc8.

Cuéllar, Mariano-Florentino. "AI Is Winning the AI Race: Success Isn't Just Staying Ahead of China." *Foreign Policy,* June 19, 2023. https://foreignpolicy.com/2023/06/19/us-china-ai-race-regulation-artificial-intelligence/.

Curtis Publishing Co. v. Butts, 388 U.S. 130 (1967).

Cutlip, Scott M., and Allen H. Center. *Effective Public Relations,* 2nd ed. Englewood Cliffs, NJ: Prentice-Hall, Inc., 1958.

Dartmouth College v. Woodward, 17 U.S. (4 Wheat.) 518 (1819).

Defend Trade Secrets Act of 2016, Pub. L. No. 114-153, 130 Stat. 376.

Dendrite International, Inc. v. Doe No. 3, 342 N.J. Super. 134, 775 A.2d 756 (App. Div. 2001).

Dennis v. United States, 341 U.S. 494 (1951).

Dhanesh, Ganga S. "Putting Engagement in its PRoper Place: State of the Field, Definition and Model of Engagement in Public Relations." Public Relations Review 43, no. 5 (December 2017): 925–933. https://doi.org/10.1016/j.pubrev.2017.04.001.

Dietemann v. Time, Inc. 449 F.2d 245 (9th Cir. 1971).

Dietrich, Gini. *Spin Sucks: Communication and Reputation Management in the Digital Age.* Indianapolis: Que Publishing, 2014.

Digital Mentor v. Ovivo, 2020 WL 550746 (W.D. Wash. 2020).

District of Columbia v. Heller, 554 U.S. 570 (2008).

Dobbs v. Jackson Women's Health Organization, 597 U.S. ___ (2022).

Doe v. MySpace, 528 F.3d 413 (5th Cir. 2008).

Drucker, Peter. "The Effective Decision," *Harvard Business Review,* January 1967, https://hbr.org/1967/01/the-effective-decision.

Durant, Will. *The Story of Philosophy: The Lives and Opinions of the Greater Philosophers,* 2nd ed. New York: Simon and Schuster, 1933.

Dworkin, Ronald. *Law's Empire.* Cambridge, MA: Harvard University Press, 1986.

Dykstra v. St. Martin's Press LLC, 2020 WL 2789913 (N.Y. Sup. May 9, 2020).

Eagle v. Morgan, No. 11-4303, 2011 WL 6739448 (E.D. Pa. Dec. 22, 2011).

Eastern Railroad Presidents Conference v. Noerr Motor Freight, Inc., 365 U.S. 127 (1961).

Eastwood v. National Enquirer, Inc., 210 Cal. App. 3d 77 (1989).

Economic Espionage Act of 1996, Pub. L. No. 104-294, 110 Stat. 3488.

Electronic Communications Privacy Act of 1986, Pub. L. No. 99-508, 100 Stat. 1848 (1986).

"Ethics." *Merriam-Webster.com Dictionary.* Accessed July 25, 2023. https://www.merriam-webster.com/dictionary/ethics.

Ethics & Compliance Initiative. "Global Business Ethics Survey." Accessed July 24, 2023, https://www.ethics.org/global-business-ethics-survey/.

Ethics Reform Act of 1989, Pub. L. No. 101-194, 103 Stat. 1760, 2 U.S.C. and 5 U.S.C.

European Parliament. "EU AI Act: First Regulation on Artificial Intelligence." June 8, 2023. https://www.europarl.europa.eu/news/en/headlines/society/20230601STO93804/eu-ai-act-first-regulation-on-artificial-intelligence.

European Parliament. "Artificial Intelligence: Threats and Opportunities." Last updated June 20, 2023. https://www.europarl.europa.eu/news/en/headlines/priorities/artificial-intelligence-in-the-eu/20200918STO87404/artificial-intelligence-threats-and-opportunities.

European Parliament, and Council of the European Union. "Regulation (EU) 2016/679 of the European Parliament and of the Council of 27 April 2016 on the Protection of Natural Persons with Regard to the Processing of Personal Data and on the Free Movement of Such Data, and Repealing Directive 95/46/EC (General Data Protection Regulation)." *Official Journal of the European Union* L 119 (2016): 1–88.

European Union. "Regulation (EU) 2016/679 of the European Parliament and of the Council of 27 April 2016." *Official Journal of the European Union* L 119, May 4, 2016.

Executive Order No. 13925. "Preventing Online Censorship." 85 Fed. Reg. 34079 (May 28, 2020).

Fair Credit Reporting Act. 15 U.S.C. § 1681 et seq. (1970).

Fair Housing Council of San Fernando Valley v. Roommates.Com, LLC, 521 F.3d 1157 (9th Cir. 2008) (en banc).

Family Educational Rights and Privacy Act, 20 U.S.C. § 1232g (1974).

FEC v. Wisconsin Right to Life, Inc., 551 U.S. 449 (2007).

Federal Communications Commission. "Obscene, Indecent and Profane Broadcasts." January 13, 2021. https://www.fcc.gov/consumers/guides/obscene-indecent-and-profane-broadcasts.

Federal Election Campaign Act of 1971, Pub. L. No. 92-225, 86 Stat. 3.

Federal Rules of Civil Procedure, Rule 47(b).

Federal Rules of Criminal Procedure, Rule 24(b)(1).

Federal Rules of Criminal Procedure, Rule 24(b)(2).

Federal Rules of Evidence, Rule 801(d)(2).

Federal Rules of Evidence, Rule 801(d)(2)(a-e).

Federal Trade Commission v. Direct Marketing Concepts, Inc., 569 F.Supp.2d 285 (D. Mass. 2008).

Federal Trade Commission v. Garvey, 383 F.3d 891 (9th Cir. 2004).

Federal Trade Commission. "Big Data: A Tool for Inclusion or Exclusion? Understanding the Issues." January 2016. https://www.ftc.gov/system/files/documents/reports/big -data-tool-inclusion-or-exclusion-understanding-issues/160106big-data-rpt.pdf.

Federal Trade Commission. ".com Disclosures: How to Make Effective Disclosures in Digital Advertising," March 2013, https://www.ftc.gov/business-guidance/ resources/com-disclosures-how-make-effective-disclosures-digital-advertising.

Federal Trade Commission. "Consumer Review Fairness Act: What Businesses Need to Know." Accessed September 26, 2023. https://www.ftc.gov/business-guidance/ resources/consumer-review-fairness-act-what-businesses-need-know.

Federal Trade Commission. "Coronavirus: Enforcement Warning Letters." Accessed September 26, 2023. https://www.ftc.gov/news-events/features/coronavirus/ enforcement/warning-letters.

Federal Trade Commission. "Disclosures 101 for Social Media Influencers." November 2019. https://www.ftc.gov/business-guidance/resources/disclosures-101-social -media-influencers.

Federal Trade Commission. "Enforcement Policy Statement on Deceptively Formatted Advertisements." December 22, 2015. https://www.ftc.gov/system/files/documents /public_statements/896923/151222deceptiveenforcement.pdf.

Federal Trade Commission. "Fashion Nova Will Pay $4.2 Million as Part of Settlement with FTC over Allegations It Blocked Negative Reviews." January 2022. https:// www.ftc.gov/news-events/news/press-releases/2022/01/fashion-nova-will-pay-42 -million-part-settlement-ftc-allegations-it-blocked-negative-reviews.

Federal Trade Commission. "FTC Chair Khan and Officials from DOJ, CFPB and EEOC Release Joint Statement on AI." April 25, 2023. https://www.ftc.gov/ news-events/news/press-releases/2023/04/ftc-chair-khan-officials-doj-cfpb-eeoc -release-joint-statement-ai.

Federal Trade Commission. "FTC Consumer Protection Staff Updates Agency's Guid-ance to Search Engine Industry on the Need to Distinguish Between Advertise-ments and Search Results." Press release, June 25, 2013. www.ftc.gov/news-events /press-releases/2013/06/ftc-consumer-protection-staff-updates-agencys-guidance -search.

Federal Trade Commission. "The FTC's Endorsement Guides: What People Are Ask-ing." Last modified June 2023. https://www.ftc.gov/business-guidance/resources/ ftcs-endorsement-guides-what-people-are-asking#SocialNetworkingSites.

Federal Trade Commission. "FTC Policy Statement on Deception." October 14, 1983. https://www.ftc.gov/system/files/documents/public_statements/410531/831014deceptionstmt.pdf.

Federal Trade Commission. "FTC Policy Statement Regarding Advertising Substantiation." November 23, 1984. https://www.ftc.gov/legal-library/browse/ftc-policy-statement-regarding-advertising-substantiation.

Federal Trade Commission. "Glossary of Scams and Legal Terms." Accessed September 26, 2023. https://www.ftc.gov/news-events/topics/glossary-scams-legal-terms.

Federal Trade Commission. "Letter Regarding Fashion Nova Settlement." January 2022. https://www.ftc.gov/system/files/attachments/press-releases/fashion-nova-will-pay-42-million-part-settlement-ftc-allegations-it-blocked-negative-reviews/generic_letter.pdf.

Federal Trade Commission. "Native Advertising: A Guide for Businesses." 2015. https://www.ftc.gov/business-guidance/resources/native-advertising-guide-businesses.

Federal Trade Commission. "Statement in Regard to Advertisements That Appear in Feature Article Format." Press release, November 28, 1967.

Federal Trade Commission Act of 1914. 15 U.S.C. §§ 41–58.

Federal Trade Commission Staff. "FTC Staff Report Concerning Enforcement Perspectives on the Noerr-Pennington Doctrine." October 2006. https://www.ftc.gov/sites/default/files/documents/reports/ftc-staff-report-concerning-enforcement-perspectives-noerr-pennington-doctrine/p013518enfperspectnoerr-penningtondoctrine.pdf.

Feist Publications v. Rural Telephone Service, 499 U.S. 340, 359 (1991).

Feitelberg, Rosemary. "Supreme Court Victor Lynn Goldsmith Talks Warhol, Prince and Celebrity Facades." *WWD*, May 19, 2023. https://wwd.com/eye/people/lynn-goldsmith-prince-photograph-andy-warhol-supreme-court-interview-1235658276/.

Finzi, Benjamin. "CEO Decision Making: Emotional Fortitude." Deloitte Insights, Spring 2021. https://www2.deloitte.com/us/en/insights/topics/leadership/ceo-decision-making-emotional-fortitude.html.

First National Bank of Boston v. Bellotti, 435 U.S. 765 (1978).

Fitzpatrick, Kathy. "Public Relations and the Law: A Survey of Practitioners." *Public Relations Review* 22, no. 1 (1996): 1–8. doi: 10.1016/S0363-8111(96)90067-3.

Fitzpatrick, Kathy, and Mark Rubin. "Public Relations vs. Legal Strategies in Organizational Crisis Decisions." *Public Relations Review* 21, no. 1 (1995): 21–33. doi: 10.1016/0363-8111(95)90037-3.

Ford, Gerald R. *A Time to Heal: The Autobiography of Gerald R. Ford.* New York: Harper & Row, 1979.

Freedom of Information Act, 5 U.S.C. § 552 (1966).

Friedman, Linda A. "Online Use of Third Party Trademarks: Can Your Trademark Be Used without Your Permission?" *Business Law Today*, American Bar Association, February 20, 2016. https://www.americanbar.org/groups/business_law/resources/business-law-today/2016-february/online-use-of-third-party-trademarks/.

Friedman, Milton. "The Social Responsibility of Business Is to Increase Its Profits." *New York Magazine*, September 13, 1970. http://websites.umich.edu/~thecore/doc/Friedman.pdf.

Frontier Technologies. "Frontier Tech: 6th Factsheet." World Intellectual Property Organization. Accessed November 3, 2023. https://www.wipo.int/export/sites/www/about-ip/en/frontier_technologies/pdf/frontier-tech-6th-factsheet.pdf.

Garner, Bryan. *Garner's Modern English Usage*, 5th ed. Oxford: Oxford University Press, 2022.

Garrison v. Louisiana, 379 U.S. 64 (1964).

General Data Protection Regulation (GDPR), art. 17.

Gertz v. Robert Welch, Inc., 418 U.S. 323 (1974).

Gilbert v. Medical Economics Co. 665 F.2d 305 (10th Cir. 1981).

Gilmartin Group, "Quiet Period: What It Means for Public and Private Companies," Accessed September 27, 2023, https://gilmartinir.com/what-is-a-quiet-period/.

Gitlow v. New York, 268 U.S. 652 (1925).

Goldwater v. Ginzburg, 261 F. Supp. 784 (S.D.N.Y. 1966).

Goldwater v. Ginzburg, 414 F.2d 324 (2d Cir. 1969).

Gonzalez v. Google LLC, 598 U.S. 617 (2023).

Gooding v. Wilson, 405 U.S. 518 (1972).

Google v. Garcia, 786 F.3d 733 (9th Cir. 2015)

Gou, Angie. "As Unanimity Declines, Conservative Majority's Power Runs Deeper Than the Blockbuster Cases." *SCOTUSblog*. July 3, 2022. https://www.scotusblog.com/2022/07/as-unanimity-declines-conservative-majoritys-power-runs-deeper-than-the-blockbuster-cases/.

Gower, Karla. Legal and Ethical Considerations for Public Relations. 3rd ed. Long Grove, IL: Waveland Press, 2018.

Gower, Karla K., and Margot Opdycke Lamme. "Public Relations On Trial: The Railroad-Trucker's Brawl." *Journalism History* 29, no. 1 (Spring 2003): 12–20. https://doi.org/10.1080/00947679.2003.12062616.

Gramm-Leach-Bliley Act. Pub. L. No. 106-102, 113 Stat. 1338 (1999).

Grayned v. City of Rockford, 408 U.S. 104 (1972).

Green v. AOL, 318 F.3d 465 (3d Cir. 2003)

Grey, Thomas C. "Holmes and Legal Pragmatism." *Stanford Law Review* 41, no. 4 (April 1989): 787–870.

Guccione v. Hustler Magazine, 800 F.2d 298 (2d Cir. 1986).

Guides Concerning the Use of Endorsements and Testimonials in Advertising, 16 CFR § 255.

Guinness World Records. "Longest Jury Deliberation." Accessed September 21, 2023. https://www.guinnessworldrecords.com/world-records/93247-longest-jury-deliberation.

Haelan Laboratories, Inc. v. Topps Chewing Gum, Inc., 202 F.2d 866 (2d Cir. 1953).

Harlow, Rex. "A Timeline of Public Relations Development." *Public Relations Review* 6, no. 3 (1980): 3–13. https://doi.org/10.1016/s0363-8111(80)80007-5.

Harper & Row Publishers, Inc. v. Nation Enterprises, 471 U.S. 539 (1985).

Hatch Act of 1939, 5 U.S.C. §§ 1501–1508 (1939).

Health Insurance Portability and Accountability Act of 1996. Pub.L. 104–191, 110 Stat. 1936.

Hirtle, Peter B. "Copyright Term and the Public Domain." Cornell University Library, last updated August 2, 2023. https://guides.library.cornell.edu/copyright/publicdomain.

Hoehling v. Universal City Studios, Inc., 618 F.2d 972 (2d Cir. 1980).

Hoffman v. Capitol Cities, 255 F.3d 1180 (9th Cir. 2001).

Holder v. Humanitarian Law Project, 561 U.S. 1 (2010).

Honest Leadership and Open Government Act of 2007, Pub. L. No. 110-81, 121 Stat. 735, 2 U.S.C. and 5 U.S.C.

Hopkins, Wat. Actual Malice Twenty-Five Years After Times v. Sullivan. New York: Prager, 1989.

Hudson, David. "Obscenity and Pornography." Middle Tennessee State University, 2009. https://www.mtsu.edu:8443/first-amendment/article/1004/obscenity-and-pornography.

Hustler Magazine v. Falwell, 485 U.S. 46 (1988).

Hutchinson, Lydia. "George Harrison's 'My Sweet Lord.'" *Performing Songwriter*, February 10, 2015. https://performingsongwriter.com/george-harrison-my-sweet-lord/.

Ibanez v. Florida Department of Business and Professional Regulation, Board of Accountancy, 512 U.S. 136 (1994).

Ikonen, Pasi, Vilma Luoma-aho, and Shannon A. Bowen. "Transparency for Sponsored Content: Analysing Codes of Ethics in Public Relations, Marketing, Advertising and Journalism." International Journal of Strategic Communication 11, no. 2 (April–June 2017): 165–178. https://doi.org/10.1080/1553118X.2016.1252917.

In re Copper Mkt. Antitrust Litig., 200 F.R.D. 213 (S.D.N.Y. 2001).

In re Judith Miller. Historical Society of the District of Columbia Circuit. Accessed October 31, 2023. https://dcchs.org/in-re-judith-miller/.

In re Signet Jewelers Ltd. Sec. Litig., 332 F.R.D. 131 (S.D.N.Y. 2019).

In re RMJ, 455 U.S. 191 (1982).

In re Trademark Cases, 100 U.S. 82 (1879).

In re Winship, 397 U.S. 358 (1970).

International Association of Business Communicators. "Code of Ethics." Accessed July 25, 2023. https://www.iabc.com/About/Purpose/Code-of-Ethics.

International Information Systems Security Certification Consortium, Inc. v. Security University, 823 F.3d 153 (2d Cir. 2016).

International Public Relations Association. *Code of Athens*. Accessed July 26, 2023. https://www.ipra.org/static/media/uploads/pdfs/ipra_code_of_athens.pdf.

International Public Relations Association. "Code of Conduct." Accessed September 26, 2023. https://www.ipra.org/member-services/code.

Italie, Hillel. "'Game of Thrones' Creator and Other Authors Sue ChatGPT-maker OpenAI for Copyright Infringement." *AP News*. Updated September 21, 2023, 2:03 PM EST. https://apnews.com/article/openai-lawsuit-authors-grisham-george-rr-martin-37f9073ab67ab25b7e6b2975b2a63bfe.

Jackson v. Virginia, 443 U.S. 307 (1979).

Jacobellis v. Ohio, 378 U.S. 187 (1964).

Jadwin v. Minneapolis Star & Tribune Co., 367 N.W.2d 476 (Minn. 1985).

J.E.B. v. Alabama ex rel. T.B.," 511 U.S. 127 (1994).

Josephson Institute. "The Seven-Step Path to Better Decisions." Accessed July 25, 2023. https://josephsoninstitute.org/med-4sevensteppath/.

JS&A Group, Inc., 111 F.T.C. 522 (1989) (consent).

Judiciary Act of 1869, ch. 22, 16 Stat. 44.

Jury Acquits Simpson: Throngs Cheer Verdict." *Los Angeles Times*, October 4, 1995. https://www.latimes.com/archives/la-xpm-1995.

Justia. "Recording Phone Calls and Conversations: 50-State Survey." Last modified October 2022. https://www.justia.com/50-state-surveys/recording-phone-calls -and-conversations/.

Karol, Peter J. "The Transformative Impact of Warhol v. Goldsmith." *Artforum*, June 5, 2023. https://www.artforum.com/columns/the-transformative-impact-of-_warhol -v-goldsmith_-252757/.

Kasky v. Nike, Inc., 93 Cal. Rptr. 2d 854 (Cal. Ct. App. 2000).

Kelleher, Tom. *Public Relations*. 2nd ed. Oxford: Oxford University Press, 2021.

Kennedy, David W. "Critical Theory, Structuralism and Contemporary Legal Scholarship." *New England Law Review* 21 (1986): 209–289.

Khan, Lina M. "Joint Statement on Enforcement Efforts Against Discrimination and Bias in Automated Systems." Federal Trade Commission, April 25, 2023. https://www.ftc.gov/system/files/ftc_gov/pdf/EEOC-CRT-FTC-CFPB-AI-Joint -Statement%28final%29.pdf.

Killion, Victoria L. "Free Speech: When and Why Content-Based Laws Are Presumptively Unconstitutional." *Congressional Research Service*, January 10, 2023. https://crsreports.congress.gov/product/pdf/IF/IF12308. Accessed August 6, 2023.

KP Permanent Makeup, Inc. v. Lasting Impression I, Inc., 543 U.S. 111 (2004).

Labor Management Relations Act of 1947, 29 U.S.C. §§ 141–197 (1947).

Lang Van, Inc. v. VNG Corp., 40 F.4th 1034 (9th Cir. 2022).

Lanham Act, 15 U.S.C. §§ 1051–1129.

"Law." *Merriam-Webster Legal Dictionary*. Accessed July 25, 2023. https://www.merriam -webster.com/dictionary/law#legalDictionary.

Lee, Jongmin, Susan Jares, and Robert Heath. "Decision-Making Encroachment and Cooperative Relationships Between Public Relations and Legal Counselors in the Management of Organizational Crisis." *Journal of Public Relations Research* 11, no. 3 (1999): 243–270. doi: 10.1207/s1532754xjprr1103_03.

Leung, Fine F., Jonathan Z. Zhang, Flora F. Gu, Yiwei Li, and Robert W. Palmatier. "Does Influencer Marketing Really Pay Off?" Harvard Business Review, November 2022. https://hbr.org/2022/11/does-influencer-marketing-really-pay-off.

Licensed Professional Counselors Association of Georgia. "Models of Decision Making." Accessed July 25, 2023. https://www.lpcaga.org/assets/ Models%20of%20Decision%20Making%202.pdf

Littleton, Cynthia. "Writers' Fear of Joining the 'Gig Economy' Fuels WGA Picket Lines." Variety, May 10, 2023. https://variety.com/2023/tv/news/gig-economy -writers-strike-1235608830/.

Livni, Ephrat, Sarah Kessler, and Ravi Mattu. "Who Is Liable for AI Creations?" *New York Times*. June 3, 2023. https://www.nytimes.com/2023/06/03/business/who-is -liable-for-ai-creations.html.

Lobbying Disclosure Act of 1995, Pub. L. No. 104-65, 109 Stat. 691, 2 U.S.C. §§ 1601–1612.

Loper Bright Enterprises, et al. v. Raimondo, Secretary of Commerce, et al., No. 22-451, docketed Nov. 15, 2022 (U.S.), on appeal from 21-5166 (D.C. Cir. Aug. 12, 2022).

Lorillard Tobacco Co. v. Reilly, 533 U.S. 525 (2001).

Lundell Manufacturing Co., Inc. v. ABC, Inc., 98 F.3d 351 (8th Cir. 1996).

"Lynn Goldsmith on Her Prince Photograph, Andy Warhol and the Supreme Court," *WWD*, May 19, 2023, https://wwd.com/eye/people/lynn-goldsmith-prince-.

MAI Systems Corp. v. Peak Computer, Inc., 991 F.2d 511 (9th Cir. 1993).

Major League Baseball Properties, Inc. v. Sed Non Olet Denarius, Ltd., 817 F.Supp. 1103 (S.D.N.Y. 1993).

Marbury v. Madison, 5 U.S. (1 Cranch) 137 (1803).

MarketsandMarkets. "Big Data Market by Component, Deployment Mode, Organization Size, Business Function (Finance, Marketing & Sales, HR, and Operations) & Vertical (BFSI, Manufacturing, Healthcare & Life Sciences, and Retail & Consumer Goods)— Global Forecast to 2027." Accessed October 6, 2023. https://www .marketsandmarkets.com/Market-Reports/big-data-market-1068.html.

Martin v. Hearst Corporation, 777 F.3d 546 (2d Cir. 2015).

Masson v. New Yorker Magazine, Inc., 501 U.S. 496 (1991).

Mattel, Inc. v. MCA Records, Inc., 296 F.3d 894 (9th Cir. 2002).

McConnell v. FEC, 540 U.S. 93 (2003).

McCutcheon v. Federal Election Commission, 572 U.S. 185 (2014).

McDonald, Tom. "Six Commonly Asked Questions and Answers about Quiet Periods." IR Magazine, September 11, 2020. https://www.irmagazine.com/reporting/six -commonly-asked-questions-and-answers-about-quiet-periods.

McKinsey & Company. "Jobs Lost, Jobs Gained: Workforce Transitions in a Time of Automation." December 2017. https://www.mckinsey.com/~/media/mckinsey /industries/public%20and%20social%20sector/our%20insights/what%20the %20future%20of%20work%20will%20mean%20for%20jobs%20skills%20and %20wages/mgi-jobs-lost-jobs-gained-executive-summary-december-6-2017.pdf.

McKinsey & Company. "Patagonia Shows How Turning a Profit Doesn't Have to Cost the Earth." Accessed July 25, 2023. https://www.mckinsey.com/industries /agriculture/our-insights/patagonia-shows-how-turning-a-profit-doesnt-have-to -cost-the-earth

"Measuring Fair Use: The Four Factors." Stanford University Libraries, Accessed October 28, 2023. https://fairuse.stanford.edu/overview/fair-use/four-factors/.

Memoirs v. Massachusetts, 383 U.S. 413 (1966).

Milkovich v. Lorain Journal Co., 497 U.S. 1 (1990).

Mill, John Stuart. *On Liberty, Utilitarianism, and Other Essays*. London: Oxford University Press, 2015.

Miller v. California, 413 U.S. 15 (1973).

Miranda v. Arizona, 384 U.S. 436 (1966).

Mitchell, Margaret. *Gone with the Wind*. New York: Macmillan, 1936.

Multi Time Machine Inc. v. Amazon.com, 792 F.3d 1070 (9th Cir. 2015).

Multi Time Machine Inc., v. Amazon.com, 804 F.3d 930 (9th Cir. 2015).

Myers, Cayce. "An Analysis of Social Media Ownership Litigation Between Organizations and PR Practitioners." *Public Relations Review* 41, no. 4 (2015): 515–522. doi: 10.1016/j.pubrev.2015.05.003.

Myers, Cayce. "Apology, Sympathy, and Empathy: The Legal Ramifications of Admitting Fault in U.S. Public Relations Practice." *Public Relations Review* 42, no. 1 (March 2016): 176–183.

Myers, Cayce. "Intellectual Property Issues and RFPs: Protecting Your Work." PRSay. PRSA, September 28, 2022. https://prsay.prsa.org/2022/09/28/intellectual-property-issues-and-rfps-protecting-your-work/.

Myers, Cayce. "The Law in Modern Society." In *Communication and the Law*, edited by W. Hopkins, 1–21. Northport, AL: Vision Press, 2023.

Myers, Cayce. "The New Water Cooler: Implications for Practitioners Concerning the NLRB's Stance on Social Media and Workers' Rights." Public Relations Review 40 (2014): 547–555.

Myers, Cayce. "Protecting Online Image in a Digital Age: How Trademark and Parody Issues Affect PR Practice." *Research Journal for the Institute for Public Relations* 3, no. 1 (2016): 1–18.

Myers, Cayce. "Public Relations Confidentiality: An Analysis of PR Practitioner–Client Privilege in High Profile Litigation." *Public Relations Review* 41, no. 1 (March 2015): 14–21.

Myers, Cayce. *Public Relations History: Theory, Practice and Profession*. New York: Routledge, 2021.

Myers, Cayce. "Public Relations or 'Grassroots Lobbying'? How Lobbying Laws Are Re-Defining PR Practice." *Public Relations Review* 44, no. 1 (2018): 11–21. https://doi.org/10.1016/j.pubrev.2017.11.006.

Myers, Cayce. "Regulating Public Relations: How U.S. Legal Policies and Regulations Shaped Early Corporate Public Relations." American Journalism 37, no. 2 (Spring 2020): 139–164. https://doi.org/10.1080/08821127.2020.1750883.

Myers, Cayce. "To Reveal or Conceal?: Introducing the Anonymous Public Concern Test for US Defamation Lawsuits." Journal of Information Policy 5 (2015): 71–108.

Myers, Cayce. "Warren, Samuel & Louis Brandeis. The Right to Privacy, 4 Harv. L. Rev. 193 (1890)." *Communication Law and Policy* 25, no. 4 (2020): 519–522. https://doi.org/10.1080/10811680.2020.1805984.

Myers, Cayce. "What's the Legal Definition of PR?: An Analysis of Commercial Speech and Public Relations.," *Public Relations Review* 42 (2016): 821–831.

Nader v. General Motors Corp. 255 N.E.2d 765 (N.Y. 1970).

Namath v. Sports Illustrated, 48 A.D.2d 487 (N.Y. App. Div. 1975).

Naruto v. Slater, 916 F.3d 1148 (9th Cir. 2018).

National Advertising Division, Better Business Bureau. "Better Business Bureau Programs." Accessed September 26, 2023. https://bbbprograms.org/programs/all -programs/national-advertising-division.

National Conference of State Legislatures. "Privacy of Employee and Student Social Media Accounts." Last modified August 8, 2022. https://www.ncsl.org/technology -and-communication/privacy-of-employee-and-student-social-media-accounts.

National Criminal Justice Reference Service. "Making Ethical Decisions: A Practical Model." Accessed July 25, 2023. https://www.ojp.gov/ncjrs/virtual-library/abstracts /making-ethical-decisions-practical-model.

National Equity Project, "SCOTUS Affirmative Action Decision," June 30, 2023, https:// www.nationalequityproject.org/blog/scotus-affirmative-action-decision?gclid=Cj0 KCQjw5f2lBhCkARIsAHeTvlhxh5W_Bbv0K55462rW-DS1_n8iR12Zn9K5aW MD87E5KD7QIuqbiy8aAto0EALw_wcB.

National Institute of Family & Life Advocates v. Becerra, 138 S. Ct. 2361 (2018).

National Labor Relations Act, sec. 7, 29 U.S.C. § 157 (1935).

National Labor Relations Board. "Employee Rights.." Accessed October 30, 2023. https: //www.nlrb.gov/about-nlrb/rights-we-protect/your-rights/employee-rights.Near v. Minnesota, 283 U.S. 697 (1931).

Newberry v. United States, 256 U.S. 232 (1921).

New York Civil Rights Law § 79-h.

New York Lobbying Act. 32 NY Leg. §§1-a-1-v (2016).

New York Times Co. v. Sullivan, 376 U.S. 254 (1964).

New York Times Co. v. United States, 403 U.S. 713 (1971).

Nike, Inc. v. Kasky, 539 U.S. 654 (2003).

Noelle-Neumann, Elisabeth. "The Spiral of Silence: A Theory of Public Opinion." Journal of Communication 24 (1974): 43–51.

Nola Spice Designs, L.L.C. v. Haydel Enterprises, Inc., 783 F.3d 527 (5th Cir. 2015).

Office of the General Counsel, Division of Operations-Management. "Report of the Acting General Counsel Concerning Social Media Cases." Memorandum OM 11–74, August 18, 2011.

Office of the General Counsel, Division of Operations-Management. "Report of the Acting General Counsel Concerning Social Media Cases." Memorandum OM 12–31, January 24, 2012.

Office of the General Counsel, Division of Operations-Management. "Report of the Acting General Counsel Concerning Social Media Cases." Memorandum OM 12–59, May 30, 2012.

"O. J. Simpson Trial." Encyclopedia Britannica. Accessed September 21, 2023. https://www .britannica.com/event Page Society, "Page Principles," Accessed November 3, 2023, https://page.org/who-we-are/page-principles/

Olson, Kathleen. "First Amendment Theory and Practice." in Communication and the Law, edited by W. Wat Hopkins. Northport, AL: Vision Press, 2022.

Paris Adult Theater I v. Slaton, 413 U.S. 49 (1973).

Pavesich v. New England Life Ins. Co., 50 S.E. 68 (Ga. 1905).

Peregrine, Michael. "State Attorney Generals' Warning To CEOs May Chill DEI Initiatives." Fortune, July 18, 2023. https://www.forbes.com/sites/michaelperegrine /2023/07/18/state-attorney-generals-warning-to-ceos-may-chill-dei-initiatives/ ?sh=58f2cc8b1583.

Petroliam Nasional Berhad v. GoDaddy.com, Inc., 737 F.3d 546 (9th Cir. 2013).

Philadelphia Newspapers, Inc. v. Hepps, 475 U.S. 767 (1986).

PhoneDog v. Kravitz, No. C 11-03474 MEJ, 2012 WL 273323 (N.D. Cal. Jan. 30, 2012).

Pizza Hut, Inc. v. Papa Johns, Inc., 227 F.3d 489 (5th Cir. 2000).

Pompper, Donnalyn. "The Sarbanes-Oxley Act: Impact, Processes, and Roles for Strategic Communication." International Journal of Strategic Communication 8, no. 3 (2014): 130–145. https://doi.org/10.1080/1553118X.2014.905476.

Poritz, Isaiah. "AI Deepfakes Bill Pushes Publicity Rights, Spurs Speech Concerns." Bloomberg Law, October 17, 2023. https://news.bloomberglaw.com/ip-law/ai -deepfakes-bill-pushes-publicity-rights-spurs-speech-concerns.

Poritz, Isaiah. "First ChatGPT Defamation Lawsuit to Test AI's Legal Liability." Bloomberg Law, June 12, 2023. https://news.bloomberglaw.com/ip-law/first -chatgpt-defamation-lawsuit-to-test-ais-legal-liability.

Privacy Act of 1974. Pub. L. No. 93-579, 88 Stat. 1896 (1974).

Prosser, William. "Privacy." California Law Review 48 (1960): 383–415.

Public Relations Society of America. "Ethics Case Study: Ethical Decision-Making Guide." Accessed July 25, 2023. https://www.prsa.org/docs/default-source/about /ethics/ethics-case-studies/ethics-case-study-ethical-desision-making-guide.pdf ?sfvrsn=8a55268f_4.

Public Relations Society of America. "PRSA Code of Ethics.." Accessed July 25, 2023. https://www.prsa.org/about/ethics/prsa-code-of-ethics.

Public Utility Holding Company Act of 1935." 15 U.S.C. §§ 79 to 79z-6.

Qualitex Co. v. Jacobson Products Co., Inc., 514 U.S. 159 (1995).

Rand, Ayn. Atlas Shrugged. New York: Random House, 1957.

Rand, Ayn. The Fountainhead. New York: Bobbs-Merrill, 1943.

Rand, Ayn. The Virtue of Selfishness: A New Concept of Egoism. New York: Signet, 1964.

Randall, Alice. The Wind Done Gone. Boston: Houghton Mifflin Harcourt, 2001.

R.A.V. v. City of St. Paul, 505 U.S. 377 (1992).

Ray, Rashawn, and Joy Anyanwu. "Why Is Elon Musk's Twitter Takeover Increasing Hate Speech?" Brookings Institution, November 23, 2022. https://www.brookings .edu/articles/why-is-elon-musks-twitter-takeover-increasing-hate-speech/.

Reed v. Town of Gilbert, 576 U.S. 155 (2015).

Rehabilitation of Offenders Act 1974, c. 53.

Rehak, Judith. "Tylenol Made a Hero of Johnson & Johnson: The Recall That Started Them All." New York Times, March 23, 2002. https://www.nytimes.com/2002/03 /23/your-money/IHT-tylenol-made-a-hero-of-johnson-johnson-the-recall-that -started.html.

Relentless, Inc. v. Dep't of Commerce, No. 22-1219 (U.S. argued Jan. 17, 2024), on appeal from the 1st Cir.

"Ren." *Encyclopedia Britannica*, Accessed July 25, 2023. https://www.britannica.com/topic/ren.

Reno v. American Civil Liberties Union, 521 U.S. 844 (1997).

Reporters Committee for Freedom of the Press. "Anti-SLAPP Laws." Accessed October 3, 2023. https://www.rcfp.org/resources/anti-slapp-laws/.

Restatement (Second) of Torts § 652B. American Law Institute, 1977.

Rivlin, Gary. "Talkative Chief Complicates An Offering By Salesforce." *New York Times*, June 5, 2004. https://www.nytimes.com/2004/06/05/business/talkative-chief-complicates-an-offering-by-salesforce.html.

Roberson v. Rochester Folding Box Co., 64 N.E. 442 (N.Y. 1902).

Roe v. Wade, 410 U.S. 113 (1973).

Roosevelt Institute. "The End of Affirmative Action?" June 29, 2023. https://rooseveltinstitute.org/2023/06/29/the-end-of-affirmative-action/?gclid=Cj0KCQj w5f2lBhCkARIsAHeTvljgNEwbux2LseZDit7VYK2ZrMYa9x2YR0LQydC3Af j5m-WSxzJA-uIaAmarEALw_wcB.

Rosen, Zvi S. "Federal Trademark Law: From Its Beginnings." Landslide 11, no. 4 (2019). https://www.americanbar.org/groups/intellectual_property_law/publications/ landslide/2018-19/march-april/federal-trademark-law/.

Roth v. United States, 354 U.S. 476 (1957).

Russell, Karen, and Carl Bishop. "Understanding Ivy Lee's Declaration of Principles: U.S. Newspaper and Magazine Coverage of Publicity and Press Agentry, 1865–1904." *Public Relations Review* 35, no. 2 (2009): 91–101.

Sable Communications of California v. FCC, 492 U.S. 115 (1989).

Santa Clara County v. Southern Pacific Railroad Co., 118 U.S. 394 (1886).

Sarah Andersen et al. v. Stability AI Ltd. et al., No. 3:23-cv-00201 (N.D. Cal. filed January 13, 2023).

Sarbanes-Oxley Act of 2002. Pub. L. No. 107-204, 116 Stat. 745 (2002).

Scalia, Antonin, and Bryan A. Garner. *Reading Law: The Interpretation of Legal Texts*. St. Paul, MN: Thomson/West, 2012.

Schenck v. United States, 249 U.S. 47 (1919).

Scheufele, Dietram A., and Patricia Moy, "Twenty-Five Years of the Spiral of Silence: A Conceptual Review and Empirical Outlook." International Journal of Public Opinion Research 12, no. 1 (2000): 3–28. https://search-ebscohost-com.ezproxy.lib.vt .edu/login.aspx?direct=true&db=ufh&AN=3236575&scope=site.

Schwartz, Brian. "Total 2020 Election Spending to Hit Nearly $14 Billion, More Than Double 2016's Sum." CNBC, October 28, 2020. https://www.cnbc.com/2020/10 /28/2020-election-spending-to-hit-nearly-14-billion-a-record.html.

Securities Act of 1933. 15 U.S.C. §§ 77a et seq.

Securities Exchange Act of 1934. Pub. L. No. 73-291, 48 Stat. 881.

Securities Exchange Act of 1934, Rule 134. 17 C.F.R. § 230.134 (2023).

Seligman, Terri, and Hannah Taylor. "Navigating the National Advertising Division." Landslide, March–April 2018–2019. https://www.americanbar.org/groups/ intellectual_property_law/publications/landslide/2018-19/march-april/navigating -national-advertising-division/.

Shelton, Colleen, and Lynne M. Sallot. "Image Repair in Politics: Testing Effects of Communication Strategy and Performance History in a Faux Pas." *Journal of Public Relations Research* 21, no. 1 (2009): 25–50. doi: 10.1080/10627260802520496.

Shulman v. Group W Productions, Inc. 18 Cal. 4th 200 (1998).

Sidis v. F-R Publ. Corp., 113 F.2d 806 (2d Cir. 1940), 807–808.

Sinai, Yuval. "The Doctrine of Affirmative Defense in Civil Cases—Between Common Law and Jewish Law." *North Carolina Journal of International Law* 34, no. 1 (Fall 2008): 111–178. https://scholarship.law.unc.edu/cgi/viewcontent.cgi?referer =&httpsredir=1&article=1863&context=ncilj.

Silverman v. OpenAI Inc., No. 2:23-cv-03416, (N.D. Cal. 2023).

Sipple v. Chronicle Pub. Co., 154 Cal. App. 3d 1040.

Society of Professional Journalists. "SPJ Code of Ethics." Accessed October 3, 2023. https: //www.spj.org/ethicscode.asp.

Sonny Bono Copyright Term Extension Act, Pub. L. No. 105-298, 112 Stat. 2827 (1998).

Soyer, Emre, and Robin Hogarth. "Fooled by Experience." *Harvard Business Review*, May 2015. https://hbr.org/2015/05/fooled-by-experience.

SpeechNow.org v. FEC, 599 F.3d 686 (D.C. Cir. 2010).

St. Amant v. Thompson, 390 U.S. 727 (1968).

Starbucks Corp. v. Wolfe's Borough Coffee, Inc., 588 F.3d 97 (2d Cir. 2009).

Starbucks Corp. v. Wolfe's Borough Coffee, Inc., No. 01 Civ. 5981, 2011 WL 6747431 (S.D.N.Y. Dec. 23, 2011).

"States and Cities Limit AI Use in Employment Decisions." *JD Supra.* January 23, 2023. https://www.jdsupra.com/legalnews/states-and-cities-limit-ai-use-in -8779184/.

Stavropoulos, Nicos. "Interpretivist Theories of Law." *Stanford Encyclopedia of Philosophy.* Last modified July 20, 2017. https://plato.stanford.edu/entries/law-interpretivist/.

Steaks Unlimited, Inc. v. Deaner, 623 F.2d 264 (3d Cir. 1980).

Sternlicht, Alexandra. "Top Creators 2022." Forbes. September 6, 2022. https:// www.forbes.com/sites/alexandrasternlicht/2022/09/06/top-creators-2022/?sh =1884fe1c67a1.

Students for Fair Admissions v. Harvard, 600 U.S. 181 (2023).

Sullivan v. Louisiana, 508 U.S. 275 (1993).

Summer, David. Fumbled Call: The Bear Bryant–Wally Butts Football Scandal That Split the Supreme Court and Changed American Libel Law. Jefferson, NC: McFarland & Company, Inc., 2018.

"Supreme Court Research Guide." Georgetown Law Library. Accessed September 21, 2023. https://guides.ll.georgetown.edu/c.php?g=316498&p=2114300.

Telebrand Corps., TV Sav., LLC, & Ajit Khubani, 140 F.T.C. 278 (2005).

Telecommunications Act of 1996, Pub. L. No. 104-104, 110 Stat. 56 (1996).

Terilli, Suzanne, Slavko Splichal, and Paul Discol. "Lowering the Bar: Privileged Court Filings as Substitutes for Press Releases in the Court of Public Opinion." *Communication Law & Policy* 12, no. 2 (2007): 143–175. doi: 10.1080/10811680701266500.

Terminiello v. City of Chicago, 337 U.S. 1 (1942).

Thaler v. Perlmutter, ___ F3d___, 2023 WL 533236 (D.D.C. 2023).

Thornhill v. Alabama, 310 U.S. 88 (1940).

Tillman Act, ch. 420, 34 Stat. 864 (1907).

Time v. Hill, 385 U.S. 374 (1967).

Toys "R" Us, Inc. v. Akkaoui, No. C 96–3381 CW, 1996 WL 772709 (N.D. Cal. 1996).

Tremblay v. OpenAI Inc., No. 2:23-cv-03223, (N.D. Cal. 2023).

Trump, Donald. @realDonaldTrump. "Revoke 230." Twitter, May 29, 2020. https://twitter.com/realDonaldTrump/status/1266387743996870656.

Twardy, Susan. "Attorneys and Public Relations Professionals Must Work Hand-in-Hand when Responding to an Environmental Investigation." *Public Relations Quarterly* 39, no. 2 (1994): 15–16.

Twitter, Inc. v. Taamneh, 598 U.S. 471 (2023).

Two Pesos, Inc. v. Taco Cabana, 505 U.S. 763 (1992).

Uniform Trade Secrets Act with 1985 Amendments §1(4).

United Mine Workers of America v. Pennington, 381 U.S. 657 (1965).

United States Courts. "About Federal Courts." Accessed July 28, 2023. https://www.uscourts.gov/about-federal-courts/educational-resources/about-educational-outreach/activity-resources/about.

United States Courts. "Federal Judicial Caseload Statistics 2022." Accessed July 28, 2023. https://www.uscourts.gov/statistics-reports/federal-judicial-caseload-statistics-2022.

United States v. Alvarez, 567 U.S. 709 (2012).

United States v. Harriss, 347 U.S. 612, 620 (1954).

United States v. Kovel, 296 F.2d 918, 922 (2d. Cir. 1962).

United States v. Rumely, 345 U.S. 41 (1953).

United States v. Stevens, 559 U.S. 460 (2010).

U.S. Copyright Office. "An Act for the Encouragement of Learning." Statutes at Large 1 (1790): 124. Accessed November 2, 2023. https://www.copyright.gov/history/1790act.pdf.

U.S. Copyright Office. "Copyright and Artificial Intelligence." Accessed November 1, 2023. https://www.copyright.gov/ai/.

U.S. Copyright Office. "Fair Use Index." Last updated February 2023. https://www.copyright.gov/fair-use/.

U.S. Department of Justice. "Use of Compulsory Process to Obtain Information from, Or Records of, Members of the News Media." July 2021. https://www.justice.gov/d9/2022-12/media_memo_07-19-2021.pdf.

U.S. Patent and Trademark Office. "Strong Trademarks." Accessed November 6, 2023. https://www.uspto.gov/trademarks/basics/strong-trademarks.

U.S. Patent and Trademark Office. "What Is a Trademark?" Accessed October 28, 2023. https://www.uspto.gov/trademarks/basics/what-trademark.

U.S. Securities and Exchange Commission. "About the SEC: What We Do." Last modified October 1, 2013. https://www.sec.gov/about/about-securities-laws#secact1933.

U.S. Securities and Exchange Commission. "The Laws That Govern the Securities Industry." Last modified October 1, 2013. https://www.sec.gov/about/about-securities-laws#secexact1934.

U.S. Securities and Exchange Commission. "Regulation S-K." 17 CFR 229 (2023).
U.S. Securities and Exchange Commission. "Regulation S-X." 17 CFR Part 210 (2023).
Valentine v. Chrestensen, 316 U.S. 52 (1942).
Victor v. Nebraska, 511 U.S. 1 (1994).
Virginia Consumer Data Protection Act. Va. Code Ann. §§ 59.1-572 to -578 (2021).
Virginia State Pharmacy Board v. Virginia Citizens Consumer Council, 425 U.S. 748 (1976).
Vlad, Iuliana, Lynne M. Sallot, and Bryan Reber. "Rectification without Assuming Responsibility: Testing the Transgression Flowchart With the Vioxx Recall." *Journal of Public Relations* Research 18, no. 4 (2006): 357–379. doi: 10.1207/s1532754xjprr1804_4.
Volkswagenwerk Aktiengesellschaft v. Church, 411 F.2d 350 (9th Cir. 1969).
Vulcan Golf, LLC v. Google Inc., 726 F.Supp.2d 911 (N.D.Ill. 2010).
Vulcan Metals Co. v. Simmons Mfg. Co., 248 F. 853 (2d Cir. 1918).
Wagner, Stephen, and Lee Dittmar. "The Unexpected Benefits of Sarbanes-Oxley." *Harvard Business Review*, April 2006. https://hbr.org/2006/04/the-unexpected-benefits-of-sarbanes-oxley.
Walters v. OpenAI, L.L.C., Civil Action No. 23-A-04860-2 (Ga. Super. Gwinnett Cnty. June 2, 2023).
Warren, Samuel D., and Louis D. Brandeis. "The Right to Privacy." *Harvard Law Review* 4 (1890): 193, 196.
Wedell-Wedellsborg, Merete. "The Psychology Behind Unethical Behavior." *Harvard Business Review*, April 2019. https://hbr.org/2019/04/the-psychology-behind-unethical-behavior.
West v. Media General Convergence, Inc., 53 S.W.3d 640 (Tenn. 2001).
"What Percentage of Lawsuits Settle Before Trial? What Are Some Statistics on Personal Injury Settlements?" *The Law Dictionary*. Accessed July 28, 2023. https://thelawdictionary.org/article/what-percentage-of-lawsuits-settle-before-trial-what-are-some-statistics-on-personal-injury-settlements/.
The White House. "Blueprint for an AI Bill of Rights: Making Automated Systems Work for the American People." Accessed October 31, 2023. https://www.whitehouse.gov/ostp/ai-bill-of-rights/.
The White House. "Executive Order on the Safe, Secure, and Trustworthy Development and Use of Artificial Intelligence." Last modified October 30, 2023. https://www.whitehouse.gov/briefing-room/presidential-actions/2023/10/30/executive-order-on-the-safe-secure-and-trustworthy-development-and-use-of-artificial-intelligence/.
Wiencierz, Christian, and Ulrike Röttger. "The Use of Big Data in Corporate Communication." *Corporate Communications: An International Journal* 22, no. 3 (2017): 258–272. https://doi.org/10.1108/CCIJ-02-2016-0015.
Wilding, Melody. "How to Stop Overthinking and Start Trusting Your Gut." *Harvard Business Review*, March 2022. https://hbr.org/2022/03/how-to-stop-overthinking-and-start-trusting-your-gut.
Williams-Yulee v. Florida Bar, 575 U.S. 433 (2015).

WJLA-TV v. Levin, 564 S.E.2d 383, 395 n.5 (Va. 2000).

Wolford, Ben. "Does the GDPR Apply to Companies Outside of the EU?" GDPR.eu. Accessed October 24, 2023. https://gdpr.eu/companies-outside-of-europe/.

Wolford, Ben. "What Are the GDPR Fines?" GDPR.eu. Accessed October 24, 2023. https://gdpr.eu/fines/.

Wolford, Ben. "What Is GDPR, the EU's New Data Protection Law?" GDPR.edu. Accessed October 24, 2023. https://chat.openai.com/c/d3ea7f12-f306-4e6e-922b-309dec15ed05.

Woo, Chang, Michael Gulotaa, and April Gulotta. "Penn State's After-Sanction Response Strategy." In The Moral Compass of Public Relations, edited by Brigitta Brunner, 28–42. New York: Routledge, 2017.

Yalof, David, and Kenneth Dautrich. The First Amendment and the Media in the Court of Public Opinion. Cambridge: Cambridge University Press, 2002.

Yoshino, Kenji, and David Glasgow. "What SCOTUS's Affirmative Action Decision Means for Corporate DEI." Harvard Business Review, July 12 2023. https://hbr.org/2023/07/what-scotuss-affirmative-action-decision-means-for-corporate-dei.

Youm, Kyu Ho. "Defamation." In Communication and the Law, edited by W. Wat Hopkins. Northport, AL: Vision Press, 2022.

Zacchini v. Scripps Howard Broadcasting Co., 433 U.S. 562 (1977).

Zeran v. America Online, Inc., 129 F.3d 327 (4th Cir. 1997).

Index

AAF. *See* American Advertising Federation

ABA. *See* American Bar Association

abortion: living constitutionalism and, 26–27; originalism and, 27; textualism and, 27

Abrams v. United States, 59

acceptable performance, 54

Accredited in Public Relations (APR), 37

ACPA. *See* Anticybersquatting Consumer Protection Act

ACPR. *See* American Council on Public Relations

actual malice, 9; defined, 243; expansion of, 67, 147–48; journalism and, 149–56; media relations and, 149–56

administrative law, 31–32; defined, 245

administrative law judges (ALJs), 31–32

Administrative Procedure Act (APA), 32

ADR. *See* alternative dispute resolutions

adversarial advocacy, 92–102

advertising: consumer perception of, 122–23; defining, 116; endorsements, 126–32; exchange of goods and, 126–27; false, 116–22; implied statements, 122; influencers, 125–32; liability for nondisclosure in, 127; monitoring, 119; native, 119–21; ordinary user endorsements, 128–32; puffery in, 122–25; recognizing, 120; regulations, 115, 116–17; substantiation and, 121–25; transparency and, 115–25; truth in, 118–19

advertising bans, 73

advocacy, 8; adversarial, 92–102; corporate social, 62–63

AEDPA. *See* Antiterrorism and Effective Death Penalty Act

affirmative defense, 145–46; categories, 70; defamation, 70

agency, 37; challenging, 32; enablement clause, 31

AI. *See* artificial intelligence

AI Act, 238–39

CPRA. *See* California Privacy Rights Act
Creativity Machine, 200
credibility, 140
Creel Committee, 80
CRFA. *See* Consumer Review Fairness Act
criminal violations, 14, 44
Cromwell, Oliver, 144
Crosby, William, 145
CSA. *See* corporate social advocacy
CSR. *See* corporate social responsibility
cultural numbness, 45
Curtis Publishing v. Butts, 147–48
Cutlip, Scott, 36; on public relations, 54
cybersquatting, 218–19

damages, compensatory, 244
damages, punitive, 244
Dartmouth College v. Woodward, 76
Data Protection Authority (DPA), 184
data protection officer (DPO), 185; requirements of, 271n52
Declaration of Principles, 36
defamation, 7, 256n39; affirmative defense, 70; artificial intelligence and, 160; Communications Decency Act and, 158–60; components of, 145; corporations and, 148; defenses to, 70, 154–56;

defined, 244; development of, 67; example, 142–43; false light differentiated from, 177; fame and, 67; fault, 143; harm, 143; history of, 143–49; identification, 143; journalism and, 146; legal process, 143; liability for, 69; medieval, 144; police power and, 146; printing press and, 144; proving, 66; publication, 143; public figure and, 67; regular negligence standard, 147; reputation management and, 142–56; Roman, 143–44; societal preservation and, 146; statement, 143
defendant, 92; defined, 246; responsibility of, 97; witnesses for, 98
DEI. *See* diversity, equity, and inclusion
deontological ethics, 40, 45; utilitarianism conflicting with, 41–42
deposition, 94
derivative works, 206
Deutsche Public Relations Gesellschaft, 37
Digital Millennium Copyright Act (DMCA), 197
disclosure: of artificial intelligence, 137; of endorsements, 126–27; FTC guidelines, 127; influencers and, 126–27; liability, 127; native advertising, 121; of

private facts, 172, 180–82. *See also* nondisclosure agreements

"Disclosures 101 for Social Media Influencers," 128

discrimination: artificial intelligence and, 241; big data and, 188

disinformation, 31, 83; Enron and, 132; for reputation management, 141

disparagement, 149

District of Columbia v. Heller, 26

diversity, equity, and inclusion (DEI), 241; design of, 49–50; ethics and, 48–51; hiring practices and, 50; outlets, 50

divinity, 251n69

DMCA. *See* Digital Millennium Copyright Act

Dobbs v. Jackson's Women's Health Organization, 18

doctrinarism, 25, 27

Dominion Voting, 148, 150

".com Disclosures," 121

DPA. *See* Data Protection Authority

DPO. *See* data protection officer

dualist philosophy, 32–33

Due Process, 26, 59

Durant, William, 16

Dworkin, Ronald, 248n26

dying in committee, 28

Eastern Railroads President's Conference v. Noerr, 79–80

ECPA. *See* Electronic Communications Privacy Act

EEOC. *See* Equal Employment Opportunity Commission

egoism, 38–39, 251n64; contemporary, 40; self-interestedness of, 40

Eighth Amendment, 24; incorporation of, 25

Electronic Communications Privacy Act (ECPA), 157–58, 174–75, 269n17

Ellsberg, Daniel, 60, 255n17

emotional distress, 256n46

emotional fortitude, 44

employee speech, 9; social media and, 160–65

en banc decisions, 260n22

endorsement: authentic, 128; disclosure of, 126–27; FTC guidelines for, 129, 131; liability for, 131; monitoring, 131; ordinary user, 128–32; strategies, 131

English Year Books, 144

Enron, 132

environment: commercial speech and, 72–73; ethical decision making and, 45

Ephron, Nora, 230

Equal Employment Opportunity Commission (EEOC), 31

equal protection clauses, 50; corporations and, 76

eraser bill, 173

erasure, right to, 10, 141, 185–87

fighting words, 7; defining, 64;
Murphy on, 63–64; Trump
and, 64
Financial Services Modernization
Act, 175
financial transparency, 132–36
First Amendment, 3, 24; case law
on, 57; case scenario, 84–85;
defined, 245; development
of, 58–59; discussion questions, 84; ethics and, 81–83;
incorporation of, 25, 254n7;
overview, 56–70; philosophical approaches to, 25; public
relations categorization under,
7; World War I and, 58–59. *See
also* speech, freedom of
first do no harm, 35
*First National Bank of Boston v.
Bellotti*, 78, 81
Fitzpatrick, Kathy, 46
fixed meaning interpretation, 29
FOIA. *See* Freedom of
Information Act
Food and Drug Administration
(FDA), 31
Ford, Gerald, 182, 211
forgotten, right to be, 10, 141,
185–87
Fourteenth Amendment, 24–25,
59; living constitutionalism and,
26–27
Fourth Amendment, 24; incorporation of, 25
Fox News, 150

fraud, 249n43
Freedom of Information Act
(FOIA), 174
Friedman, Milton, 40, 251n66
FTC. *See* Federal Trade
Commission
FTCA. *See* Federal Trade
Commission Act
fully protected speech: corporate
social advocacy and, 62–63;
corporate social responsibil-
ity and, 62–63; defined, 61;
requirements for, 62
future legal issues, 234–42

General Data Privacy Regulation
(GDPR), 33, 184, 186–87, 238;
key areas of, 185
Gertz v. Welch, 146, 178
gig economy, 230
Gitlow v. New York, 57, 59
Glass-Steagall Banking Act of
1933, 133
Goldwater, Barry, 150–51
Gonzales v. Google LLC, 159–60
good Samaritan provision, 157
Gramm-Leach-Bliley Act, 175

Harrison, George, 206
Hatch Act, 77
hate speech, 83
Health Insurance Portability
and Accountability Act
(HIPPA), 175

Hellenic Public Relations Association (IPRA), 37
HIPPA. *See* Health Insurance Portability and Accountability Act
Hippocrates, 35
Hippocratic Oath, 35, 250n45
hiring practices, 50
Hobbes, Thomas, 39
Holmes, Oliver Wendell: on freedom of speech, 58–59, 63; pragmatism and, 26
honesty, 16–17
Hong Kong Christian Industrial Committee, 74
Hustler Magazine v. Falwell, 68

IABC. *See* International Association of Business Communicators
ICCPR. *See* International Covenant on Civil and Political Rights
image control, 178
impermissibility, 43
inclusion, 50
indictment, 92
individuality, 42–44
influencers: business model of, 125; disclosure and, 126–27; disruption through, 125; FTC and, 126–28; regulations, 126; transparency and, 125–32
initial public offering (IPO), 31; quiet period, 134

insider trading, 135
Instagram, 125
intellectual property (IP), 10; artificial intelligence and, 197–98, 236–37; case scenario, 226–27; Constitution and, 196; content access, 223–24; defined, 245; discussion questions, 226; ethics, 223–26; European Union and, 225–26; global considerations, 225–26; history of, 196–98; misconceptions around, 198; substantial similarity and, 206. *See also* copyright; trademark; trade secrets
intentionality, 40–41
internal communication, 9; social media and, 160–65
International Association of Business Communicators (IABC), 17
International Covenant on Civil and Political Rights (ICCPR), 83
international law, 32; importation of, 33
International Public Relations Association (IPRA), 37; transparency and, 114
internet of things, 277n9
interrogatories, 94
intrusion, 172, 182–83
intuitive decision making, 44
Investment Company Act, 135
Investors Advisor Act, 135

endorsement, 131; for false advertising, 118; protection, 9, 56

libel: chain, 146; per quod, 67, 145; per se, 67, 145; proof plaintiff doctrine, 155–56; trade, 149

litigation, defined, 245

living constitutionalism, 25; abortion and, 26–27; Fourteenth Amendment and, 26–27; overview of, 26–27

lobbying, 8; public relations differentiated from, 79–81

Lobbying Disclosure Act, 79

Locke, John, 82, 251n69

Marbury v. Madison, 18

Masson, Jeffrey, 267n20

Masson v. New Yorker Magazine, 151

McCain-Feingold Act, 78

McConnell v. FEC, 78

McCutcheon v. FEC, 78–79

mediation, 102

Memoirs v. Massachusetts, 65

Mickey Mouse, 273n22

Mill, John Stuart, 38–39

Miller, Judith, 106, 261n28

Miller v. California, 65, 247

mini room model, 230

Miranda v. Arizona, 18

Model Rules of Professional Conduct, 16

monism, 33

moral and ethical interpretivism, 27

morality: ethics and, 16; religion and, 42–43; transparency and, 136

mortification strategy, 103

Murphy, Frank, 63–64

NAAPD. *See* National Association of Accredited Publicity Directors

NAD. *See* National Advertising Division

Nader, Ralph, 183

NARB. *See* National Advertising Review Board

Nash, Laura, 46–47

National Advertising Division (NAD), 116–17

National Advertising Review Board (NARB), 117

National Association of Accredited Publicity Directors (NAAPD), 36

National Association of Advertisers, 117

National Association of Public Relations Counsel, 36

National Electric Light Association (NELA), 36

National Labor Relations Act (NLRA), 9, 142, 161–65

National Labor Relations Board (NLRB), 31; concerted

About the Author

Cayce Myers is professor of public relations and director of graduate studies at the School of Communication at Virginia Tech. He is the author of *Money in Politics: Campaign Fundraising in the 2020 Presidential Election* (2021).